M000206190

Born in 1898, Paul Brunton travelled extensively in the East and published thirteen books between 1935 and 1952. He is generally recognized as having introduced yoga and meditation to the West, and for presenting their philosophical background in non-technical language. He died in Switzerland (where he lived for 20 years) in 1981.

Praise for Paul Brunton

'Paul Brunton was surely one of the finest mystical flowers to grow on the wasteland of our secular civilization. What he has to say is important to us all.' – Georg Feuerstein

'. . . a great gift to us Westerners who are seeking the spiritual.' – Charles T. Tart

'A person of rare intelligence . . . thoroughly alive, and whole in the most significant, "holy" sense of the word.' – *Yoga Journal*

'Paul Brunton was a great original and got to a place of personal evolution that illumines the pathways of a future humanity.' – Jean Houston

'A simple, straightforward guide to how philosophical insights of the East and West can help to create beauty, joy, and meaning in our lives. . . . His keynote is balance, and his uplifting message encompasses all phases of human experience.' – *East West Journal*

'. . . sensible and compelling. His work can stand beside that of such East-West bridges as Merton, Huxley, Suzuki, Watts, and Radhakrishnan. It should appeal to anyone concerned personally and academically with issues of spirituality.' – *Choice*

'Any serious man or woman in search of spiritual ideas will find a surprising challenge and an authentic source of inspiration and intellectual nourishment in the writings of Paul Brunton.' – Jacob Needleman

PAUL BRUNTON

A HERMIT IN
THE HIMALAYAS

The Classic Work of Mystical Quest

RIDER

LONDON • SYDNEY • AUCKLAND • JOHANNESBURG

7 9 10 8 6

First published in 1937
This edition published in 2003 by Rider, an imprint of Ebury Publishing

Ebury Publishing is a Random House Group company

Copyright © Estate of Paul Brunton 1983

The Random House Group Limited Reg. No. 954009

Addresses for companies within the Random House Group can be found at
www.rbooks.co.uk

A CIP catalogue record for this book is available from the British Library

The Random House Group Limited supports The Forest Stewardship
Council (FSC), the leading international forest certification organisation. All
our titles that are printed on Greenpeace approved FSC certified paper carry
the FSC logo. Our paper procurement policy can be found at
www.rbooks.co.uk/environment.

Printed and bound in Great Britain by
CPI Antony Rowe, Chippenham, Wiltshire

ISBN 9781844130429

Copies are available at special rates for bulk orders. Contact the sales development team on 020 7840 8487 or visit www.booksforpromotions.co.uk for
more information.

To buy books by your favourite authors and register for offers, visit
www.rbooks.co.uk

CONTENTS

CONTENTS

INTRODUCTION

Much has changed in the world since Paul Brunton wrote *A Hermit in the Himalayas* – and PB (as he is known to his followers) himself changed a good deal after writing this third and last of his travel books. At the same time, many things remain the same.

When PB began this journey, he hoped to spend some time in Tibet, but was prevented from doing so by governmental authorities. Nowadays, it is quite possible for tourists willing to ignore China's Human Rights record to enter Tibet – but it is either dangerous or impossible for a Tibetan to do so. PB's reflections on the British Rule of India – written years before India's independence – may seem like a faint footnote to a bygone era. However, today's news reminds us of the karma, challenges and fate awaiting a Western empire that supplants the culture and regime of an Eastern nation. The harsh clamour of contrasting cultures, politics and fates continues throughout the globe. Taken in this light, PB's comments and suggestions are *very* relevant today.

I call the second theme 'PB's Responses'– his comments on a wide, and wild, variety of topics, including divorce, sex, UFOs, astrology, tea, and my favourite, shaving! As *The Notebooks of Paul Brunton* show, PB's thoughts on some of these topics changed quite a bit over the years (except for tea, which he loved to the end of his days). Why, then, keep these older opinions around? Simply because the Paul Brunton of these pages is still a student of the Overself, as are we, which means we can immediately benefit from the perspective he brings to these various issues.

The third theme occupies the most space and is written beautifully. Indeed, much of it is about space and beauty: the grand solitary spaces of the Himalayas themselves, and the interior space of the indrawn mind. PB's previous 'travel' books primarily explored the remarkable places and peoples of India and Egypt. Here he turns heart and pen towards Nature, recording the elegant simplicity of a hermetic retreat from the world. PB moves easily amongst the gentle and dramatic elements of his mountain home, at one moment absorbing the silence of a starry night, at another confronting a panther, protected only by his self-control. Yet his is no world-denying retreat. Instead we find PB establishing the parameters, purpose, and practices of retreat which will free us for a time from our secular entanglements, and return us to that world better able to meet it. This, then, is the core of the book: a pathway into the deep stillness of our higher self through sacred communion with nature herself.

Although PB himself first found his higher self on a mountaintop, it can also be found in a city park, or in one's own back yard. So take this book outside, find a place of daily retreat, and, for a moment or two, feel the cool clarity and solemn silence of those distant mountains speaking their lesson in your heart.

Timothy Smith
Co-Editor, The Notebooks of Paul Brunton

Note: the state of Tehri Garhwal is today much as it was when PB visited it. Interested in learning more? Check out these websites:

> http://tehri.nic.in/
> http://www.gmvnl.com/districts/tehri/
> http://www.garhwaltourism.com/tehri/

FOREWORD

By

PRINCE MUSSOOREE SHUM SHERE
JUNG BAHADUR RANA

of

NEPAL

It affords me much pleasure to write these introductory words to this, the latest[1] of my friend Paul Brunton's books. The scene is set amid the long and famous range of mountains which separates India from Central Asia. The ridges and peaks which the author describes, as he saw them in Tehri State, are but a continuation of my own beloved Nepalese Himalayas. Born as I was in these mountains, I have a strong affection for the Himalayas, and the moments spent reading about them in Brunton's original and attractive prose have been happy ones.

Only those who have been reared among the forest-clothed ranges and snow-clad heights of Himalaya will know that he has not over-praised them but done them simple justice. They must remain the most stupendous sight in all Asia, nay in all the world.

Prior to leaving the mountains the author visited me for a few days and during his stay showed me the manuscript of "A Hermit in the Himalayas". It was then only that I discovered therein a few pages devoted to my own sudden visit to his retreat, when I crossed the ridges on horseback through friendship for one whom I regard as a spiritual prophet of our time. Had I known that his retentive memory was making silent and secret notes of all that I said, I might have been a little more careful in my utterances! For I did not know that he was keeping a journal in which he recorded some of the thoughts, events and conversations at odd intervals. Fortunately I can trust his discretion not to publish matters which are not the public's concern.

This new book, being but a journal, is to me more interesting than a studiously composed work, for it necessarily bears an air of intimacy and frankness which can usually be found in diaries and journals alone. It admits one into the most secret thoughts of the gifted writer. He told me that when he looked through the pages before showing them to me he found them to be

[1] This was written in 1936.

7

"*horribly egotistical*", and felt inclined to consign them to burial under the mountains where they were written. But I assured him that egotism is an essential part of every memoir, and that these memoirs of his life in the Himalayas cannot escape from a quality which gives added interest and attraction to literature, even though it may be repulsive in society.

During the sojourn which is the subject of this book, Paul Brunton was, I believe, the only white man living in the little-known State of Tehri. Certainly few Europeans would care to go and isolate themselves amid wild and rugged mountains far from the haunts of civilized society, as he has done. Nevertheless I feel sure that he gained his reward, for even during the short period when I was his companion I must say that the days seemed marvellous : one was wafted away from all the awful realities of humdrum life to a world of dreams, peace and spirituality.

On this last theme it seems to me that his ideas in general, as expressed here and in other books, are specially fitted for the guidance of Western people and of those increasingly numerous Orientals who have taken to their mode of living and thinking. I personally find it easier to understand many intricate subtleties of our own Asiatic philosophies and spiritual techniques, including Yoga, when explained by Brunton in his scientific, rational, modern and unsectarian manner than when expounded in the ancient ways, which are so remote from twentieth century understanding.

One comes across many passages in the scriptures of most religions where mention is made of the Spirit speaking in different ways, through different tongues and different men. I am convinced that Brunton is one of the chosen instruments to re-interpret the half-lost wisdom of the East to those caught up in the mechanical life of the West, and thus serve His cause.

A book like this is intended for those who have either sympathy or yearning for the inner life of the Spirit. I can gauge the profound ignorance of the reviewer who, in a certain European-managed newspaper of Calcutta, denounced the author's earlier work "A Search in Secret India" as false, denied the existence of any spirituality in India, and finally ridiculed the author's competency to conduct these researches. All the best Indian journals and leaders of opinion have, nevertheless, given the highest praise to that book, thereby bringing out in contrast the lack of understanding and experience betrayed by the Western-born reviewer of the country in whose midst he lived.

His opinion was as much worth accepting as that of an uneducated pugilist on a priceless Chinese vase of the Ming dynasty.

I can personally testify that there are not only the Yogis in India as described in Brunton's book, that is, men of supernormal attainments, marvellous powers and lofty spirituality, but others equally unusual whom he has not mentioned. Yet the average European and Western-educated Indian look with indifference, scorn and contempt upon his statements—thus proving that they have not been initiated into the world's most valuable knowledge and Asia's most treasured secret tradition.

8

As a *Nepalese, belonging to a people who have rigidly maintained their land in absolute independence and proud exclusiveness, I can also testify that these ancient traditions of a mystic wisdom have been preserved in the mountain fastnesses of Nepal far better than even in India itself. But those only who seek as earnestly as the author can hope to penetrate into the society and secrets of the true Sages of Asia. His Calcutta critic would be beneath notice were it not that equally unfair prejudices constantly manifest themselves. Thus I have heard Europeans describe his Egyptian researches and Great Pyramid spirit-experience as "a mere journalistic stunt"! Once again they betray ignorance. Either they have never met Paul Brunton, or if they have, they were not permitted to share his inner life as I have shared it. Those who really know him—a difficult matter, I must admit—know that his sincerity is unquestionable and that his material sacrifices for the sake of discovering the elusive truth behind life have been great. Few really know him, and misunderstanding seems to be his ordained and accepted lot.*

I am glad to have the opportunity of rendering my friend the little service of writing this introduction. May the much-needed message whose inner light flickers through the following pages bear the blessing of the hidden Sages of the Holy Himalayas!

PREFACE TO THE FIRST BRITISH EDITION

LEST readers wrongly believe that this is a new book, that I have broken the silence of several years with the following utterance, I must hasten to tell them that it is not. It was written more years ago than I like to remember. The sheets were struck off the press in Madras, near where I was staying at the time, and circulated in book form. A small number of them was sent to England and here issued in the same form but soon disappeared. *A Hermit in the Himalayas* was never reprinted, despite demands.

Although I did not return to the same Central Himalayan region which it describes, the tides of war did bring me to these stupendous mountains, first to the extreme Eastern end, on the frontiers of Sikkim, and later to the extreme Western end, overlooking Little Tibet.

It has never since been possible for me to forget the breath-taking grandeur of those endless rows of summits, gleaming in the sun as they half-lost themselves in the sky, nor the happy sound of rushing streams dancing on the floors of steep, rocky valleys.

It was inevitable that some of the points of view from which the reflections in this journal were written should become modified by the inner development and wider experience of passing years. But the general point of view remains substantially the same, and that is the need of gaining spiritual peace by regaining control of the mind and heart. It is not long since I came back from Oriental travel and tropical life to live in the Western hemisphere again, yet everything I have seen and heard here convinces me that this need is more urgent and more imperative than it was when the journal was written. If the world stands bewildered and confused in the face of its troubles, it is partly because we Westerners have made a God of activity; we have yet to learn how to *be*, as we have already learnt how to *do*.

We need these oases of calm in a world of storm. There are times when withdrawal to retreat for such a purpose is not desertion but wisdom, not weakness but strength. If we withdraw for a while so as to reconsider our goals and survey our courses, if we use the time and leisure to calm our agitations and sharpen our intuitions, we cannot be doing wrong.

However, I do not advocate rural or monastic retreat for the purpose otherwise than as a valuable temporary and occasional help, for the real battle must be fought out within one's self, just where the aspirant now stands. Every successful passage through the tests provided by worldly life gives him a chance to make a spurt not only in consciousness and understanding but more especially in character. It offers him one quick way of changing his character for the better. The error which deems mystical belief and meditation practice as suitable only for, and confined to, ascetics, monks and holy men, or cranks, neurotics and freaks, is a serious one.

The old easy-travelling pre-war world has gone. Despite aeroplanes, Himalaya seems farther away to most Britons today than it was when I first entered its many-coloured domain under a turquoise sky. He who seeks a retreat cannot go far nowadays, perhaps no farther than the next county. Indeed, in these days of housing shortage, sometimes he cannot even get the undisturbed privacy of a room. Is the way closed, then? No. It is still open for all men, albeit differently. A half-hour, stolen from the day's activities or the night's rest, set apart for meditation in his own house, will in the end yield a good result. A useful suggestion for those who cannot get the right conditions at home or in the open air, is to try a church outside of service-hours. It is admittedly harder than trying the same exercise in a peaceful mountain valley, but wherever he is it is his mind alone that counts.

The tranquil passivity he sets out to reach, will eventually deepen and deepen until a point is felt where thinking is still and the mind emptied. Into this inner silence there enters, we know not how, the Overself's godlike consciousness.

Those who spend sufficient time on the mystical quest, and with sufficient keenness and guidance, find it infinitely inspiring because it links them—however remotely weakly and momentarily—with an infinite power, an infinite wisdom, an infinite goodness.

The fruit of such meditations comes in the form of brief glimpses of the soul's flower-like beauty. Although it comes only for a few minutes in most cases, its bloom endures and recurs in memory for years afterwards. Only the adept, he who has travelled far on his inward journey, is able to return at any time, and at will, to the serene beatitude of this high consciousness.

P. B.

January, 1949.

GOOD-BYE!

Good-bye, proud world! I'm going home;
Thou art not my friend, and I'm not thine.
Long through thy weary crowds I roam;
A river-ark on the ocean brine,
Long I've been tossed like the driven foam;
But now, proud world! I'm going home.

Good-bye to flattery's fawning face;
To Grandeur with his wise grimace;
To upstart Wealth's averted eye;
To supple Office, low and high;
To crowded halls, to court and street;
To frozen hearts and hasting feet;
To those who go, and those who come;
Good-bye, proud world! I'm going home.

I am going to my own hearth-stone,
Bosomed in yon green hills alone,—
A secret nook in a pleasant land,
Whose groves the frolic fairies planned;
Where arches green, the livelong day,
Echo the blackbird's roundelay,
And vulgar feet have never trod
A spot that is sacred to thought and God.

O, when I am safe in my sylvan home,
I tread on the pride of Greece and Rome;
And when I am stretched beneath the pines,
Where the evening star so holy shines,
I laugh at the lore and the pride of man,
At the sophist schools and the learned clan;
For what are they all, in their high conceit,
When man in the bush with God may meet.

—*Ralph Waldo Emerson.*

CHAPTER ONE

*The Philosophy of Friendship—On Pony-back in the Himalayas—My
Bungalow on a Mountain-top.*

THE last lap of my journey will soon be over. After weeks of fitful
travelling since I left the torrid triangular patch of South India,
tonight I shall take to my bed with the pleasant consciousness that it
will probably be a long time before the roll of brown blankets and
white sheets is strapped up in its canvas covering again.

Not that the journey itself has not proved a welcome change.
Even the gradual fall of the thermometer helps the sun-baked body,
while the extensive panoramic succession of pictures and places stirs
even the curiosity of the jaded intellect. There is a sense of freedom, a
zest of relief, for a weary European who arrives here after the
suffocating plains, where the summer heat lies like a shimmering
pall.

Best of all, one has had the pleasure of meeting old friends and
making new ones. It is true that a man who bases his friendships on
spiritual affinity, rather than on the ties of self-interest or of worldly
associations, cannot hope to count many, for the dictates of the
Overself must be obeyed and the different degrees of understanding
—as well, I often find, of misunderstanding—themselves erect
unscaleable barriers between those whom God hath not joined
together in the pleasure of friendship.

When I reflect now over the variety of some of the external
appearances beneath which I found this affinity during the present
journey, I am astonished at the possibilities with which life presents
us once we begin to walk in the shoes of the Overself, however
intermittently and however weakly.

A bespectacled merchant in costly silks whose shop fate has set
in a crowded Bazaar; a shrewdly intellectual assistant editor of a
newspaper who talks politics and economics while I sip an iced
drink; an illiterate workman who labours from dawn till night
throughout the week for a meagre wage, and whose tragic poverty
illustrates for me the truth that those who have perspired in the
battle of life, but never bled, do not really know what it means;
a middle-aged noble-minded Maharajah who belongs to the
Victorian epoch in his earnest regard for moral restraints and in his
melancholy observations upon the decadence which is fast over-
taking today's younger generation; a young English headmaster

who is trying, with fresh eyes and fiery enthusiasm, to lift educational methods out of the antiquated ruts in which he found them; a forceful and dominant Minister whose abilities have made him the central figure in the Government of a large Indian State and whose fluent conversation provides me with an intellectual stimulus; a Spiritual Head of an Indian religious fraternity who benignantly ignores differences of belief in the deep regard that ties us to each other; a penniless and possessionless Yogi who meditates on mysterious forces the while he sits upon the Ganges bank beyond Rishikesh, that unique town where recluses, monks and pilgrims make their permanent or temporary abode; with great calmness he tells me how he separated the spirit from the body and found himself witnessing scenes in far-off Calcutta or even hearing the noise of London traffic as he looked down upon it! Then there is a young Bengali lady who has achieved an exceptional height of spiritual realization, and whose face reminds one of the beatitude-filled face of St. Teresa, the while she sits with half-closed eyes surrounded by a large group of devotees; a lean, bent old Muhammedan grey-beard who takes me through dingy Delhi alleys and bazaars to the Jumma Masjid, India's largest mosque, where he discourses to me of his youthful adventures upon the Mecca pilgrimage, and then tells me how he is preparing himself for another kind of pilgrimage, to wit, his exit from this world. He is likeable, this grey-beard, for he does not hesitate to mix a little fun with his philosophy.

There are several others, both known and unknown, who touch my trail so intimately; they are perhaps more mundane in mind, but that does not prevent us being completely at ease with one another. A man must be ready to touch life at many sides if he would really live; even as a great Exemplar did not disdain to consort with the world's rejected and despised sinners; yet always he should do so where the inner attraction is mutual and spontaneous, not otherwise. Not seldom the most startling life-changes come about in this way. One of the first people whom Christ induced to price life at its proper value, or, in common parlance, whose soul He saved, was not a respectable prop of civic authority and civic virtue, but a harlot.

When I was revisiting a certain city after some years' absence abroad a friend there offered to give a little party in my honour to enable me "to meet the leading men of the town". I flatly refused. I had no desire to meet the leading men of any town. Besides, why all the bother! I had done a bit of journalism, a bit of editing, and a bit, I hope, of finer writing in a few books. I had made a few uncommon researches. That was all. Lots of men have done that, and more. Time to give a party when I shall have accomplished something worthwhile, when I shall have climbed the Himalaya of the soul and reached its white summit. And if that ever happens I fear the leading men of the town will not then want to meet me!

There are still others whom I would have liked to meet again, but, alas, time will not tarry. I dare not dally on my northward way. For I have a goal, an objective, one too which is of the highest importance to me.

*   *   *

And so now I am sitting in the saddle astride a sturdy ash-grey mountain pony, listening to the chime of its jingling harness-bells and moving at walking pace up the steep slippery trails that are leading me into the rarefied air of the Himalayan[1] ridges. It would be untrue to say that both of us are not tired and will not welcome the final halt when it comes, nor that the string of coolie-porters who are moving half a mile or so behind me in single file under the leadership of my servant, bearing baggage and provisions, will not be glad to take their agreed pay and last dismissal. Even the pony has developed an unfortunate and unpleasant habit of wandering stupidly to the extreme outside edge of the narrow trail, where a dangerous, sparsely timbered ravine of three thousand feet depth awaits it like a yawning abyss; on the inner side, the path leads against the perpendicular face of the ridge out of which it is carved. It would be extremely easy for the animal to go down the fearfully abrupt slope infinitely faster than it came up, and finally measure its length upon the ground. The idea of sliding all the way down to the ravine bottom does not make much appeal to me. The feeling remains and returns that I must check my steed firmly. I therefore pull frequently at the left rein, but the obstinate pony just as frequently makes for the precipice's edge the whilst I sway in the saddle! I cannot see what attractive bait lures it towards utter destruction, but I have no intention of sharing its impending fate down that precipitous glen.

Why it should want to forsake its subsolar existence at the prime of life I do not really know, but this afternoon it deliberately dangled its right foreleg into space over the precipice edge, with the result that it slipped and stumbled, sending me to the ground with a thud, a bruised hip and painfully dislocated shoulder. I thought that the time had now arrived for the two of us to have a serious, heart-to-heart talk and I endeavoured to point out to the melancholy creature the obvious error of its ways in skirting precipices so obstinately.

[1] Pronounced *Himm-ahl'-yan* (accent on second syllable). The word means "Abode of Snow".

Apparently the conversation did some good, for it raised its sad but handsome head a little higher and thereafter kept its feet on *terra firma*. It set its hooves down with greater care and no longer did a mere hair's breadth separate us both at times from the terrifying drop. I rewarded the pony later with a couple of spoonfuls of my precious sugar, once, alas, so common that it grew thickly in the plains around me, but now to be carefully conserved and thriftily ladled out, lest my supplies should run out before their estimated calendared month and my tea thereby rendered totally unpalatable.

The leader of the coolies has told me that the pony's undesirable habit has been inherited from a Tibetan pack-pony parent, which used to carry huge loads in sacks swung so broadly across its back as to force it to keep away from the inner side of tracks, so that the load might clear the rocks on that side.

The sun has shone directly down all day with a heat that surprises me, yet it is a tolerable and not trying heat, something indeed like the temperature of good August summer weather in Europe. In comparison with the terrific enervating heat of the broiling plains, it is certainly paradisaical.

At a turn in the ever-winding cliff trail, which is climbing higher and higher, a whole new panorama of breath-taking scenic beauty is displayed before my wondering eyes. That Nature could pile up cyclopean peaks and mountain ridges with such a generous hand and in such indiscriminate shapes is something which tame European eyes can scarcely believe. Look where one will, in every direction, one is hemmed in by her Himalayan giants. To the north-east, a realm of perpetual frost, the colossal towering barrier that keeps Tibet a suspicious and secluded alien in a world knit into friendly communication by every conceivable means, rears its crevassed grey flanks, white snow-mantled shoulders and bluish icy head to the sky from the shadowed ravines at its base. Enormous masses of smooth shining snow glitter upon it. To the east, a long irregular line of forest-covered heights and spurs stretches away, tier over tier, until it loses itself in the distant horizon. To the west, I look down into great rugged gorges of greyish olive-green blended with rich brown that meet and unite in a vast bowl of rock and earth thousands of feet below. To the south, I can but raise my head and crick my neck, as I gaze at the uplifted summit of the lofty purple granite cliff which towers above my pony only a couple of feet away from the animal's side, and which dominates the immediate landscape.

All this plethora of camel-backed ridges split by deep chasms, soaring peaks and sharply cut ravines lies strewn confusedly with one branching out of the other or running parallel with it for a length and then twisting off at a tangent to meet it suddenly again.

The map-makers must have had a hard job, here, methinks, amid this heap of endless confusion, harder than amongst the level farms and unfenced fields of the plains. The heights have been thrown up haphazard, just anyhow. There is nothing Euclidean here, not a sign of the straight geometrical layout of New York.

It is strange to remember suddenly that all Himalaya whirls with this ball of ours around the sun at more than eighteen miles per second.

Yet the rugged charm of this display makes it more attractive than any other natural scene I know. I take Nature's gift thankfully. The Gods who made this land must have been beauty-drunk. The wild beauty of the scene outsteps imagination. It inspires the mind and uplifts the soul. Were I a Shelley I would quickly become lyrical over this region, but, alas, I am not. For the lordly Himalayas exist within an aura of complete solitude which is ineffably peaceful and inspiringly grand. In these Himalayan highlands there arises the true charm of mountaineering; civilization is so remote, towns so distant and serenity so prevalent. They carry the suggestion of eternity, although there are hill ranges in the south which, geologically, are far older. The tremendous heights are, perhaps, chiefly responsible for this suggestion. Here one is face to face with the universal mystery itself, hiding behind no man-made façade of gregariously built cities but revealing its calm challenging face directly and assuming its wildest form. Himalaya embodies the grand forces of Nature.

*　　　*　　　*

We continue climbing the narrow track. The steep paths of Himalaya are akin to the steep paths of life itself. But I adventure up the rugged trail with music sounding in my ears. God is luring me on. I am riding, not merely into Himalaya, but into heaven. I have forsaken one world only in order to find a better. No hardships have come to me, none can come to me, for they would first have to penetrate into the region of my heart, and they cannot do that. The air is sweet with love that emanates from the Supreme Being. The mountains are flushed with beauty that belongs, not to them, but to God. The entire journey has become a glorious poetic symbol. The quest of the Holy Grail is its divine reality.

My pony's feet move unsteadily upon the flinty stones, crumbled rock and dislodged granite fragments which intermittently litter the way, having fallen from the slopes above. Fitful patches of grass occasionally survive the stony ground. Sometimes the trackside proudly flaunts a few flowers even. Both mint and marigold are here.

17

On the way I pass a curious sight. A coolie is carrying a lady in a queer conical wicker basket which is tied around his back. The passenger's husband walks behind. Both are pilgrims to some holy Himalayan shrine, although they have not taken the customary route. The lady is not infirm, but the labour of walking steep trails is too much for her.

A mountain spring bubbles slowly across the track out of a rocky cleft in the massive wall of forest-covered slope. It creates a shallow puddle and then drops over the side of the chasm. The pony suddenly stops, drops its head to the ground, and thirstily sucks the puddle. Had I not sensed what it was going to do, I might easily have been tumbled out of the saddle again and down into the gaping ravine. But I take the precaution of dismounting in advance!

From this point the trail keeps fairly horizontal and we move at a faster pace. Nevertheless, because of the winding nature of the country, we have to make considerable detours around the outside of peaks and the inside of valleys; no short cuts are possible.

Fir trees flourish hereabouts upon the mountain side and are held in the tight-coiled grasp of creepers which climb in spirals around their bark. Once I see a solitary rhododendron-tree ablaze with red blossoms, and again a few clustering stars of flower-blooms.

Eventually the sun begins its fated decline, the heat rapidly diminishes, a lustrous yellow pallor sinks over the landscape as the sky turns to transparent amber.

Occasionally a gliding vulture and circling eagle sweep through the turquoise blue sky to their eyries. I notice how the vulture does not fly jerkily like other birds, but with movements exactly like those of an aeroplane. It balances flat on its wings and glides evenly up or down.

Once I hear the cuckoo. Its call makes me think of spring's sure recurrence in Europe.

Sundown brings a rapid change of colours. The peaks and crags of ethereal white which rise to the sky are now warmed by the waning beams into masses of coral and pink; but this is only temporary. The descent of the dying sun transforms the frosted silver of the snows from colour to colour, while suffusing the lower forest-covered ridges with saffron. The red drifts into gold and the gold returns once again to yellow. And when the final rays take their leave, the warm colourings also abandon the range and the snows assume a chalky whiteness. The pallor becomes more pronounced and ends in greyish-white.

Sunset, alas, is but a short interval 'twixt day and night in the East, but these colourful moments are most precious to me.

Soon a shroud of vagueness envelops the whole countryside. But the moon rises early from behind the range and fortunately it is a thick crescent, so that we can see our direction clearly enough under its beams as soon as my eyes become accustomed to the spreading darkness. Nevertheless, when our route takes us, after much twisting and turning, along the top of a forest-clothed ridge, we find ourselves surrounded by blackness and can scarcely pick our way through the trees. At last we emerge into the silvery light once more and then my pony has a three-mile stretch of level visible mountain-side track before it.

The chief practical advantage of such a path, I reflect dryly, is that you cannot possibly lose your way. No signposts are provided merely because no signposts are needed. You may go forward or turn back and retreat, but you cannot go anywhere else—unless, indeed, you know how to scale perpendicular cliffs or to descend abrupt precipices. This is far better than wandering through a strange city, where nothing is easier than getting oneself lost.

Yes, it is the last lap of the journey. We ride through a monstrous yet beautiful ghost-world. Leaves turn to silver in the moonbeams and tree-trunks seem to be carved out of frosted stone. There is something indescribably weird in the picture of pale moonlight on the world's giants. I judge the time to be about nine o'clock, but I cannot tell with exactness, for my wristlet watch has been smashed in the unlucky accident and henceforth I must exist timeless until my return to civilization. Not that it will be any noticeable loss, I decide sardonically, for time and I can well part with each other for a few months. The earth must henceforth turn in its diurnal course unheeded. Moreover, it was better for me to have fallen a few feet than three thousand.

Silhouetted against the black background of the sky, which is now rapidly filling with the first multitude of trembling stars which arrive with their jewels as ambassadors of the night, stands the rising terrace of peaks that crosses the far end of our route transversely and blocks the valley. It is like a line crowded with pyramids. Each is now a wraith-like titan, grand, grim, yet undeniably beautiful. Each mocks at this puny pony-mounted creature that dares to invade its silent realm. For the Himalayas, in this weird light, has become the fabled land of the giants. Here, those fairy stories which cheered our childhood may well come true. It is fitting that I should suddenly detect, on the western horizon, the beautiful star-cluster of the Pleiades in the zodiacal constellation of Taurus. Not an ancient people exists but has its legend of these seven daughters of Atlas who were raised to the heavens and transformed into stars.

I push on more eagerly. It is fortunate that we have sufficient moonlight to guide us, because I see that the forest-hidden nature of the country might quite possibly cause me to miss my destination and override the pony unnecessarily. And this, I am ashamed to confess, does happen. We travel a quarter-mile too far when an uneasy and growing sense of being wrong completely overwhelms me and forces me to dismount and turn the pony's head in the direction whence we have come. My electric torch lies thoughtlessly packed in my baggage. There is no help for it but to make a slow and careful exploration on foot. And after I have done this I discover that the trail almost skirts the top of the ridge at one point, where a little clearing has been made in the dense forest and covers the mountain-side from top to bottom.

I tether the animal to a tree and clamber up the short steep bank to the summit. There, gleaming palely in the moonbeams, are the whitewashed walls of a solitary bungalow set amid a wild yet Arcadian region upon the very crest of the mountains! I have reached my new home.

A few paces beyond the building brings me to the edge of another deep gorge, which abuts on the southern face of the ridge. It is clear that I shall have to walk warily hereabouts in future!

Once more I reward the pony which, despite its legacies of painful injuries to my person, has carried me successfully to this unique and attractive domicile. On this occasion I plunge a hand more deeply into my pocket and it eagerly gobbles up the liberal helping of sugar.

A cold wind comes blowing off the snows, and I turn up my jacket collar.

Overhead, the sky scintillates with its wealth of beauty. Planets wander through the firmament with unnatural brilliancy. The stars, in their high heaven, are like clusters of diamonds upon the crowned hair of night.

And now I sit down beside the path to wait patiently for the party of bearers whom I have outdistanced some hours previously. I fall into a reverie of the night until, after a time, I am awakened by hallooing shouts and cries of welcome. Once again the gregarious sense reasserts itself and I feel pleased that we are all together again. I count my train of coolies, add the servant, and note that all are safe after their journey. Their jolly faces smile in accord with mine when I inform them lightly, "We are seven!" and add a few lines from a certain poem, but they miss the subtle Wordsworthian allusion. Perhaps they imagine I am chanting a prayer to my strange gods, in thanksgiving for our arrival, but I do not know.

The baggage is hauled up the bank and deposited inside the bungalow. Bags are opened, candles and matches are found, and the ceremony of paying off the bearers gone through. They are wiry, well-knit little men belonging to the hill-tribes. They are remarkably strong and sturdy. Coolies drawn from their class can carry a hundredweight load on their backs day after day—not that I have ever given them such an inhuman load, fifty pounds being their average. Yet their diet is often nothing more than rice and parched peas—and not much at that—with a little milk to wash it down.

One wonders how much meat and how many meals a day a European porter would need to eat to support such work. My own coolies have their chief meal in the morning, and only an extremely light one later. These tough tribesmen can stand more heat and cold, weight-carrying and height-climbing, than their slimness suggests as possible.

I forestall their demands for *baksheesh* by giving them a sum which silences their garrulous leader. They will have but a short sleep, they tell me soon, and be off before dawn, taking the pony with them.

My servant opens the bedrolls. Tired and dusty as we are, unfamiliar with our location, we have no time to take further stock of our surroundings but disregard all else and throw our bodies into that mysterious yet ever-welcome condition which the world calls sleep.

CHAPTER TWO

Projected Expedition to Mount Kailas in Tibet—Magnificence of the Snowy Mountain Scenery—I Discover "The Sanctuary".

ONE day a scientist will give us the mathematics of slumber, working out to precise fractions the ratio of the degree of fatigue to the period of unconsciousness. But whatever ratio he produces for the delectation of the curious, I am certain that he will need to revise his figures in the case of the dwellers on the Himalayan highlands.

For both of us awake after a briefer sleep than we normally enjoy, yet more refreshed and more vital than heretofore. It may be that the clean crisp air, when inhaled, assists the body to restore its worn-out functions more rapidly than under other conditions. At any rate, we set about the day's activities at an early hour and light a lamp whilst awaiting the coming of the dawn, when the peaks will show indistinctly against a dark blue sky and rays of the rising sun will then tinge the snowline.

I wander through the bungalow. It is a simple, elementarily furnished place, as befits a lonely abode on the mountains. Three sets of double doors open into my room, one leading from the dining-room, another to the bathroom (no tiled walls and porcelain bath affair, this, but just a bare room holding a zinc tub for cold water), and the third opens directly on the forest. Light enters through glazed panels in the last door.

So this is to be my new home. Suddenly I remember a warning hint that it is haunted, but I take the thought lightly. Even if it once were justified, it cannot be now. I am ready to believe that the departed did show himself in a faintly phosphorescent form once or twice in an effort to retain his foothold on this familiar earth, but I am not ready to believe that he is still here. No ghost can flourish long in this healthy mountain air nor exist without becoming miserably lonely and utterly bored by the lack of appreciation. What encouragement can a poor ghost expect in this lonely dwelling, shut up unused as it is for a few years at a time? A self-respecting ghost needs an audience. And what audience can he expect here— unless it be the pine trees, the shaggy bears or the penetrating winds? No—he needs company, society, if he is to keep his nerves in order. I am sure that I shall find the warning groundless.

And of what shall my activities consist? The principal one is just sitting still! I am quite serious. It is indeed, I must admit, a queer kind of work, the queerest which I have yet undertaken ever since my ship weighed anchor and turned its bow from the British shore; it is certainly not the kind for which anyone will care to pay me a single rupee in remuneration. Yet that is the absolute truth, the sole purpose of my cutting adrift from the generality of men and settling for a while in this unfrequented Himalayan kingdom. I expect no excitements, no hair-raising situations, no perils, in this new adventure of mine.

A mixture of different feelings passes through me. At one and the same time I am exhilarated, awed and reassured. Exhilarated, because I believe that some part of me "belonged" here, has indeed dwelt happily here in some former earth-life. Awed, because I remember that there are more than sixty peaks in the grand chain of the Himalayas over 25,000 feet high, that the tremendous roll of staccato thunderstorms and the restless flickering of bluish lightning constantly disturb these snow-capped gods standing in icy detachment from the human world. Reassured, because although Nature is notoriously inhospitable to man in these regions, a sense of divine protection imperiously sweeps away every fear as it arises.

It will be hard, amid these eternal mountains, to appreciate the value of time and consequently to let the mind rush restlessly about. *"Be still and know that I am God!"*

That is the phrase from the Hebrew Bible. It bids me go to the Himalayas, not as an explorer nor as researcher, but simply to cease my external activities and to tranquillize my mind to the point of utter placidity. I am not even to continue my ancient labours of self-conscious meditation, it counsels, but just to be still!

I am to seek no outer adventures, nor even any inner ones, I am to take Nature as my tutor, to merge my spirit into the absolute silence of her surroundings, and to let every thought lapse away into mere nothingness. I am to become a living paradox, seeking attainment of a higher order of being by the curious method of making no effort! In short, the Psalmist's saying, which I am obeying like an injunction, is to be taken in its literal fullness.

So, in my hunger for the divine presence, I set out on my journey northwards, hardly knowing where my feet will come to rest. For the great range of the Himalaya mountains must be close on fifteen hundred miles in length from end to end. Where, in that strange world, can I find a spot solitary enough yet suitable enough to permit me to merge my inner being into its surroundings?

From time immemorial the best of India's Yogis, sages, and saints have resorted to the forest-clad ridges or icicle-studded caves of Himalaya, to meditate and dwell amid harmonious scenes. It is therefore in line with a good tradition that I imitate their example.

My first thought is of icy Mount Kailas, on the Tibetan side. It is the most sacred spot in all Asia to both the Hindus and the Buddhists of that continent. What Rome is to the Catholic Christians, what Mecca is to the Muhammedans, and what Jerusalem is to the Jews, Kailas is to them. It is their mountain of salvation, the home of their gods and the habitation of their angels. Nirvana is enthroned upon its icicles. I know that this is no mere superstition on their part, for there are profound esoteric reasons in its support. Has our fancy grown so poor and narrow that it can give no place in life and no space in the world for the old gods? Is Mount Olympus but a barren deserted spot to us, which was so well peopled to ancient men? The gods change their names with peoples, but not themselves. Moreover, it has been recommended by the Buddha himself to his disciples as a spot worthy of being chosen by those who want to meditate and attain Nirvana. Just as the cloud-capped top of Olympus hid the Hellenic gods from profane eyes, so the ice-strewn top of Kailas is believed to hide the spirits of departed Buddhas.

The Tibetans name it Kang-Rinpoche, "the Ice-Jewel". Their famous mediæval Yogi, Milarepa, practised his meditations in a grotto on this mountain.

There is a pilgrim route to Kailas through Almora, but I choose a longer and harder route because it is less frequented and more variegated. To travel through its calm solitudes, so far removed from the tensions of peopled places, will be to travel into sanity and serenity out of an insane and uneasy world.

It is true that there will be certain dangers upon the journey amidst the wildness of Trans-Himalaya, but they trouble me for no more than a moment. I have learnt in the school of first-hand experience that the protective aegis of Providence accompanies the man who sets out upon an enterprise at a bidding higher than his own.

*   *   *

Kailas becomes my Canaan, my land of promise. But in New Delhi, where the red tapes of the Central Government meet and are tied into an orderly unity, I discover that I shall not be permitted to cross the Tibetan frontier. Mount Kailas is far too sacred to the Tibetans to allow infidel Europeans to visit it, and under some article of the Treaty of 1908 the British have guaranteed that they will withhold the grant of such permission from Europeans desirous of violating its sanctity by their presence.

Time is precious. I appeal to the Viceroy.

His Excellency has read my book *A Search in Secret India* and, as a direct consequence, paid a visit of inspection to Dayalbagh, the co-operative town on a spiritual basis about which I have there written a chapter. Moreover, His Excellency was so pleased with what he saw that the creator of the town, Sahabji Maharaj, was duly knighted when the next New Year Honours List was published.

But the reply to my request for a special permit is a courteous expression of regret because the Tibetans are so strongly opposed to any European visiting their most sacred spot.

I telegraph to the Secretary of State for India, in London. I have talked to him about my researches; he has expressed his sympathy and he knows of my tact, understanding and discretion in dealing with the religious feelings of Orientals.

The reply is frank and sincere. It will be embarrassing to the Government to make a request to the Tibetan Authorities which will certainly be refused. Moreover, even the making of such a request to them will do nothing to assist me in performing the journey.

The Government will be prepared, however, to obtain a permit for me from the Tibetans to cross the frontier and make an expedition from Kalimpong, near Darjeeling, along the trade route to Lhasa, but only as far as Gyantse, and no farther.

I am disappointed. That the mere colour of one's skin should debar one from making a pilgrimage (for that is what it really amounts to) to Asia's most sacred spot seems to be a fit Nemesis for the colour-prejudice sins of the white race itself. I know more about Buddhism than most Tibetans themselves, for I have studied it long and deeply under one of the most learned and spiritually advanced Buddhist priests, yet I am to be classed as an infidel because my skin happens to be white and theirs yellow!

The permit to travel as far as Gyantse is useless to me. Gyantse lies well inside Tibet and is an important town for the Tibetan traders who come down from Lhasa to India. It is in east central Tibet, whereas Mount Kailas is in the western part of the country. But I am neither trader nor geographer. I do not want to go to Tibet merely to see a few sheepskin-clad traders and a few sleepy beflagged monasteries. I have a higher purpose than that, and Kailas lies at its very core. My time, which is part of my life, must now be utilized for the sake of that purpose, and no other.

I telegraph my news to a Yogi friend who has already been to Mount Kailas. He replies that there is still one way whereby I may make the journey with perfect certainty.

His suggestion is that if I disguise myself as a saffron-robed Yogi, stain my face and hands an appropriate colour, and wear the yellow robe he will himself arrange the rest and accompany me throughout the journey. He guarantees to get me safely across the frontier into Tibet and as far as Mount Kailas, as he has friends along the route.

I refuse his offer. I feel it will not be "playing the game" with Government friends who trust me. The pilgrimage must be made honourably or not at all. Besides, it might lead to awkward political complications.

There exists one last hope, one final card which I have kept up my sleeve.

A Tibetan friend, who is sympathetic to my work and researches, possesses a certain amount of influence in the councils of the Government of Tibet. He has, indeed, already provided me with letters written and sealed in the Tibetan language, introducing me to the Head Lamas of all the monasteries on my route and requesting all local officers to assist me in obtaining the necessary fuel and food, so confident is he that I will be able to make the journey. I have hoped to stay for some time in a monastery situated at the foot of Mount Kailas, and there pursue my meditations in peace.

I send him an urgent message explaining what has occurred.

The suspense of waiting is eventually brought to an end by a pink telegraphic slip. It reads:

Much regret. Consulted Government. Unable influence Lhasa present juncture due internal trouble there.

I accept the words as the fixed fiat of destiny.

"Mount Kailas is within you," my Master has said cryptically a day or two before my departure. Does he know that I shall not reach it? Thenceforward the white cone of Mount Kailas recedes from my objective and I turn my head in another direction.

My acceptance is a sensible if helpless one. For destiny has truly prepared a special place for my meditations and when I search the long rugged line of the Himalayas on the map and let my finger rest on the kingdom of Tehri-Garhwal, where India's sacred river, the Ganges, takes its rise, I feel, as by inspiration, that here must be my substitute for Mount Kailas.

Between the hot plains of British India and the frozen plateau of Tibet lie a chain of States all almost entirely enclosed within the natural boundaries of the great Himalayas. These include Bhutan, Sikkim, Nepal and Tehri-Garhwal. Few white men visit them, for, apart from the lonely, wild and extremely mountainous character of these countries, there are barriers which tend to keep Europeans away. Nepal is almost an entirely independent kingdom, Bhutan the same, while Sikkim is a British protected State. Tehri-

Garhwal, although politically under British protection, has never attracted English residents and remains, under its own Maharajah, to all intents and purposes, as conservatively Indian as it has been for centuries. It is remote from all railways. No tourist and no tripper yet cheapens this land. Moreover, a special permit is required by any European to enter that part of the State which abuts on Tibet. The difficulties of access and travel, the absence of civilized amenities, the lack of modern transport, and the unfamiliarity of the inhabitants with Western ways are things which keep white travellers away, except perhaps for a few rare and ultra-keen sportsmen intent on hunting wild game. But those are the very things which will now attract me. Moreover, the most sacred shrines of India are here. Many stories of the deities, sages and Yogis who have lived in this secluded kingdom have come down from the mists of tradition. Here, if anywhere, I may find a fit spot for my meditations, for it is set amid the world's grandest scenery.

* * *

The cold grey shade that precedes the sun's rising has disappeared. Dawn has spread over the East like a pinkish pearl. When the music of twittering, chirruping, singing and jubilant birds, excited over the event, has somewhat subsided, I get the bags opened. What a varied mass of things have been jammed and welded together! It is really wonderful how much can be stowed away inside a military pattern kitbag! Suits, shirts, shoes, food, papers, lamps and what not disappear down an eyeletted yawning mouth into its voluminous stomach and still it asks for more!

Next I set forth to explore the environment, to make myself more familiar with it, and to select a spot where the onerous task of doing nothing in particular might suitably be undertaken!

Here I am at last, perched on top of a narrow ridge, the dividing barrier between two deep valleys.

My first view is of the forest, my second of the snows. It is a striking and superb scene. My bedroom possesses a back door which opens out to the north-east, and to sight of the grandest heights on the globe. There, above the tops of the fir and deodar trees which literally grow within a few inches of the door, and which are rooted down below on the mountain-side, the long and rugged barrier of snow-covered peaks and pinnacles which separates Tehri State from Tibet towers high above the whole countryside. Some of these slopes are too steep even to afford hold to the snows and these show grey against the prevailing white.

A veritable conflagration of colours blazes across the heavens.

In the slanting rays of the early sun the sky colours reflect themselves in the snows, which assume a delicate rosy tint, then tones of pale pink and old gold. Soon they settle, after a few kaleidoscopic changes, into silver-white masses, freely dappled with grey patches of bare rock, which shine transparently like mother o' pearl.

For one hundred and twenty miles, and, out of the range of my vision, more than one thousand four hundred miles beyond, the line of icy heights can be seen in one vast view stretching to the right and left. It runs in my sight from the Buranghati Pass at sixteen thousand feet, in the north, all the way to Nanda Devi at twenty-five thousand feet, in the east, where it finally closes. Nanda Devi itself towers to an incredible height above all the other peaks like a monstrous church steeple. Here is a solid wall of granite—the loftiest upon this planet—reinforced by a casing of snow and ice hundreds of feet thick, presenting such a formidable face to beholders that one understands readily why the world lets Tibet alone. These massive ridges are the Gibraltar of the plateau beyond them; they are impregnable and, except at a few points, impassable.

White smoke seems to float off a few peaks, as from volcanoes, but it is only the powdered spindrift of feathery snow being driven by the wind across the sky.

Jutting up out of the irregular whitish line I see at once several immensely high summits which crown the range. Nothing much lives, nothing much can live, at their exalted altitudes. Nature has set them like proud monarchs upon their white thrones. No plebeian creature of the animal or human species dare approach and make its home in that regal though sterile domain, save in its valleys. For their snowy heads rise twenty thousand feet and more boldly above the sealine, and they have been generously given to this territory. In the north-east, no less than a group of such giants are clustered together near Gangotri, where the sacred Ganges finds its glacial source. Closer to me is Bandarpunch, another twenty-thousand-feet giant, west of which rises a second of India's mighty rivers, the Jumna. The sacred, sun-kissed peaks of Badrinath, Kedarnath and Srikant continue the jagged skyline and glitter against a cloudless sky.

It is a curious and startling thought that a visitor from another planet who was approaching our earth would notice first of all this serried Himalayan range. For, with hundreds of peaks, at least, more than twenty thousand feet in height, the Himalayas become the most outstanding object on the surface of our own planet! Even the North American Rockies cannot match it, for they possess only a single twenty-thousand-feet mountain—Mount McKinley.

Mantled in forest and snow the heights rise into heaven. I regard them with reverence, with awe and with admiration. But in that blizzard-swept world of deep crevasses and dangerous avalanches, of slithering snow glaciers with boulder-strewn wastes and huge hanging ice blocks, which stretches to right hand and left, there is no place for someone who wants to sit still, untroubled and undisturbed.

The dense forest of straight dark firs and stately deodars stretches away almost from my feet into the deep ravine down below.

What luck! To have an entire forest of Christmas trees at one's door! And each tree carries a load of gifts upon its needled branches —gifts intangible and invisible, maybe; gifts of serenity and quietude! · The tops of these towering trees reach almost to my very door, but their roots are forty or fifty feet down the mountain-side. What the firs lack in girth, they make up for in height. They are lordly and grand in their vivid green garments.

Lichen coats their barks. The ground is thick with fallen brown fir-needles. The creeping plants which entwine themselves around a few of these trunks in front of my door show snow-white blossoms of faintly scented little flowers which brighten the shadowed scene. They spangle the dark foliage like a firmament of shining stars. Among these silent tree-shadows I may find, doubtless, what the towns cannot give—peace, depth and healing. But the gradient is set at an exceedingly steep angle and one can scarcely descend into it without clinging with both arms to each trunk as one passes. Moreover, the sun does not yet penetrate the thick foliage of the innumerable branches; the forest is cold and gloomy; and I, as a sun-lover, must bask in the golden rays. Once again I turn away.

These forests in the kingdom of Tehri provide almost the sole income of the State, so little land being fit for cultivation. They are therefore the State's most valuable possession; and the lumber that is hewn out of them is floated down the rivers during the monsoon rains into British-ruled India for sale to the railways. Forest-inspection officers travel on circuit to supervise this property. In order that they might have some decent shelter and proper accommodation during their circuit, bungalows have been built in lonely parts. Such a bungalow is the one I now occupy, through the courtesy of the State Authorities. An officer is unlikely to use it more than two or three times during the entire year, and then only for a night or two on his travels.

Leaving the door, I walk in the cool crisp air around the bungalow. The narrow ridge on which it stands continues its eastward way for half a mile beyond the clearing and then rises abruptly into a seven-hundred-feet hillock, part of which is bare and stony and the other part freely dotted with small trees. That hillock does not attract me either.

I proceed to the edge of the bluff overlooking what I had thought last night to be a gorge lying behind the bungalow. I peer down and discover that it is really an immense natural basin of terrifying depth. To slither over the side into vacancy is an easy matter. Yet it is singularly beautiful. I feel pleased that my new home should overlook a scene of such grandeur. The declivity is covered with thick deodar forest almost down to the bottom. It is the meeting-place of two dark Scotch-looking glens, whose precipitous sides here widen out to form a circular valley large enough to hold a great peak, should Nature, in a whimsical fit, decide to drop one here-abouts. Thick dark-green forests alternate with brown and purple stretches of bare granite scattered upon its sides. Ridge upon ridge rises in magnificent parallel terraced formation along the eastern side, like gigantic battlements built to repel intrusive man, while tangled hillocks and scarped spurs, more thinly afforested, form the western boundary. Gazing down into the deep and vast gorge-like hollow and letting my eyes rest on its wild rugged slopes, I realize that I need not search farther. Somewhere around this mountain-ringed bowl I shall surely find the ideal spot for my meditations.

A few strokes with a woodman's knife and I convert a fallen five-feet piece of pine into a stout and excellent Alpine hill-stick. The secret lies in sharpening the end, not into an exact point, but into the shape of a boat-keel. Then the final phase of my quest is entered.

Making my way with slow caution up a hillock on the western side, for the climbing of its slippery slope requires a little care, and then clambering over some rocks stuck into its precipitous face, I gradually round the hollow, and pass through a clump of mossy sycamores. The aromatic odour of some mint growing by the way-side reaches me. I halt, bend down and inhale more of this pleasant air. At last I attain the summit. Here, to my astonishment, I find the place freely carpeted with dead autumn leaves. How have they got here? Has some Himalayan whirlwind blown them hundreds of feet into the air and then deliberately deposited them here?

At any rate, these leaves provide a magnificent natural carpet for the hill-top, one which is as comfortable as a thickly woven, hand-made Mirzapur, and certainly not a whit less artistic. An odd cowslip and a few tiny violets flourish into decorative existence among the leaves.

I know that I need travel no farther. The gods have led me to this perfect retreat. The Hindus, like the Tibetans, firmly believe that the Himalayas are the secret abodes of the gods, as well as of those spiritual supermen whom they call the Rishees, who today are supposed to dwell there in invisible etheric bodies. Yes, one of them has brought me hither. It may even be that this unimaginably beautiful and secluded spot is his very dwelling-place. Enchantment creeps upon me.

It is a fact that the broad mountains of this kingdom of Tehri are holy precincts. The Hindus believe that these Himalayan shrines, set in the colossus among mountain ranges, are even more sacrosanct than their holy cities of Benares, Puri and Nasik. Shiva and Krishna and all the other deities have moved here, and something of the spell which they exerted on former men lives on.

Here then is my entrancing brown and emerald mountain sanctuary. And there, among the massed leaves, my waiting, topaz-coloured prayer-rug! Twice a day, at the favoured times of dawn and dusk, I shall climb its steep face with the aid of my stick, and then settle down to learn how a man might arrive at the art of being still and, perchance, even ultimately know God.

Himalaya shall be my novitiate for heaven, and in these grand solitudes I may prepare myself for the sublimer solitude of God.

CHAPTER THREE

A Meditation on British Rule in India and on Political Strife—Necessity of Spiritualizing Politics—The Control of Thoughts—A Secret of Concentration.

LATE in the afternoon I return up the steep gradient to my sanctuary. The hill-stick serves its purpose well even if it is not so perfect as a regular mountaineer's staff with iron-pointed tip. I pick out a spot where I may sit down and think quietly, as a prelude to the inner stillness which I hope to invoke with the eventide.

I take my seat close to the very edge of the cliff, for thence one can look down into the great tree-girt valley and see most of its sublime grandeur. The place suggests cloistral peace. If serenity can be attained anywhere on earth, this is indeed one region among the few. This unspoilt border State, where the ancient Hindu gods have walked, seems quite apart from the rest of India.

My gaze comes to rest at last upon the curving branches of a lofty deodar, whose aged trunk is heavily covered with brownish-green dank moss and with long tufts of ragged lichen like a beard. It grows but a few feet away from and below my seat, and leans forward at a slight angle from the cliff-side. The sunbeams filter through its foliage. There is not very regular symmetrical growth of the branches, as with pine-trees, and the clustered needles which form the foliage droop sadly towards the ground. Nevertheless there is quite an air of faded aristocracy about the old dark tree, while its leaves still waft the peculiar fragrance which betrays its primal relationship with the Syrian cedar. I remember that the Mogul Emperors used the wood of deodar trees to heat the water for their baths, and for the baths of their harem favourites, because of its unusual scent. Two tiny mountain flowers kiss the venerable foot of the deodar with their fresh young petals. Most spiritual of all trees, legend makes the deodar the favourite of the gods.

I fancy that we shall get to know each other well, this tall graceful deodar and myself, and even attain an intimacy of firm friendship which my inevitable departure one day shall be unable to break. At any rate, we must henceforth companion each other for a long time, for such are the dictates of destiny. I shall whisper my heart-hidden secrets to you, O patriarchal deodar, and tell of those vanished joys and terrible tribulations which a man can never commit to public gaze, writer though he be. And you too shall speak to me, albeit in tones so low that the world will sneeringly say that I am deluding myself. But we shall both laugh pityingly at the world and forgive it, because we know well that although Nature is the common mother of us all, the world still remains darkly ignorant of her tightly held secret.

My thoughts drift back to sultry India, to the land which I have left behind. In the cities of the distant plains, where one's hand placed upon a stone parapet in the sun has to be hastily withdrawn, so scorched is it, and where the few white sun-stewed men who cannot escape from feet-imprisoned duties are reeling in the haze of summer heat and being pestered by voracious mosquitoes, the stress of political agitation has temporarily diminished, because it is difficult. to work up enthusiasm for far-off ideals in a temperature of one hundred and ten, no matter how much you may fancy yourself to be an idealist.

The mystery and meaning of the British conquest of India is something that no Briton and no Indian has ever explained satisfactorily, because none has ever examined it with inner vision but without racial prejudice. I think that if British rule is as black as it is painted by many Indians, emigration is the only resource for them! I equally think, however, that if the subject race is such a difficult one as it is painted by British officials, emigration is the only thing for them too! Time alone, through the amplitude of its perspective, may help both to understand why this huge sub-continent was the meeting place of such widely different races.

Life is unlikely to have thrown the two people across each other's path in this strange manner without some purpose.

Have they a service to render each other?

The couple of centuries during which Western civilization has been lapping at the shores of India must be rounded out by a couple of decades more before the world shall see the answer.

Meanwhile politicians have created a new profession for young educated India, and the cry for independence, for the British authority to leave the shores of their country, makes itself vociferously heard wherever they forgather. The young cultured Hindu who dresses like the moderns but thinks like the ancients is fast disappearing. The trouser which he wears today becomes a symbol of the titillation to which he is subjecting his religion, his Government, his customs and his environment. On the other side, in the military cantonments and civilian clubs, in the red sandstone buildings of the Government Secretariat at New Delhi, scornful Anglo-Saxons, with all the stubborn courage of their race, are determined to hold the bridge during their generation, anyway. Destiny, as usual, will have the last word to say in the matter. She will write her own

33

solutions, which, upon her dark mysterious scroll, again as usual, will be the wisest. "Time's the king of men," says wise Shakespeare. "He's both their parent, and he is their grave: And gives them what he will, not what they crave!" For there is a higher Power which over-rules the ambitions and aspirations of men.

I possess my own prophetic anticipations of what is going to happen in India, but in a world where national and racial prejudice is king it is not always tactful to tell the truth. I do not wear, and I do not want to wear, any political label. It is true that to be un-labelled nowadays is deemed heresy and weakness, is to invite neg-lect, but to don the prophet's mantle is full of danger. Both Britisher and Indian would mistake and narrow down my attitude, and certainly misunderstand my prediction. Therefore it is better to bide my time and keep silent. Meanwhile I want to see East and West appreciate each other more, and I try, in my humble way, to be a harbinger of goodwill between both. Why should I waste my time, with millions, in railing and ranting against the defects of established society? Rather should I do a little constructive work.

There is another risk for me should I venture to make political prophecies in this country, which seethes with Oriental intrigue and suspicion. I am reminded of a little-known incident of the last war as I think of this danger.

That much-admired, much-maligned and much-misunderstood man, the late Colonel T. E. Lawrence, reached a critical period of his campaign in Arabia, encountering stubborn obstacles that were not to be overcome easily.

But by a flash of his famous genius he hit on the novel idea of sending a request to London for professional stage magicians to be sent out to travel among the tribes on the borders of the Red Sea and Mediterranean. They were to be, if possible, of Arab birth themselves, and familiar with the customs and beliefs of the tribes-men. Their work was to pose as native wandering fakirs, to perform magical feats and thus gain a reputation for their supernatural powers. On the strength of this reputation they were to assume the gift of prophecy and predict the sensational defeat of the Turks, thus inducing the Arabs to throw in their lot with the British. Five men were accordingly sent out to the Near East on this mission, three being of Arab birth, one an Arabic-speaking Frenchman, and one an Arabic-speaking Englishman specially trained in stage magic for this part. They did good work for Lawrence and helped to influence many Arabs, but the Frenchman and another member of the party were detected and paid the penalty of their lives.

* * *

Not that there is any real end to the turbulence of political clashes and the harassments of racial differences. We shall have a pacified world when we have pacified hearts—not before. The ancient sages who gave this simple formula to mankind are nowadays denounced as impractical idealists. But if the final test of a policy is its results in material affairs, we must confess that this peaceless world has not improved on them. The spiritual emptiness of our epoch and the poverty of our inner resources express themselves clearly enough in the chaos, the distress we see everywhere around us, and the dolorous servitude which we give to unworthy ideals and unworthy men.

The world's development of egotism and intellect has given it a fictitious sense of practical wisdom. But the sages who spoke to former times spoke out of a knowledge of humanity's history profounder and more accurate than any which our book-delving historians can ever hope to have. For the paltry few thousand years which we can record—and that with much guesswork—represent but the tail-end of mankind's lengthy past. When a man—he never pretended to be anything more than that—like Buddha proclaims and re-proclaims that "Hatred ceases not by hatred; hatred ceases only by love", he is not a mere sentimental idealist voicing his well-meaning but futile emotions. He is every whit as practical as the business man who keeps his ears glued to the telephone and his eyes to the papers on his desk. For Buddha, like all great sages of his status, sees the pitiful tangle of wars without end that dismayed the prehistoric epoch as it has dismayed the historic epoch. He sees these things in the universal vision of the planet's past which the gods hold before him, as in a mirror. And he is shown how the threads of cause and effect in humanity's affairs are tied by invisible hands in such a way that an inescapable justice, an equalizing readjustment, is forever at work. He sees, too, that a spiritual Power is back of the universe whose expression in one form is a sublime benevolence, and that this power is eternal. He knows that hatred brings pain, both to the hated and the hater, and that therefore both hatred and its corollary of suffering can never cease until benevolence takes its place. And because the Power which prompts us ultimately to practise benevolence is an eternal one, and above all an inescapable one, he preaches the advisability of yielding to it now and thus saving much needless suffering. Is he or the hater unpractical?

Precisely the same vision of life is given to Jesus. In a world of dry formalists and barren religionists, given over to the doctrine of an eye for an eye and a tooth for a tooth, Jesus condenses and reaffirms this truth. He, too, is shown the vision of the universe and the laws which secretly govern the beings who dwell upon it. Not for nothing has he disappeared into the mountains, where he sits in the paralysed immobility of meditation. And not long after his return he rebukes the visionless Pharisees and heals the man with the withered hand; he says, in impassioned and inspired words, to the multitude which has gathered around him:

"Bless them that curse you, and pray for them which despitefully use you. . . . Judge not, and ye shall not be judged: condemn not, and ye shall not be condemned: forgive, and ye shall be forgiven. *For with the same measure that ye mete withal it shall be measured to you again.*"

He knows.

But the world of surface-seeing men does not know, does not understand, and so blunders on its blind pain-bringing way. Bitter antagonisms will yield to wise co-operation only when this unwritten law is understood, that whatever a man does towards another is ultimately reflected back to him from some source or other. Universal benevolence is therefore the wisest and most sensible policy. In this troubled age it is our immediate and intimate concern.

Yet who wants moralizings and preachings today? They can only earn an easy laugh against me. It is futile to preach to the converted, for those who believe these things do not need to be told, whilst those who lack the faith will not listen anyway. Destiny will take charge of the nations and teach them what they need to learn. The most practical course open to me is, therefore, to concentrate my energies and direct my attention into a channel where they can be most economically used.

Such a channel exists in myself. The best starting-point from which to reform the world is undoubtedly my own self. The best way to spread the spirit of benevolence is to begin with myself. Let me, then, compose my thoughts and silently repeat the Buddhist formula for world well-being, whose spirit if not whose words is:

"To the four quarters of the world, I send compassion. To the north, south, east and west, above and below, I send compassion. To all living creatures upon the earth, I send compassion."

My mind softly dwells upon this gentle theme; the emotion of pity passes through me; and when the final benedictory word is pronounced, I feel no less blessed myself.

The face of one of my bitterest critics rises suddenly before me. I hear her speak her acidulous words as plainly as though she were physically present, yet I am aware she is in a different continent. Knowing what I know and keeping my secrets well, I generally refuse to dally words with misunderstanding in whatever garb it appears, and pass it by with silent indifference. But today I smile forgivingly at her lack of comprehension, and wish her well. I gaze into her eyes and bid her bitter soul find truth, and with it, sweetness and light. Three times I bless her and then interpose a psychic wall between me and her thoughts.

A dragon-fly glides by me on gossamer wings.

* * *

And now the chilling of the air which preludes dusk warns me to cease my meditations and to match my physical stillness with a mental one. I look around—the sun has begun to dip behind the mountains, which lose their warm flush and return to shadowed pallor.

I sit in rigid repose, the while I let the world drift slowly out of the field of awareness, the while I turn attention inwards. Somewhere within me dwells the Overself, the eternal essence, that divine being whence I draw my life-force.

"Be still," my Master has adjured me, "and then you will know the Overself, for God and the Overself are as one."

My breathing slows. For a single minute I fix all my attention upon the movement of the respiration. The effect of controlling it purposefully is to bring the in- and out-breaths into rhythm, into cadence and quieter activity, gentler and less abundant.

The brain is like a wheel which endlessly revolves, picking up fresh thoughts with every revolution. Now I watch the wheel slow down. The more I hold to my resolve to press attention deeply inwards towards a central point, the more my thoughts diminish in frequency and length. I know that I may find, in this repose of the intellect, a way towards wisdom.

I remember what a powerful Yogi teacher, of whose attainments I possess an extremely high opinion, once said to me. He lives in a little room inside an ancient and picturesque temple. Whilst I sit chairless on the floor, he reclines with half-closed eyes upon a cotton-covered bench, from which he seldom moves. We are talking of the difficulty which beginners experience when attempting to learn how to concentrate the mind. The adept remarks:

"If we assume that the average number of thoughts which pass through a man's brain during a given period is one hundred, and if he succeeds in reducing it by constant practice in regulation to eighty, then we may say that he has gained the power of concentration of mind to the extent of twenty per cent. Therefore the most direct way to obtain such concentrative power is to practise the lessening of the number of one's thoughts."

37

And with the slower working of my brain, yet with all attention not a whit less alert, I begin to feel a profounder peace enveloping me. The prolonged concentration of thought has ultimately induced a finer state to arise inside. How sorry I feel for the city dwellers who are subject to turmoil without end! Why should they make the intellect supreme? Yet their way of escape cannot inwardly be different from mine. Minds, exasperated by the inevitable frictions and disappointments of daily life, may find in the respite gained by mental quiet a soothing and healing serenity that will anóint their wounded nerves with balm.

The intellect is but an instrument and not the essential being of man. It is not self-sustained. It is an automatic and routine faculty. Modern man represents the triumph of mechanistic intellect over mere instinct, just as future man will represent the triumph of divine intuition over mere intellect.

Reason, which may be a good guide at times, may also be our betrayer at other times. Not always by prudent forethought may we best be led, but also by the spontaneous upwelling of inspiration. Reason is purely arithmetical, whereas intuition is an unfoldment from we know not where. The advance of intuition upon our thought is not mathematically measurable. It enters the mind unannounced, as by a private door. It is not a thought but an influx from a superior realm which seeps into thought. It is not an emotion—unless indeed it be emotion utterly purified from the personal. But alas, most of us attach little or no importance to the faint heralds of dawning intuition.

The comparative stillness which surrounds me now may not be, nay, is not, the utter stillness which I long to attain, for not a few slow-walking thoughts contrive to meander around inside the emptied halls of my brain. To be really still is to be centred. Nevertheless, I shall be contented with it today and not attempt to cross the mystic frontier.

I know that these intruders are alien to the essential being of man. I know that when all thoughts are let go, when they die off like lotus flowers in midwinter, the divine reality begins to arise. The mere resolve and consequent effort to turn one's attention inwards immediately arouses them to a fierce struggle for their own existence. Their grip on man is more tenacious than he normally realizes, for it is the result of long hereditary ingrained habit passed down through the race. They hold him mercilessly, enslave him in a manner which he rarely understands, and deprive him of the liberty that already exists in his unknown inmost nature. I have watched in myself the processes by which thought moves and I have discovered them to be mechanical.

I have come to the Himalayas to declare further war on these invisible antagonists. Not that I cannot keep them at bay when I set out determinedly to do so; not that I am unaware of those theoretical and practical secrets whose application may give me a good victory; not that I even lack powerful personal aid in these undertakings. But I have kept these invaders at bay only for a time, whilst my victories have never given me more than a temporary respite. Such is their ancestral power over man. The spiritual summit of my life has yet to be attained. The time has come, however, to stage another pitched and continuous battle with them until one or the other combatant retires from the field.

No better setting for this battle may be found than these remote and lonely Himalayan wilds. In none of the many countries which I have visited—for I only feel at home when I am abroad!—have I found an atmosphere so conducive towards spiritual tranquillization as in these mountains to which my destiny has finally brought me. Here, best of all, can one realize, make real, the saying of the Psalmist, "Be still, and know that I am God."

No better method may be practised—for me, at any rate—than sitting down and being still. No Government permit is necessary to enter the divine domain which lies just beyond the Himalayan barrier of intellect. No greater help is procurable from men than that which has been promised me by my Master. His power is such, I know, that the two thousand miles or less between us dwindle to a mere two feet at his will.

What more can I require?

But the shadows of twilight have crept in the sanctuary like a shy maiden creeping into her lover's house. Even the pink after-glow of sunset has disappeared. Day has wearied and soon the starlight will kiss the summits to sleep.

What, I wonder, is the mysterious quality in dayfall which makes it so attractive to me? Why, when all the great teachers and great Yogis of the past counsel men to meditate at daybreak do I follow my own instinct and select the opposite pole of the day for my favourite period of mental quiet? Every scientific fact, every esoteric principle, every rational argument is on their side. Yet dusk is the hour that helps me most. I must accept the beauteous revelation which comes at this still hour, and not be a mere copier of others.

The twilight, then, shall one day provide my destined moment of final liberation. The exile has begun his homeward journey.

I rise, for it is time to return to my forest-embowered bungalow.

CHAPTER FOUR

My Quest of Inner Stillness—The Remembrance of Former Births—A Buddhist Method of Tapping Pre-natal Memory—Nature's Purpose with Mankind—On Unity with Nature.

FOR several days now I have been making my ascent to the imposing natural amphitheatre which is my sanctuary, despite the constant pains in my back. I have faithfully kept my tryst with stillness. The deodar begins to unbend from his aristocratic stiffness and welcomes me as our acquaintance grows. Before long he will admit me into the sacred circle of friendship, without a doubt. The russet leaves have made a little clearing for me, as though to intimate to the world that this place is specially reserved for someone who wants to be still. The few tiny-headed mountain flowers glisten in the sunlight and their yellow and heliotrope discs of petals vie with each other to dispel their faint scent and make the air sweeter. Even the finely antlered hind, which fled with extreme fright but a week ago, has now peeped at me for a full minute, twitching its broad ears and moist nose, before making off into the lonesome forest. Yes, I am getting on.

Nevertheless, I have made no undue effort to crush my recalcitrant thoughts at one fell swoop. I take my meditations quietly and when I relax after them I let the thoughts simmer down without abnormal pressure on my part. I feel that there is no need to hurry, despite the time limit set to my sojourn by the Himalayan climate itself, let alone by my duties to the world. "Patience is the key of joy, but haste is the key of sorrow," my leisurely Arab friends used to say rebukingly, when I moved among them with all my Western speed. Here, somehow, I see that they are right. I feel that there will never be any need to worry about the result of my little adventure, because even if it should be complete failure to attain my aim, there will yet be a Higher Power which has taken me into its care, and its decisions may unrebelliously be accepted.

I do not want to strive for further growth in spirituality. I feel as poor lung-racked Keats felt about his art when he said, "If poetry comes not naturally as leaves to a tree, it had better not come at all."

Today the prelude to my meditation takes a trite theme—trite, that is to say, for the East, but perhaps unfamiliar to the majority of Western people. The doctrine of successive re-embodiments of the

40

soul, which Pythagoras called metempsychosis and which the Buddhists and Hindus of Asia call rebirth, is as old as the oldest prehistoric people which ever existed.

Hardly an Asiatic—unless he happens to be a Muhammedan—but accepts this doctrine as a fact in Nature, such is the power of inherited belief! Hardly a Westerner but imagines that his single earth-life is the be-all and end-all of his physical existence; such again is the power of inherited belief!

In the realm of spiritual and psychic mysteries the Oriental people have an immense fund of knowledge which has been handed down by tradition, a fund still superior to that which exists in Europe and America, partly for the simple reason that the latter continents have raced ahead in material and intellectual development and have had to disdain the less tangible things in consequence, and partly because the Eastern races are so much older in point of time. It is true that the Oriental traditions have now become inextricably intertwined with the parasitic creepers of superstition and fable, but the original tree is still there. Not that this knowledge was broadcast to the masses, for it was kept in the hands of the few.

Even in India, despite her degeneration and abasement, spirituality still exists among more than a few.

So long as a mere sense of colour snobbery debars us from entertaining the thought of accepting instruction from a teacher belonging to the brown race, so long we Western folk shall be unable to find the highest teaching. For, as in ancient times, from the days of Buddha to those of Jesus, the best wisdom has enfleshed itself in a few Oriental bodies.

At first glance the notion that he has lived on earth before strikes the average Western man as ridiculous, although the Oriental has never dreamt of disputing the correctness of his forefather's knowledge on this point.

The learned Buddhist monk who instructed me in Buddhism told me once of a psychological method which had been originally taught by the Buddha himself and which had been practised in his own monastery with definite results. By this method it was possible to discover one's former embodiments. Part of the daily practice consisted in turning memory backwards from day to day, from week to week, from month to month, until the events of a whole year were thus recovered. Later, the preceding years were similarly brought back to memory, little by little. Finally, a marvellous power of both memorizing and visualizing was thus developed and flung back to the years of infancy. Incredible though it seem, everything leading right back to the birth-date could then be remembered.

Psychologists, hypnotists and psycho-analysts have almost made

a fetish nowadays of declaring that the whole of our past life lies
etched in the memory of the subconscious mind. If that is true, then
a mental exercise which drags out the earliest infantile events into
the light of remembrance is not so far-fetched after all. The dis-
coveries of Abnormal Psychology are clearing the way a little.

But my Buddhist monk did not stop there. He said that the
abnormally sharpened faculty of remembrance was then flung
across the gate of birth, in their practice, and lo!—it brought the
memory of quite another person, of the previous existence on earth!
Every detail, from the former death to the former birth, could be
traced out by continuing this queer psychological process.

The monk admitted that the concentration involved was fearfully difficult and that few Buddhists were ever able to go far with
the method. He had himself practised the meditations for twenty
years and could testify to their effectiveness. But the most prolonged
efforts were needed to wrest these memories from reluctant Nature.

I have neither the desire nor the competency to dogmatize in the
matter, but in the light of this explanation one must smile satirically
at the crop of Queens and Cleopatras which has swiftly followed the
trail of this doctrine of re-embodiment, since the latter has appeared
in the West. Every half-baked psychic steps in where the more
experienced Oriental fears to tread! Remembering bygone existences
is not so easy as that. Nature has not put a thick veil over them for
nothing.

Hardly anyone in the lands from whence I come is likely to give
the Buddhist method a trial, because hardly anyone is prepared to
sacrifice some hours daily for half a lifetime merely to revive dead
memories. The game, quite frankly, is not worth the candle. Like
Nature, we realize that the vanished past is less worthy of our
deepest efforts than the living present. It would be unprofitable to
drag these pictures out of their shadowed cave.

But this is not to say that such memories may not come as a gift.
I have had them, most unexpected, extraordinary, and strangely
apposite. Yet, because such memories can never provide valid proof
for another, it is futile to talk about them. In this connection the
aphorism of the almond-eyed Chinese sage may well be applied:
"Those who know, do not speak; those who speak, do not know!" I
can say only that if, by the grace of God and the Peninsular and
Oriental Steam Navigation Company, I tread Asiatic soil today, I
have also trodden it in anterior lives.

*　　　*　　　*

My thoughts are disturbed by a strange swishing sound. Something or someone is moving up the cliff-side towards me. I cannot tell,

by the mere sound, whether it is human or animal, but I remain perfectly still. Soon a pheasant advances into my line of vision. Its body is azure blue; its tail light brown. The bird takes a single glance at me and turns affrightedly, rushing down into the valley at tremendous speed. It makes a great clucking and screams with excitement. Callers, evidently, and especially human ones, are quite rare here!

Because this doctrine of re-embodiment comes generally linked up with the uncomfortable notion of fatalistic retribution, many Western people shy at it like a frightened horse. "What!" they exclaim, horrified. "You expect us to suffer for the sins of others? How unjust!"

Why not?

The whole question hinges on who we are.

If we are nothing more than physical bodies, then the objection is perfectly fair. If we are merely flies fluttering across this planet for our brief day and gone, then the West is right. If, however, we are souls revisiting this world again and again, then the request to settle up in one earth-life the sins we have committeed in another possesses a certain rough justice about it. Then, the destiny which puts its imprint on our lives becomes no blind arbitrary force.

I believe, nay, I know, that man's destiny is with God, and not with the worms. The brain does not generate thought, the body does not generate the soul, any more than the wire generates electric current. Both brain and body are only conduits, carrying a finer and subtler force into this dense material world.

If we are mere flesh-beings, and nothing more, then it would certainly be unfair to ask our atoms, slowly transformed and redistributed after death into other beings, to atone for our wrong-doings.

But we are that, plus something more. That something more is Consciousness. Really, we are conscious minds interwoven with the bone and flesh of the body.

Those minds represent the summation of our characters, tendencies and capacities. They are the real sources of our acts because they are our real personalities, not the bodies. If we believe that they do not vary greatly from birth to birth, then it is not difficult to see that the personality which has to adjust agony given out in one embodiment by agony received in the next is suffering for its own sins and not another's.

But a doctrine which declares that every action must bear its fruit, and that personal embodied life must continue again until the consequence is worked out, is quite reasonable. It dovetails well with all the other natural laws which every scientist detects in the physical

43

world. It certainly is more consoling than the idea that life is but a lottery where prizes are few and pitfalls are many. There is a tide of events which flows resistlessly above our personal wills. The higher laws put themselves into execution; we need not worry. What is unreasonable is the lamentable and listless hopelessness into which the Indian people often fall, aided and abetted by the relaxing enervating effect of tropical climate.

The futility of a merely physical view of things becomes more apparent when this question of life's justice or injustice is reflected on. We ignore the mental side of life as being of lesser importance when all the time, in Nature's eyes, it is the *causative* side.

Nature certainly seems "red in tooth and claw", as the materialists say. But Nature is our mother. What mother punishes her children except educatively? Nature is as real and as living as any human mother. For this planet has a directing Intelligence back of it, as the slightest glance at the mineral, plant and animal kingdoms will show. And what have we done to Nature that she should wish to chastize us for other than educative purposes? And how could her scheme of education be carried out with only a single earth-life?

Then what is Nature's aim in this scheme? Dare I say it? Is it too far-fetched for the ears of flesh-framed minds? How can this all-too-distant goal be described in words that shall make it seem at all attainable and at all rational?

Suffice to hint that Nature's effort is to detach us from entrapment in the material world and to restore us to the primal places of the spirit whence we have descended. Or, in Biblical allegory, to admit us once again to the Garden of Eden.

If we have tied ourselves to this wheel of existence which Destiny turns, we may also untie ourselves. That is Nature's desire and will constitute our happiness. Our worldly worries may drag us back to pessimism, but Nature draws us to peace. We must retire from the periphery of this earthly case of ours to the centre, from complete extroversion to a balanced introversion. But so long as we have not found our centre, we lie ever at the mercy of coming events. Those alone dwell upraised above care and fear who dwell in the centre.

These words sound platitudinous. They are. For, since the world's earliest epochs, they have been repeated in some form or another by every great Seer, every great Sage, and they will be so repeated until the last day of the æon. No other explanation of Nature's aim has ever endured or can endure so long, because it is the answer which she herself gives to those who know how to query her aright. One fact is preferable to forty hypotheses; this is Nature's fact.

The material frame of this universe must one day dissolve, and our bodies with it, yet *we* shall remain.

But sufficient unto the day is the writing thereof!

*   *   *

It might do some men, including myself, good to model themselves after these skyward-soaring rocky heights, to find their stability, their fixity, their strength. Do not these mountains rise in symbolic significance as a lesson to weak mortals?

Lately, my excursions into stillness have led to a distinct sense of closer touch with my surroundings. In the poet Shelley's phrase, I feel "made one with Nature". When I sit on my cliff-edge with untimed patience, letting the beauty and serenity of my surroundings seep into my being, I begin to feel that I, too, have become a part of the quiet landscape. I am absorbing into my nature the stillness of Himalaya. My body seems to grow up out of the brown stony earth much as some small tree might have grown up. I squat on the ground rooted like the deodar tree before me. The life which throbs through my veins seems to be the same life which runs in the sap of the plant world around me. Even the solid mountain itself is no longer a mere mass of hard crystalline rock and thin patchy soil, but a living growth obeying directive laws no less than my fleshly body obeys them.

And as this unifying spirit penetrates me more and more, a benign sense of well-being appears to be one result. I and all these friendly trees, this kindly earth, those white glistening peaks which rim the horizon, are bound up into one living organism and the whole is definitely good at its heart. The universe is not dead but alive, not maleficent but benevolent, not an empty shell but the gigantic body of a Great Mind. I feel sorry for those materialists who, quite honestly but upon limited data, find Death to be the king of the world and the Devil to dwell at the heart of things. Could they but still their over-active brains and align themselves with Nature's panoramic personality, they would discover how wrong they are.

Nevertheless, with the latest findings of advanced scientists in our hands, only dullards and doctrinaires can support the theses of materialism.

The mysterious manner in which this growing sense of unity commingles with a sense of utter goodness is worth noting. It arises by no effort of mine; rather does it come to me out of I know not where. Harmony appears gradually and flows through my whole being like music. An infinite tenderness takes possession of me, smoothing away the harsh cynicism which a reiterated experience of

45

human ingratitude and human treachery has driven deeply into my temperament. I feel the fundamental benignity of Nature despite the apparent manifestation of ferocity. Like the sounds of every instrument in an orchestra that is in tune, all things and all people seem to drop into the sweet relationship that subsists within the Great Mother's own heart.

I begin to perceive why my honoured Master makes no suggestions for a special kind of meditation and gives no mystic formula to be pondered upon and unravelled. He wishes me to make no effort to arrive at some higher position, but simply to be effortless. He does not hold up some picture of what I have to become, but merely says, *be*! In short, it is a matter of doing nothing in order to allow something to be done to me.

We humans have become so self-important and so self-conceited in our own eyes that it does not occur to us that the Great Mother who bears us so patiently upon her earthy breast, feeds us with such abundant variety of foodstuffs, and takes us back again when we are sufficiently tired, has a purpose of her own which she wishes to achieve in us if we will but let her. *We* have set up our schemes and projects, *we* have decided what we want to get from life, and *we* are thinking, striving, struggling and even agonizing in our efforts to obtain the satisfaction of our desires. If, however, we devoted a quarter of our time to ceasing from self-efforts and quietly letting Nature's mind permeate our own, we might make a wise revision of the catalogue of things wanted, yet at the same time secure Nature's co-operation in obtaining them.

The world is but an enlarged hotel, where we are lodged and fed by Mother Nature, pay our bill and then pass on.

For Nature has a will to outwork in us and only by desisting for a time from the continuous exercise of our own wills can we acquaint ourselves with her purpose. If, however, we do this we may learn with surprise that she also has a way of silently yet forcefully attaining this end before our eyes, once we help her by such selflessness. And then her aims and our aims become one, interblent. Ambitions are then transmuted into aspirations and the things we once wanted to achieve for our own individual benefit alone become achieved, almost effortlessly, *through* us for the benefit of others as well. To co-operate with her in this way is to give up carrying the burden of life and to let her carry it for us; everything becomes easy, even miraculous.

I have seen these truths before, but now, in my mountain sanctuary and in closer tie with the Mother, I see them with startling clarity.

A poet has said that Nature is the garment of God. Yes, but to me

Nature is indistinguishable from God. I know that when I am revering Nature I am not soliloquizing; someone receives my reverence. If God is the Grand Architect, then Nature is the Master Builder of this universe, in the Freemasonic system of our world.

My Master explains the futility of separative self-effort by an effective simile. He asks, "What would you think of a man who entered the compartment of a railway carriage whilst carrying a trunk on his head, and who then sat down on his seat but refused to put the trunk down on the floor? Yet people refuse to surrender the burdens of their existence to God, insisting on carrying them themselves under the delusion that no one else can carry them, just as the man in the train was under the delusion that it was not the train but himself who carried the trunk. So, too, God who supports this earth supports us and our burdens and carries all along with Him."

How many of our sufferings arise, then, from our resistance? Nature places a gentle finger upon us at first but we turn roughly away. The call to entrust our lives to a higher Power comes in the softest of whispers, so soft that unless we withdraw for a while and sit still we can hardly hear it, but we stop our ears. Submission, which would bring us peace, is farthest from our thoughts. The personal self, with its illusive reality, deceives us, and, deceiving, enchains us.

All of which is but the price we pay for our desertion of Nature's way. With her, harmony; without her, discord and consequent suffering.

I cannot adequately explain the reverence in which I hold Nature. It is to me the universal temple, the universal church. I hear in South India much ado and much agitation by the pariahs and the depressed castes because the Brahmins will not admit them to their temples. The worst forms of "untouchability" are rampant in the South as nowhere else in India. The old caste system was a perfectly sensible arrangement in the old days. The scholar formed the head of the social body, the warrior was its arms, the tradesman and peasant its body, the labourer its feet. We cannot be all head or all feet. But today that arrangement of castes has lost its force, has become disorganized and oppressive, so that there are many millions subjected to cruel and contemptuous indignities. If the Brahmins were sensible they would turn their prohibitions of the outcaste into social or hygienic ones, but not religious. We may understand and accept the refusal of a duke to sit with a dustman in a public building, but when he says that he refuses by order of God and not by that of his sense of refinement, it is time to call a halt to nonsense. Were I the leader of these unfortunate Hindu outcastes, I would say to them: "Cease this degrading agitation and insufferable heartburn

47

over something which may not be worth having. Nature has given you a real temple, where God is just as much present as in that old pile of greasy shrines and rite-ridden stones yonder; come away into the forests and the hills or even into a bare room, and I shall show you a God these others rarely find!"

Nature's voice is to be heard within; her beauty may be discerned without; but her beneficent harmony lives both within and without us.

If I did not feel this by present experience and know it by past experience, I would not dare to write such optimistic words to mislead both myself and a blinded world. But because the sublimity which steals into me as I sit upon this lonely cliff in the Himalayas is a genuine, heart-ravishing fact, I let my pen write them down.

I have suffered too much and lived too long to wish to dally with sugary sentiments which are mere fictions. But if I die tonight, then let these words be found in my journal and published broadcast to the whole world:

Nature is your friend; cherish her reverently in your silent moments, and she will bless you in secret.

CHAPTER FIVE

Unexpected Visit by Two Yogis—Pilgrims and Shrines in the Himalayas—Power out of Stillness.

MY solitude has been invaded. The first visitors have arrived. And their unexpected visit provides me once again with ample proof of the smallness of this sublunary world. Wherever one goes, whether among the boulevards of crowded continental cities or into the single narrow street of a poky little Oriental village, one must ever be prepared to run into someone one knows, or else someone who swears he knows you. Three times I have been stopped in Central and Northern India by humbly-dressed wayfarers, who call me by name and salute me with such ceremony, although I know neither their faces nor their own names. In Delhi I lunch unexpectedly with a retired major who is revisiting India on a sudden whim after an absence of fifteen years, and with whom I had last lunched in his cosy London flat eighteen months before. In Dehra Dun I pick up the threads of an old conversation, again, unexpectedly, with a scholar of Oxford University, where I last met him. And so on.

Here, in the isolation of the heart of the Himalayas, until today it has seemed to me possible to obtain absolute seclusion. Now I know better. Do what you will to run away, invisible hands are tying all sorts of threads between you and the world which you have left.

For while I sit late this morning on the small patch of stone and grass next to my bungalow, with the fir branches hanging over me, trying to sort my medley of papers, notes and letters into some kind of order, the servant appears suddenly, grins broadly, and announces two visitors!

I look up—and there they are, immediately behind him, having ascended the short bank which runs up to meet the building.

The midday sun stares down at two men who wear the yellow robe, a garment which proclaims them to be either Yogis, monks, ascetics, holy men, tramps, vagabonds or thieves, for in modern India anyone who does not want to work for his living can put this convenient garment around his lazy body, no less than a sincere, world-scorning saint who wishes to devote his life entirely to real prayer and deep meditation. Both may then beg for their food and so on, or if they are lucky, find some patron who will undertake the entire burden of supporting them.

The two men before me seem to be of a superior type. The elder

49

man is well-built, pleasant-faced, and aristocratic-looking. He wears his hair in long raven locks down to his shoulders. His companion is younger, slighter in build, but equally pleasant-looking. He, too, affects the abnormally long hair of his type. He is the first to speak, for he greets me by name, and, to my surprise, prostrates himself upon the ground.

I do not know him and tell him so.

He replies smilingly that he knows all about me and that he knows my Master too. Then he gives me his own name and I learn that he comes from the Malabar coast of South-West India. His companion, he tells me, hails from Gorakhpur in the North, the United Provinces, to be precise. The latter is a *guru*, that is, a spiritual teacher, of some influence in his own territory. The speaker himself is a kind of unattached pupil.

All this information is elicited only after repeated questioning on my part. Then the elder man approaches nearer, touches me, and produces a large mango-like fruit, whose name I forget, but which I know to be costly. He offers it smilingly, but says not a word. Thereupon his companion explains that the man is "keeping silent" and has not spoken for twelve years.

I thank him but refuse, saying he will need all the food he can get in this lonely region.

"Oh no!" exclaims the vocal one, "we have some coolies following us with all our needful provisions, for we are going on pilgrimage to Gangotri."

But I know well the hardships involved in the journey and refuse to accept the fruit, declaring frankly that I should be unable to forgive myself if I deprived them of the smallest quantity of much-needed food.

Then both men become somewhat excited and exert their utmost pressure to make me accept. The younger one declares that the fruit is their special sacrificial offering to a fellow Yogi, as dictated by custom, and that they would feel much hurt if I still refused it. As I see that they will really be hurt, I accept it reluctantly but on condition that it is straightway cut up and shared among us all. While the servant is peeling and cutting the fruit, I protest half-jokingly that they have made a mistake, and that I am not a Yogi as they can easily see by my clothes.

The *guru* gravely replies:

"It is not the yellow robe that makes a Yogi; that is nothing; it is the heart, and you are one of us."

"Then this is the first time, perhaps," I retort jocosely, "that a Yogi has come into the Himalayan forests wearing a sun helmet and creased trousers, sat himself down on a waterproof ground-sheet, tapped the keys of a portable typewriter and sipped hot tea from a vacuum flask strapped over his shoulders!"

The elder man is so overcome at my trifling sally that he roars out suddenly with tremendous laughter, which continues for a full minute. Apparently his vow of silence permits laughter. Whether laughter is not really a kind of speech is a fit problem for hair-splitting philosophers, upon which they might well engage themselves. But I have not finished questioning them. Whilst we eat the slices of delicious fruit I ask:

"But how did you know that I was staying here?"

"We did not know, but we were guided," comes the calm reply.

"By whom?"

The spokesman smiles and points upwards. And with that I have to be content.

I make one last attempt, nevertheless.

"If you are going to Gangotri you know this is not the usual pilgrim route. That way lies up through Dharasu and Uttarkashi. Here you are being taken out of your route and making it unnecessarily longer."

"But we wanted to meet you," is the gentle smiling response.

And then they rise to take their leave. They are going off to meet their coolies and to eat their lunch. The teacher, through the medium of a pencil and paper, invites me to have evening worship with him and to be his guest at dinner, as he intends resting here for one day and then to get off before dawn. This time I express my gratitude and feel impelled to accept. I realize that he is honouring me by thus sharing his necessarily limited supplies.

Some while after lunch the younger man pays me a second visit. His name is Bhandu Sharma. I suggest a walk and take him towards the top of a peak about a mile off, where yellow asters grow brightly against their austere background. On the way, as we creep along a narrow rock-shelf, which pants up the mountain-side as though eager to get to the top and be done with it, we talk of higher things and he drops into an autobiographical mood. Fragments of his life-story drop from his lips.

For six years he has wandered the length and breadth of India, amid the seething crowds of bazaars and the lonely huts of the jungles, in temples whose altar shrines reeked with rancid butter and in pure-aired mountain valleys, studying the wisdom of the Spirit and the art of Yoga at the feet of different teachers. We compare notes, for some of the latter are familiar to both of us. He says that the Mystic of Tiruvannamalai is the man who has made the profoundest impression upon him. "In his presence I instantly felt peace," says the Yogi, "and during the four days I stayed in his hermitage I received spiritual experiences which I had never had before. One day I shall return—nay, I must return."

I ask him about the kind of life he is living and how he endures it.

"It suits me well because I have the freedom to study and meditate, a freedom which I could never get in the old days when I was employed in a Government post, even though that was well paid," he replies.

"It is a hard life, though, for a man of your class."

"It would be if I had to beg for my food; that is a degradation I could not at all pass through. But I am fortunate enough to get all the food and shelter I need from the teachers with whom I stay. Thus, on this pilgrimage to Gangotri, the teacher who is taking me is also providing for all expenses."

"Is it true, as so many people assert, that most of the wandering ascetics and holy men are good-for-nothing tramps? You are moving amongst them and can speak more authoritatively than we who, after all, are outside those ranks."

The Yogi shakes his head sadly. His eyes grow grave.

"Yes, unfortunately it is only too true. I would go farther and say that more than ninety per cent of them are mere idlers, mendicants or vagabonds. I have seen them in every part of India, and lived amongst them, and I assure you that not more than five per cent are sincere spiritual seekers."

Our path skirts the forest and is flanked on the other side by a low slope. As we walk, we come upon the fresh unmistakable traces of a bear, which has turned up the soil quite freely in search of edible roots.

I tell him of an incident I witnessed while I was waiting for a train at Gwalior Station. A wandering holy man, owning nothing more than a waterpot and a stick, had terrorized the ticket-collector and railway police into allowing him to get on the train without a ticket. Before his loud-voiced, mysterious threats all were afraid to move a finger, and it was quite certain that he would repeat the performance at his destination and thus add one more to the numerous army of ascetics who travel free on India's railways. Moreover, I could see from the man's eyes that he was strongly under the influence of recently-taken hashish.

Bandhu Sharma expresses his disgust in a melancholy voice.

"My travels and pilgrimages will be over within another year," he informs me, "and then I shall throw off the society of such wastrels for ever, I hope. I shall then settle down somewhere and live in utmost simplicity on a tiny income I hope to secure from friends. I shall devote myself to study."

It seems clear to me that the wandering holy men of India are simply the wandering friars of mediæval Europe. The modernization of India will cause them to disappear as the modernization of Europe has driven out the friars.

The rare few who are real Yogis may go, too, but never completely. I deem myself fortunate to have gained a footing in their exclusive ranks, for their society is more exclusive than that of aristocracy.

He tells me of the point he has reached in his inner life. He can sit still in meditation for two or three hours and completely forget the outside world; he can enter into mystical ecstasies of the Spirit; and he has brought his power of concentration of thought to a very advanced degree. He has found a certain amount of inward peace and is consequently happy.

We discuss two problems which he cannot satisfactorily deal with alone, and finally I feel an urge to put forward certain explanations. He receives the latter joyfully and exclaims:

"Now I know why I had to come and see you. Those are the exact answers which have been eluding me!"

I tell him that the credit does not belong to me, but to my Master, for it is to him that I am indebted for this particular bit of knowledge.

We rest awhile on the peak-top. The place is festooned with ferns, which enlace themselves around the fir trees. On our return journey, under a sky patched with faded rose and with the snows glowing in the sunset like metal in a furnace, I come across a few wild jasmines with delighted surprise. They are large exquisitely perfumed flowers, as white as snow, and remind me of a certain Gwalior garden where my host had helped Nature to provide me with some remembered moments.

My companion hints at the high inspiration which he finds here. Almost all Hindus turn with devout awe to "the mighty Himalchan", as their books call it, as the last abode in our benighted era of real sages.

In the evening, under the pale glow of a kerosene lantern, I join him and the teacher at evening worship. After they have chanted their hymns, they remain bowed to earth in reverent prayer. When it comes to an end, the dinner is produced. Everything is laid out on a huge brass dish, so that all courses from first to last appear simultaneously before my gaze.

I am surprised at the comparatively varied and excellent assortment of food which is offered. All the little titbits which Indians are so fond of are there—from *chapatis* (bannocks) to *rasigullas* (treacle cakes). The *guru* has several coolies and a couple of servants and is evidently well-to-do, as pilgrims go.

Dinner over, I invite them into my bungalow for a final chat, as they will be off on their journey before dawn. We discuss those ancient topics of the spiritual life which have been discussed so many times in India, and the teacher, with the aid of his quick-moving pencil, explains a number of minor points connected with his own particular branch of spiritual culture. And then he rises, we all smile at each other, touch palms in salutation, and they pass from my ken to retire for the night. That is the last I see of these two yellow-robed wanderers.

*   *   *

This is the pilgrim season. During the four months of summer the Himalayan trails and mountain paths can be safely negotiated, but afterwards they are buried in snow four, five and six feet deep, and travelling becomes a dangerous and often impossible task. So the pilgrims make their appearance only during the summer. Most of them are holy men, fakirs and monks.

I admire the determination, the bravery and the religious devotion of these people who come from the plains of India, from regions of fiercely-burning steamy heat to an austere region of precipices, ice and snow. For the temple of Gangotri itself is right in the perpetual snow-line. It is easy enough for a European, who is fairly inured to the cold winters of his own continent, to endure Himalayan cold, but it is a matter of painful acclimatization and some suffering for these thinly-clad Hindus to penetrate into such a region.

Hundreds of men, and even women, come up on pilgrimage through canyon-like scenery to these snow-clad mountains every summer, for their religion teaches them that here their fabled gods and famous teachers lived and, invisibly, still live.

Himalaya is the holy land of the Indian sub-continent. It is to the Hindus what Palestine is to the Jews and Christians.

Here, in the grove of Badarikasrama, lived the famous sage-scribe Vyasa, who wrote the *Mahabharata*, India's greatest religious epic. There at Rishikesh by the Ganges bank the *Vedas*, her sacred scriptures, were given their final fourfold form. Vasishta, sage and seer, the recluse writer of an immense Yoga compendium, lived in this Tehri kingdom before the days of Christ. High up on a snow-surrounded natural throne, Shiva, the god who took the body of a Yogi, is still believed to be lost in one eternal aeon-old meditation. In the little tree-shadowed valley of Agastyamuni the great Seer named Agastya had practised his Yoga in ancient times. The sacred river *Bhagirathi* which flows across this kingdom is mentioned in the holy books, the *Puranas*, for it is really the chief feeder of the Ganges. Its name is associated with that of King Bhagirath, a royal Saint. The temple of Badri Narayan in a glacier valley is sacred even to the Buddhists, no less than the Hindus, and even now some Tibetan monasteries send it tribute.

When the pilgrim reaches these shrines he believes he is in the presence of deities who inhabit the place. To Kedarnath Badrinath, and even Gangotri and Jumnotri the pilgrims plod patiently on foot along the narrow winding paths, living on simple rice and lentils, ecstatically singing sacred hymns and constantly repeating prayers. They struggle up steep slopes and down slippery trails, these tired slight figures, enduring various hardships in the six to eight weeks of their return journey, and risking accident and disease. And when at last, almost exhausted, they reach the temples which have been erected ages ago at sacred points among these mountains, their faces light up with smiles, for they receive—or imagine they receive—the blessing of these gods.

I believe they are right.

Whether temples are useless collections of mere stones, or whether the gods are figments of primitive man's imagination, to live in the Himalayas for a while is itself a memorable blessing!

Overhead, the stars in their high vault have fully emerged from their coffins of daylight and glance hither and thither with their twinkling beams. Hydra, named after the monstrous serpent slain by Hercules, stretches its long straggling shape below the ecliptic. Orion, another of the southern constellations, appears on the equator. The Giant Hunter is the most striking figure among the starry forms. His belted dagger contains the nebula which is one of the sky's beautiful sights. To the south-east of Orion sparkles Sirius, famed star of first magnitude. My last look is at the shining constellation of Leo, fifth of the Zodiacal groups, which commands the zenith, and then I retire for the night.

I have enjoyed my silent communion with the distant array of stars.

* * *

A curious experience has come over me today. Whilst I sit cross-legged upon the cliff, with right foot resting upon the left thigh, with gaze fixed upon the far side of the gorge, with breath restrained by degrees into semi-inactivity, the gentle absorption into which I fall is suddenly broken by a violent surge of *power*.

No effort of mine brings it on, for I rest on the ground as effort-less as a stone. Yet an electrifying impulse rushes unexpectedly into my body and sets the spine as taut as a bow-string. Dynamic power flies all over the flesh so that I grind my teeth to keep it in restraint and plunge the nails of my fingers into the palms.

This sudden accession of strength, seemingly out of nowhere, is both physical and moral. My slight body is transformed and feels capable of performing herculean feats of labour, achievement and endurance, whilst my character absorbs fresh courage, determination and aspiration.

I feel that legions of guardian angels and helpful spirits have trooped up to support me, and will aid me to bring to successful fruition whatsoever I attempt. I feel a second Signor Mussolini, with the invisible world as my Abyssinia. I feel like that Army officer who once described to me his sensations whilst "going over the top" at the head of his troop of men. "The consciousness of having twelve hundred men behind me, all of them utterly ready to obey my slightest word of command and to follow wherever I led them, gave me a prodigious self-confidence which I normally do not possess," he confessed.

This mysterious mood continues for a whole hour or more. Then it gradually takes to its heels, not, however, without leaving a mark upon me. I realize that I have accidentally loosed some subtle psycho-physical-spiritual force, though how, why, and where is less easy to ascertain with exactness.

Suddenly a sharp wind blows up and sweeps across the gorges. The yellowed leaves dance madly around me and then hurtle before the wind into the drop. A crow calls to its mate, which answers from a nearby tree.

A peculiar premonition then takes possession of me. It predicts the frequent return of this mood, with a consequent raising of the whole vibration of living in every sphere. With this indescribable force that has welled up from I know not where gripping me, I know that the future can be faced optimistically, fearlessly, even triumphantly. These ideas of victory will help me in the future, I feel sure.

I remember that the Yogi masters of old used to talk of a power that lay hid in the etheric body of man, which although invisible was yet closely ramified with his physical body. They pictured this power under the symbol of a serpent and said that it lay coiled up at the base of the spine. Once uncoiled, awakened and forced upwards, it would regenerate a man and bestow upon him incredible psychic, magical and spiritual powers, they said. Ultimately, it might help him to break into the kingdom of heaven by violence.

But anatomists can find no trace of the habitation of such a marvellous power. Whether it be fact or fiction is immaterial to me. I have made one discovery, anyway.

I have found that stillness is strength.

A modern Indian master, since dead, has said that by sitting in one place in meditation he had put the world between his feet! His implication was that he who can command his thought may command the entire universe also.

Instead of weakening, I am today stronger; therefore those who regard meditation as an expression of feebleness do not know what they are talking about.

I glory in this stillness which grows gently and daily within me like a flower.

The delicate poise which arises during meditation may be a fountain which gushes forth power.

The high gods are still, so still that the ancient Egyptians always pictured them in their system of hieroglyphic writings as squatting down! Yet masses of men unconsciously move at their behest, whilst even great planets swing catastrophically from the vertical to an angle, or back again, at their will.

The most deceptive thing in the world is to imagine that they alone are strong who are noisy, or that they alone possess power who are fussily active.

The big-business executive of a mammoth concern sits quietly in his revolving chair, whilst his underlings rush hither and thither and make all the sound.

The hub of a giant flywheel which drives the machine-belts for a vast factory wherein thousands of men labour is silent and fixed, but the circumference creates most of the noise and whirls through the air. Yet all the activities of the factory ultimately centre in the hub.

In the terrible whirlwinds of the African tropics, which can be so devastating to life and property, at the very centre there is absolute stillness. They rage outwardly but are still inwardly.

These analogies from both Nature and life dispel the delusion that calmness is necessarily weakness. It is not.

The most powerful Being in the entire universe—its Creator—is likewise the Ever-Calm, the Ever-Still. The Supreme Being dwells within the motionless Absolute, yet all movement, all creation, all world-working, proceeds out of that Divine Stillness.

And if man is "made in the image of God", then the most dynamic element within him must also dwell in stillness. This is a primary truth of life and we would do well to acknowledge it.

If the Power which drives the entire machinery of our universe is ultimately secret and quiet, then man, who reproduces within himself in miniature all the principal elements of the universe, must also be animated by a Power which is likewise secret and quiet.

I perceive, therefore, that I have nothing to lose by persisting in my exerci.es in stillness; I need fear neither feebleness nor degeneration. On the contrary, I have everything to gain, to wit, contact with that vital creative Force which has really made me. Such contact may even impart something of that unique force to my conscious self. Yet outwardly there may still remain nothing but serenity. The world could go on regarding me as insignificant. That would not matter in the least. I would sense the unleashment and act with its co-operation from a profounder plane than the physical.

Ancient people have always possessed their fables of such possibilities. No race but has had its exaggerated stories of sages, wise men, wizards, magicians and prophets who have forced both men and Nature to move at their will. Where they had unselfish motives they were good, where they had grossly selfish ones they were classed as evil.

To throw the world back into stupid ancient beliefs and revive superstition would be retrogressive, but to throw the world back into what was true in those beliefs could only be progressive.

Applied science has shown the way. It throws an invisible beam of subtle electrical rays by wireless into space; the rays move swiftly, silently and unseen; and lo!—aeroplanes travel pilotless hither and thither, street traffic is controlled by self-working lights, alarm bells are set ringing, self-opening doors are operated, railway signals move up or down automatically, steamers find their direction accurately in a fog, and soldiers fall dead from instantaneous electrocution.

In the universal storehouse there are other forces than electricity, which may work just as secretly and just as invisibly and yet be none the less potent in their own way. Such forces may dwell, dormant and unused, within man himself.

Why not?

CHAPTER SIX

A Cross-section Through My Mail—A Would-be Suicide and My Answer—
Telepathic Aid to Students.

THE messenger who periodically brings the mail from the nearest
postal point in heated India must be one of the world's champion
walkers. Day in and day out he does nothing but walk! He does his
twenty to twenty-five miles a day, by the grace of God and his sturdy,
shoes, but thinks little of them. He invariably arrives after nightfall,
generally soaked to the skin by one of those storms which now
attack this region almost daily, opens his valise and deposits the
usual budget of letters upon the table. Then, after a meal and a
drink and a night's rest, he is off again early the next morning,
walking the long lone mountain trails with my own despatches for
civilization. And so he passes his life, a simple primitive soul, faithful
and devoted to his service, ever walking!

He is a man who might have given Charles Lamb the meat for a
well-turned witty essay, had he been born in England and in the
early nineteenth century. But destiny had reserved him for my
service upon these thread-like tracks, and for sight of a world
where aeroplanes buzz deafeningly in the air like giant bees and
smart coaches run like lightning without a single horse to pull
them!

To me he is a valued necessity for he keeps open my line of
communication with the outer world. Such a service might well
have been scornfully disdained by the ancient or mediaeval hermits,
but to a twentieth-century hermit like myself it is a welcome one.
Modern habits for modern hermits is my slogan.

Thus I live secluded but not isolated.

Once I looked upon these strangely varied epistolary missives,
which pour in from the four points of the compass, as disturbers of
my private peace. When an author has written his fifteen hundred
words for the day on his next book, and possibly a few paragraphs
of a newspaper article, he is in no mood to take up his pen again and
write a further two or three thousand words in the form of answers
to unknown correspondents or news-letters to acquaintances and
friends, especially if he must keep a daily period inviolate to his
Goddess, meditation. If anything, he will dislike letter-writing as an
irksome and fatiguing treadmill.

Certainly I could not toil like French Flaubert for three days merely to write a single perfect sentence! Only a genius or a million-aire can afford such colossal expenditure of time. I shall never be a millionaire, and I have long to live yet before I can proudly tell the customs inspector, as Oscar Wilde told him on entering the United States, "I have nothing to declare except my genius!"

Even a secretary, although a valued and essential help, cannot relieve the pressure sufficiently to diminish the burden markedly, where the correspondence is so peculiar and so personal as is mine. Yet the passage of time has mellowed my outlook and I have come to take a more tolerant view of these letters. After all, except for the few who are scarcely sane or mere autograph-hunters or common curiosity-seekers or religious hysterics, most people do not break their natural reserve and write to a stranger about the difficulties in their outlook on life or pose him their troubling spiritual problems, or, perplexed, appeal for some inner guidance, unless there is a strong and genuine urge to do so. There exists, however, quite a pleasant side to the life of an author. A fair percentage of his letters intimate what intellectual pleasure or spiritual help his readers have derived from his literary efforts. No writer is so modest that he does not like to receive such complimentary letters. They encourage him to go on with such work and keep him from abandoning a precarious pro-fession when far more lucrative activities are placed temptingly before him. And when hostile reviewers denounce his books in print as "literary offal" or as "nauseating nonsense", as they have de-nounced mine, or impugn his truthfulness, as they have impugned mine, he can smilingly forgive them and answer them with the silence of indifference, whilst he picks up the large package of letters wherein unknown readers have sent him their deepest grati-tude and even heartfelt blessings for having written those books.

Not that many critics use such unflattering epithets as those which I quote. Precisely the same work which receives such low estimation from them has received high commendation from the two best-respected journals in the world, *The Times* of London and *The New York Times*. One can well suffer the former for the sake of hearing the latter. But in any case I have built no altar to public opinion. If the world can receive my thought, it shall surely please me; but if not I shall remain undisturbed.

And now a fresh budget of mail has arrived. I cannot drag my secretary here to share the utter loneliness of this isolated Himalayan retreat, and so I must deal with every letter and every matter entirely unaided. Indeed, I am sorry I have brought a temporary servant even, for he, poor fellow, is getting a little restless and, reading his thoughts, I see that he has begun to count the days till our departure. I shall not receive a shock therefore if he stammeringly announces one morning that he would like his pay, and thereupon desert me for the more sociable and civilized city of Delhi, where I engaged him. I can very well attend to my meals with my own hands—alas that even mystics must eat!—and would even prefer that to having the calm atmosphere of these mountains disturbed by troubled thoughts. The preparation of a savoury supper is not at all beyond my culinary capacity. "Peace at any price"—once the favoured motto of a certain English political party—has become my motto also. Those Yogis who retired of old to these Himalayan recesses took none but devoted disciples with them into their solitary retreats to attend to their worldly needs: now I understand why. And although I am not a Yogi—at least, in the orthodox sense—my purpose here is very much like theirs.

The revelations which I receive from my post-bag are sometimes extraordinary. Here is a man in Czecho-Slovakia who tells me that more than two thousand people have quietly been banded together in his small country, purposely to study the secret wisdom of the Spirit and to practise meditation regularly as a means of attaining thereto. Here is a letter from an Indian barrister practising in the High Court of a large city, who is attempting to organize a spiritual retreat in the Himalayan foothills as a place whither he and other professional men may fly for vacations and still their overworked minds.

Here is an invitation from a European psychic research committee to witness and investigate a demonstration of walking on red-hot coals. Alas! distance prevents my attendance, but in any case I would prefer to witness and investigate the setting of the sun amid a blaze of golden light.

Here is a journalist friend, who, plunged for twenty years into every kind of misfortune and who with proud head but empty purse tried to make a show before the world, suddenly finds his fate reversed and all the gifts of destiny begin to pour into his lap.

Here is an eighty-year-old Hindu disciple-hunting charlatan in Madras, who offers, in a duplicated letter, to give me "initiations for God (*sic*) and to revive those Greater Mysteries which have been so jealously guarded, and to be put freely and openly before the eyes of men who deserve the same". But "as it is necessary to find a permanent building and facilities requisite for doing this work and also for my daily prayers, I charge a nominal fee of 108 rupees for the rich, 40 rupees for the middle class, and 9 rupees for the poor". Thank heaven, I can receive an "initiation for God" here in the silent mountains without paying a penny, and it will be a better kind of initiation than that old rupee-hunter is ever likely to give. But I wonder why he sent that letter to me? I am sufficiently well known

61

in India to refuse disciples rather than become one. Clearly Darwin's terse definition of the fool as a man who never makes an experiment does not apply to him.

Here is a faithful friend's letter, telling of the political troubles in which far-off Europe is plunged and bewailing the ever-present threat of a great war. She is naturally depressed, for she is a General's wife, and begs me to emerge from my solitude and do something about it! But who am I, my dear friend, an insignificant itinerant scribbler and a weak and faulty mortal, to tackle what a thousand worried politicians and a hundred thousand bewildered pacifists can tackle far better? Europe has made its own destiny and, under the watchful eyes of the gods, Europe must shoulder it. Every calamity brings its unseen spiritual compensation. Do not despond, however, for there *is* a Plan back of things, and at the appropriate hour the presence of higher powers will be clearer before the surprised audience of our world. Our race is being carried through a transitional phase in its lifetime. For the great powers of fate, the unseen guiding forces of history, mobilize at critical periods the human instruments necessary to accomplish both our pre-destiny and their will, whether for pain or pleasure or both.

Who are the real masters of the world anyway? Are they the unconscious puppets whose names appear in the public prints, or are they the divine beings who have had watch and ward over mankind since immemorial days?

Meanwhile root your life in the sacred Overself and you shall have nothing to fear. It is exceedingly difficult for the modern mind to conceive of a state wherein the personal ego melts into submission to the impersonal Infinite. It seems, at first sight, impossible that one's entire life, with its joys and sufferings, its fears and hopes, its follies and failures, should become held in suspension, as it were, by a deeper life that arises from a divine source within oneself and transcends it. In this state there are no yesterdays and no tomorrows, for so only can peace be attained. But we must try, and if we try in faith and rightly, we shall eventually not try in vain. Take this truth into your head, madame, as you would take a lantern into your hand.

* * *

Here, too, is another letter from a lady. She is old and has sought for spiritual truth for thirty years, but "alas, all my efforts were in vain. I found only disappointment and utter disillusionment in my quest, which has led to scepticism and embitterment". In a tortured mood, she appeals for my advice. You shall have it, poor lady. Sorrow is but the preface to wisdom. You shall renew your vanished hopes and pick up again your faith in a Supreme Being.

Here is a political friend whom I have helped with advice. He writes to ask if I will become a candidate in his party for the next elections. Thanks and regrets. I have already become a candidate in a higher kind of election, one conducted by Mother Nature and yielding to the successful no other prize than repose, no other honour than truth.

A further letter comes from a friend in Egypt, giving me all the news from a group that plays its part in the social life of that sunny land, and then demanding my own. A railway official writes of the problems that have arisen during his efforts to practise meditation. A doctor in England sends his thanks for my elucidation of certain psychological points in one of my books, and then propounds a question somewhat difficult to answer. A keen American business man says that some of my paragraphs have revolutionized his outlook on life, but will I deal with certain delicate personal problems? A few scattered groups, who may one day become vital exponents of the gospel of inspired action and who are willing to work selflessly for the higher welfare of mankind, send their informal news and wish to take counsel on various points. My youngest student, a dozen years old in body but dozens of centuries old in soul, sends an affectionate note about his progress at school. He can do already, with ability and assurance, what many adults are still struggling to do—sit still and relax, with thoughts successfully attuned to the Infinite. A Yogi who begins and ends his letter with the Sanskrit symbol for God; an engineer who is trying to keep a secret sensitivity to diviner things amid his busy activities, albeit his spiritual impulses flow unevenly and disjointedly; a company director who is now learning to direct himself as well; an unemployed carpenter who begs for my benediction upon his efforts to find work; a countess caught in the social whirl yet not forgetting her higher duties—all these and more contribute their quota of correspondence for the day.

My last letter is a harrowing one. It tells of a series of terrific tragedies which have broken the writer's heart. Can I give him some crumb of comfort, he asks, some explanation which will enable him to hold on to life and not end it violently?

I give him what explanation I can, but there is not much to say when confronted by the mystery of destiny. To unravel it properly is a task for an Adept. But there are a few words of cheer to follow: "When the great troubles descend and life seems black with woes, do not mutter mournfully, 'This is the end!' but rather say hopefully 'This is the beginning!' The occasion should be seized as the opportunity to start a new life, to show forth the positive, courageous and constructive qualities that lie latent within you. It should be an opportunity to reconstruct your existence on a finer basis, a proper basis—on those qualities that ought to endure. Conquer your difficulties in the mind first, and then they too will gradually reshape themselves in external circumstances anew. Let each sorrow, when it comes, be the starting point for a diviner kind of life. You are made in God's image—oh yes, deep inside you really are—then live up to it. When you refuse to recognize the evil in another person or in a set of circumstances, you diminish its power to affect you. Make of your trouble a means of looking at life from a fresh angle and think about it in a stronger way, a positive way. Be without bitterness concerning that which might have been; rebellion cannot help you; wise resignation may. Begin afresh, by becoming a fresh personality. Try, thus, to disarm destiny. Make a list of the things you still possess, both material and spiritual, and you will see that you are not really lost. At the very worst, you will be lost only when you lose all hope, all courage, all trust in the divine healing powers that rule us. The agony of letting go of things is great, yes, but the agony of letting go of hope is greater. Do not submit to that; it is uncalled for. God still exists and He still cares. I assure you I have earned the right to write that last sentence, for I have earned it in anguish as keen as your own."

And now I must take my little typewriter out of its much-travelled case and begin to tap out replies, a few, for I lack time to write more. There are other people with whom an inner voice that must be obeyed debars all communication: it has ample reasons for thus commanding me and time generally gives striking endorsements of its vetoes. I do not always know why I should obey, for the deeper mind possesses reasons of its own, yet I obey. Malignant critics, for instance, are best answered by silence. Thus one opens no channel of communication with those hostile invisible sources which use them as their unconscious tools. Malignity must be met by fearlessness, but that is not to say that it need be met by foolishness. When Jesus told his followers to be as harmless as doves but as shrewd as serpents, He knew well the existence of those dark evil powers.

There are others who make impossible demands upon my limited time and energy. Their answer, too, is blank silence. They will misunderstand, of course, good people although they may be, but I cannot cram forty-eight hours into twenty-four.

One gets also the usual crop of begging letters, for the world—particularly the Indian world—always imagines that wealth is a necessary accompaniment of fame. It never dreams that poverty may sometimes be fame's shabby sister. Others ask glibly for a complete set of my books free. They are under the illusion that an author travels with a publisher's warehouse in his trunks, whilst they are ignorant of the fact that he, too, has to pay his pennies for every book he gives away. There is nothing free in this universe.

Yet if some mistake an author to be a publisher, others take him to be an employment bureau!

And lastly, because one writes of subjects which have long been the preserves of the unbalanced and the wild-eyed, and which were therefore once ridiculed but are now beginning to receive an overdue respect, many a crank descends upon one in the belief that he or she has found a fellow-crank! Despite such cajoling, I refuse to budge from my position of plain common sense and enlightened enlarged realism.

* * *

In the evening, however, I enter into another kind of correspondence. It works without pen and without machine, yet it is infinitely more satisfying to me. For there exist a very few who have offered devotion and loyalty without ever being asked for anything, and whose offer has been tested and redeemed. They call themselves my students, but I want no students. The Overself within each of us is quite capable of giving all the teaching and all the help we need— if we reach aright for it. No other teacher than this inward light is really necessary, but the world of aspirants is too weak to grasp this truth and must find someone who has gone a little farther on the way and lean on him. Let them lean if they wish, so long as they do not lean overlong and lose the virile capacity for spiritual self-reliance which is both their birthright and destiny. In the last finding the words of wise Marcus Aurelius remain true: "A man must stand erect, not be kept erect by others." But the universal law which reflects back to us whatsoever we give out is more binding on those who believe in it than on others. Should I ever acquire a spiritual fortune, these friends shall be the richer for it too. One cannot express formal gratitude in formal words when faced by devotion, this rarest of all gifts. It turns the wilderness that is social life to me, who feel alien and kindredless therein, into a blossoming flower-garden.

The few who have given such tried devotion must have their rewards. I can give them neither pence nor posts but I can give my best—myself.

Their faces flit before me at dusk, like a long gallery of portraits, as I sit in the sanctuary whilst a crow overhead flaps heavily to its roosting-place. Whatsoever I have found in these elusive realms of spiritual being I share with them. If I enter into peace profound, it is not alone for me but for them also; if I discover the benignity back of Nature, the high mood wings its way silently towards them. When the exquisite pulsation of the sacred silence overwhelms me with its sublimity, I telegraph it, as by telepathy, to those faithful souls. They may not always be aware of what is being done for them, because the heavy bars of insensitivity are not easily lifted, but in odd ways and at various times the accumulated despatches are ultimately delivered. Sometimes these latter receive no admittance until a sudden sorrow descends to afflict and to harass: then strength, wisdom and consolation trickle into the being of the sorrowful and enable them to endure what might otherwise be unendurable. Sometimes an unexpected mood of serenity visits the addressees in the midst of a crowded street, a busy office or a noisy factory. Then, too, the diurnal activity has not been in vain. But in some way or other a powerful concentrated thought must eventually reach its goal.

The outside world will laugh at these foolish notions. Let it laugh. We who have built up a sincere affectionate spiritual link, which defies space and survives trials, can afford its laughter. For it is a link which depends neither upon the appearances of social status nor the appurtenances of worldly property, and is therefore fit to become immortal.

CHAPTER SEVEN

*Reflections Upon the Future of Tibet—Sir Francis Younghusband's
Experiences—Destiny of Orient and Occident.*

EARLY this morning the sky is a heavenly Wedgwood blue, as clear as the sky of Italy, delicately silvered white by regular streamers of mottled chalky cloud. It is on these clear days that one sees the precipitous massifs of the Himalayas at their best. Every detail of the glorious landscape becomes lit up by the slanting rays of the young sun, while the vivid light turns the great glaciers of ice into gigantic prisms, which reflect back the loveliest fiery welter of colourings.

From west to east one's eye travels along the formidable horizon of jagged peaks and wavy snowfields, a view of such purity and magnificence as to arouse and satisfy the profoundest aesthetic sense. Indeed, the austere purity of the snows would rebuke any intruder who brings a worldly breath with him. The metallic grey crevasses which streak the glaciers and the black islands of rock which protrude through the snows give the needed contrast, and the sky offers a perfect blue background to the entire iridescent scene.

I think, by way of contrast, of the green paddyfields in South India which I know so well, of the picturesque coconut groves, of the dusty plains.

I can scarcely gaze out of my back door without feeling a rapturous uplift and exquisite enlivenment. These pyramidal summits which thrust themselves so majestically above the long white ridge must make the most town-stupefied man a Nature-worshipper. They are so grand, so numerous and so resplendent. Dawn, with its pallors, and sunset, with its purples, create pictures that can be watched a thousand times without any sense of monotony. What though these shining slopes of the Himalaya are often blizzard-swept and avalanche-marked? Their faces possess a perfect beauty. They are the most exquisite productions of the Grand Architect and the Master Builder.

And yet how jealously these giant ranges of grey ice and bare snow defend the barren black plateau which lies behind the immense magnitude of their perspective! At fifteen thousand feet it is the roof of the world. Tibet has lain secure under the fortress-like barrier of the Himalayas for centuries. It seems as if Nature has deliberately

67

raised these scores of frigid giants to girdle and guard the land. It holds itself aloof from the rest of the world for very good reasons.

But how much longer can it maintain this suspicious seclusion?

Applied science and technical invention can conquer even the peaked Himalayas. A cunningly built aeroplane has already nosed its way around and over Mount Everest—the world's highest peak. Consular Officer Sir Erich Teichman's epic flight from Kashgar in Central Asia to Governmental Headquarters in New Delhi has shown what twentieth-century man can do to traverse even the snowy wastes of the Western Himalaya within less than a couple of days.

When I visited Hardwar, the ancient town at the mouth of the gorge through which the Ganges enters the plains after cutting its way through the mountains, I received a tremendous surprise. From Hardwar a path leads into the Himalayas as far as the famous shrine-temples of Kedarnath and Badrinath. These places are so closely associated with the Hindu religion that each year hundreds of pilgrims make their way to them on foot, or, if they are well-to-do, in small crude palanquins. But this year I found a new means of travel for these pious folk.

Some enterprising Hindu engineers had formed a small company and started an air transport line which was already functioning briskly. Wealthier pilgrims were offered seats in a smart little monoplane which covered the distance from Hardwar to the nearest fit landing-points in a single hour. From these points the pilgrims had but a four-day pony journey to reach the temple of Kedarnath or a seven-day journey to Badrinath. Yet the poorer folk who toiled their tired way up the mountain paths usually took three to four weeks to cover the same ground.

If aeroplanes are now buzzing into the very heart of the Himalayas and transporting the pious to its sacred shrines, the arctic barrier cannot remain unscaleable much longer. I may yet do my "hop" across to Mount Kailas and startle the Buddhist monks in one of the five monasteries around it with a totally unexpected request for hospitality.

Imperilled by petrol plus the brain of man, Tibet's long security may go. Its frozen fastnesses and lofty strongholds cannot remain untouched in this century. The coming of the aeroplane may and must bring the sound of whirling propellers across its high tableland and through the very windows of the Potala, Lhasa's great palace.

The Everest Flight, Teichman's "hop", and the pilgrim plane are but the heralds of what is yet to come. Even Ethiopia's conquest is also a portent. Her seclusion was as old as Tibet's, albeit not so harsh. But nearly three thousand years of reserve and freedom have gone, broken in seven months. But for the aeroplane the Italians would have needed seven years to conquer those dreary deserts and rocky purple mountains which support the tablelands.

Why are these narrow-eyed, high-cheeked Tartars of Tibet so obstinately and deliberately keen on keeping their frontiers closed? Why do they reinforce Nature's majestic mountainous isolation with their own unyielding determination? Why do they cling to such excessive suspicion as tenaciously as the immaculate snows cling to the sides of the ranges that keep guarded watch over their land?

The reasons are twofold—religious and material.

The rulers of Tibet are the priesthood. The high Lamas are all-powerful. They appoint the sovereign—the Dalai Lama—and compose his Council of Ministers. They hold the mass of people within their material and spiritual grip.

They know that the coming of foreigners will be fatal to their rule. They regard the foreigner as the bearer of materialism or alternatively as the bearer of a strange religion—both of which are antipathetic to their own faith, and consequently dangerous to their own power.

They hold his fancied materialism in bitter scorn and do not hesitate to apply the epithet "barbarian" to the Western intruder, who knows so little of the psychic and religious mysteries whose secrets are written down in the guarded libraries of the great monasteries.

More vital, in these matter-of-fact days, is the little-known fact that there is probably as much gold within the frontiers of Tibet as within the frontiers of any other country in the world. There may even be a great deal more, for no trained geologist has ever been allowed to make a proper survey of the country's untouched lodes. Even the gold-mines which are being worked today, under guards of troops, lie in a forbidding and most difficult region, and are being worked by the most primitive unscientific methods. The methods which were used two thousand five hundred years ago are still good enough for the modern Tibetans. They are scarcely worthy the name of mining. No one knows with any accuracy how vast are the hoards belonging to the great lamaseries, nor how immense are the lodes of gold lying still unmined in the mountains. There is more than one temple with a roof of solid gold.

Will the white faces seek to rifle Tibetan earth of its gold? Will Western avarice remain forever content with being kept out?

*   *   *

Far greater than the Lamas are the forces which today force East and West together and make the old mingle with the new.

Tibet cannot resist successfully the oncoming of the white faces, be it for good or for ill. Already its heads have been reluctantly forced to drop a little of their conservatism, and to admit a few of the white man's inventions. Even now the Government are putting up a broadcasting station chiefly for the purpose of enabling it to issue orders more quickly to the governors of certain provincial towns. Electric lights glimmer in the palace of Potala. And a telegraph line has linked the capital with Darjeeling in India. When the Tibetan officer interceded on behalf of my Mount Kailas expedition with the authorities at Lhasa I did not have to kick my heels in New Delhi for three weeks while a yak-rider crossed the high passes and a horseman traversed the plateau of Southern Tibet to and fro with the messages. No, thanks to the Lhasa telegraph line to Darjeeling I was able to get the final decision through my friend within a few days.

It is in the line of evolution today that East and West must meet, if not marry. Although I am somewhat sympathetic to the desires to be left alone of Oriental peoples who, in the past, were naturally suspicious of the white man's imperialism, the calendar has moved and those desires are now antiquated. The whole world is being welded by transport, communications, trade and culture. I am not of those who foolishly assert that the Western peoples bring nothing but materialism with them to the East, nothing good. On the contrary, they bring both good and bad. And they find both good and bad.

Holiness is not the sole prerogative of the Orient. The latter, I confidently claim, needs a spiritual revival no less than the Occident. Both hemispheres are spiritually in a bad way.

And as we are living in a material world, because we possess material bodies, it is right and sensible to make the most of this world, to use all the conveniences, comforts and inventions which the brain of man can devise. Therefore the meeting of the progressive West and the conservative East must awaken the latter to exploit and develop the resources of Nature more fully. Such a result will not hurt it, only benefit it.

The West, too, benefits. The first and obvious benefit is purely material. The second, and slower, is purely cultural.

But let these meetings of different peoples come about through friendly intercourse. The methods of mediaeval Spain in opening up Central America and raping her gold will not be admired by the world today. East and West should meet in good fellowship. Let their ideas be exchanged and material improvements brought about by means of mutual co-operation, not by means of the bullet and the bomb!

These last words remind me of a significant anecdote which was related to me some years ago by Sir Francis Younghusband. More than thirty years ago he was placed at the head of a small British military expedition which was sent across the snow-cloaked shoulders of the Eastern Himalayas into Tibet to negotiate a political and commercial agreement with the Lama-King's Government.

The main object of the army's mission was to change the latter's hostile attitude and to compel the Tibetans to adopt a more reasonable view towards Indian trade. With its entry Tibet's isolation would begin to leak.

Sir Francis gave the Tibetans the fullest opportunity of arriving at a peaceful settlement but they were obdurate. A hastily gathered army barred his passage on the treeless road to Lhasa. The opposing force was armed only with ancient and rusty matchlock guns, with bows and arrows, and with swords. The British leader knew how childish was this opposition to his well-equipped soldiers, with modern rifles, machine-guns and mountain artillery. He therefore requested the Tibetan commanders quite a few times not to resist his advance and be massacred, as he sought only to get a treaty signed and then he would immediately evacuate Tibet and return to India.

But despite their ill-armed and ill-disciplined body of men, the Tibetans would not budge and affected scorn for the enemy, whom at last they attacked. Colonel Younghusband (as he was then) was compelled to give the order to fire, with the result that the withering shells of his artillery poured into the Tibetan ranks, whilst his quick-firing rifles were repeatedly pumping bullets into the enemy when the latter took a few minutes to reload each wretched muzzle-loading flintlock musket, with the flint often missing fire.

The inevitable occurred. Hundreds of Tibetan soldiers were quickly shot down and the survivors fled in disorder. The way to Lhasa lay open.

The point of this story is that the real reason of the Tibetan army's opposition in the face of a force with such superior weapons lay in its superstition. Its soldiers had trusted to the sorcery of their reputed magicians and to the spells of their famous priests. They had been told that, with the aid of specially-prepared amulets and talismans which were freely distributed in their camp, they would be rendered supernaturally invulnerable against the shots of the enemy. And such was their unthinking faith and blind superstition that these poor ill-fated men did attack the British army with complete and complacent confidence that no British bullet would be able to penetrate their bodies! But the laws of Nature will not be suspended, even for any Lama!

The episode illustrates the habitual mixture of ridiculous superstition and profound wisdom which one finds in Oriental races. Yet no people can afford to go on believing in arrant untruths. The coming of the white races in the East is like a clean strong wind which blows away the repulsive cobwebs of outworn beliefs and barbarous customs. For the whites bring sanity, common sense and scepticism. There is room and necessity for these things in life also.

Civilization has almost destroyed our faith in the supernatural. Yet let it not be thought that the superstition of the Tibetans is all arrant nonsense. It is not. There is fire behind the smoke. Truth continues amid the distortions in which we find her engulfed. The Lamas cannot suspend Nature's laws but they can take advantage of laws which to us are unknown, to them long known. Men with genuine magical powers do exist there, but they are not to be found in the monasteries. Such men always disdain the herd of common monks and take themselves off to isolated places or high up in the mountains. And naturally they are very, very few. They are not at all interested in impressing the masses with displays of their super-normal gifts. But the boasters and pretenders, the blindly credulous among the orthodox Lamas, even as in India, acquire and keep a hollow reputation for miracle-working which would crumple up with the first touch of scientific investigation.

I have met more than one pretender in India and Africa who offered to provide me with amulets that would make my body bullet-proof!

Nevertheless, not only is there some residue of truth behind Tibetan claims (and Indian claims) for the existence of psychic powers and of forces, otherwise inexplicable, but there is also something behind the tradition of high spiritual wisdom in the bleak plateau. I believe, from my varied researches, that Mount Kailas and its vicinity, including Lake Manasrowar, possesses a magnetic atmosphere of intense spiritual vibration, as does Mount Arunachala in South India. I am sure that any genuinely sensitive person would automatically find his thoughts being caught and held in reverence, at least, when he approached this mountain, which is Asia's spiritual centre and Tibet's spiritual pride.

When the British army under Colonel Younghusband's command did succeed in reaching Lhasa eventually and the treaty which was the subject of this little war was finally obtained and signed, a curious thing happened to its leader. He told me that the day following this event he obeyed a profound urge and went off alone up the steep rocky hill which overlooks Lhasa. After climbing for some time he sat down on a boulder and rested. Quickly there came to him the most overwhelming spiritual experience of his life. His whole being was uplifted into a kind of mystic ecstasy. Utter serenity seeped through his soul. There was nothing personal in the experience, for all his desires sank into nothingness before the wonderful impersonal peace that enveloped him.

He came down from that hill with a memorable event engraved on his memory for ever. Tibet had given him more than a military conquest; it gave him spiritual illumination.

Who or what in that snow-laden land was responsible for the gift?

*　　　*　　　*

But I must return to my theme. Contact in every way between the Occident and the Orient is inevitable. Tibet cannot close its high passes against the inflow of Western ideas. But it has had to wait for the twentieth century to discover and disclose this truth. The last forbidden land cannot hold out very much longer. Its fear of Western imperialism is baseless today, although it might have been well-grounded fifty years ago. Of the three great Powers whose dominions lie nearest to Tibet, England is no longer an annexationist country but wisely seeks her conquests now through trade, Russia has sufficient land to satisfy her and wants chiefly to concentrate internally on building up her own economic and industrial structure, while China is an empire in a state of sad disintegration.

And if the High Lamas fear Western greed for Tibet's rich goldfields, it would be a better business move on their part to lease these fields to European concerns, with expert mining engineers, up-to-date scientific equipment and modern transportation methods at their disposal. In that way the Government would get more profit out of the mines and the future ownership of the latter would be better safeguarded.

Let them also forgo short-sighted political fears and construct a motor road up a Sikkim valley and along a river, the best natural trade route between India and Tibet, and thus save both men and animals the fearful journey over the high snow-passes.

To keep men always immersed in the doctrines and doings of the centuries before Christ is not entirely healthy. If the Tibetans were wiser, they would let their brightest young lamas absorb what is useful in Western knowledge, particularly scientific knowledge, and yet insist on their holding fast to the essential truths of Buddhist wisdom. The two can easily be made complementary, although not by the narrow-minded orthodox spirits. And while maintaining their strict independence and sovereign authority over their own

73

country, they should mix some common sense and wise discrimination with their rules forbidding the entry of foreigners. On the contrary, if they can get foreigners of the best type and finest character or with expert abilities and technical knowledge to enter their frozen and unattractive land, whose valleys alone are higher than the highest of Switzerland's Alps, whose bleak plains are shelterless and treeless and whose length and breadth are swept nightly by Arctic gales, the latter should be made welcome and not driven away. Let the undesirable trouble-makers and the unsympathetic possessors of superiority-complexes and the unscrupulous exploiters be ruthlessly kept out by all means, but let the country be opened up to useful Europeans who are sympathetic and sincere well-wishers.

It is because I fully believe in the basic truths taught by the Buddha, and am therefore sympathetic to every Buddhist people, that I always suggest to them the advisability of adapting themselves voluntarily to modern knowledge and modern ways. Thus they can save their ancient wisdom and yet progress with the progressive twentieth century. It is not that I suffer from the vanity of time and always imagine that the substitution of the twentieth century for the seventeenth is necessarily the substitution of a higher for a lower form of civilization; it is because although our use of scientific inventions is conscienceless, the inventions themselves are not therefore to be despised.

But alas, today the real followers of Buddha are becoming almost as rare in their own lands as the real followers of Christ in Christian lands. That is one reason why the gods are now tearing down the barriers which divide peoples and races and countries.

The future is foreseeable. In the unified world which shall arise, in the welded East-West civilization which is coming to birth, the path will be clear and ready for the message of the universal higher spiritual awakening that is yet to come. No creed exists but stands in dire need of a fresh impulse of divine life. And it shall come because it must come.

A shaven-headed imperturbable Buddhist monk once told me of an old prophecy which is current in Tibet and known to the higher lamas and which is curiously appropriate to present conditions. He said that the prediction, made two or three centuries ago, concerned the Dalai Lama (or Grand Lama), Tibet's King and Pope combined. It was foretold that the thirteenth Grand Lama would be the last of his line and that some time after his death Tibet would be thrown open to the white "barbarians", whose "materialistic" civilization would thenceforth penetrate the country.

According to the old belief, the next king will be a reincarnation of his spirit. It is the duty of the Grand Council of High Lamas, which is convened at Lhasa, to find the child in whom the spirit of the deceased Priest-Ruler has reincarnated.

Their theory is not reincarnation in the ordinary sense but rather that an emanation from a mystic heavenly Being, nearly akin to the Buddha, enters into the particular new-born infant which is destined to become a future Grand Lama. Hence one of the titles of the latter is "The All-Knowing", as he is presumed to possess divine knowledge.

The Grand Council always consult the State Oracle when it has to find guidance in its search for the child. After finding a number of male infants bearing certain traditional signs, it orders their names to be inscribed on tablets which are placed in a golden urn, and the one thus drawn out by lot is selected.

After it finds the boy, he has to be educated and prepared for his high office. That means about fifteen to twenty years must pass before the child reaches maturity and real rulership. Meanwhile the country is governed by the Council of Regents.

I do not remember the name of this particular native prophet who foretold the disappearance of Grand Lamas and the entry into Tibet of the whites.

I believe, however, that part of it will be fulfilled and that this sealed country will be thrown open eventually and will suffer the impact and inevitable influence of the forces of the new era, whatever they may be.

CHAPTER EIGHT

A Correspondent Decries My Retreat from the World—The Virtues of Idleness and Solitude—My Religion—The New Testament—Jesus and His Critics.

THREE and a half weeks have silently slipped by since I penned in my journal the last of these paragraphs, which come so disjointedly from my pen. For after all, I did not come here to these primeval forests and snow-covered summits to write but to rest. If I am to remain faithful to the charge which has been laid upon me, to be still must remain my principal aim. Whether I take up the transparent barrel of pen on some days, or tap the glistening glazed keys of my typewriter on others, or ignore both writing instruments for weeks on end, that need not be a matter to trouble me here, as it might have troubled me in the old days in Europe. The solemn pettiness of worldly existence has disappeared under these trees.

I perceive that labour is an excellent thing and, indeed, a necessity if one is to justify one's existence, but I perceive also that a time must come when to learn how to *be* is no less excellent, no less necessary if one is to obey the supreme law of life.

For I have had a sight of the far-off goal. I have seen the wonderful way which stretches to the summit before all men, the way which leads to the kingdom of heaven about which Jesus spoke and to the peace of Nirvana which Buddha described. We may resist its oncoming for a hundred thousand years, if we will, because amid all the tribulations and exaltations of daily living we prefer the delights of material sense-existence. We may resent the intrusion of those prophets who voice its gospel, because they throw the icy water of doubt upon our comfortable orthodoxies which feed us with illusions.

But the truth remains that Nature holds us in her grasp: there is no ultimate escape. On some fated day we shall all be called, with an imperiousness that will brook no dispute, to our true home.

Let me, then, not waste all my days in insensate devotion to labour without end. I have earned the right to call a brief halt to this existence of constant toil and up-piling studies. I have burned more midnight oil than most men, and have awakened many a time to greet the cold grey dawn with my bald editorial head lying upon the table amid a mass of papers. It was once my boast that I could toil like a galley-slave and eat up work as ravenously as a hungry dog would eat its biscuits: today I reject and repel the remunerative tasks which are constantly proffered me.

Not that I regard my solitary existence here or my hermitage life in the South as the only sort of existence worth having; on the contrary, I believe in rhythm, in withdrawal only if followed by activity, in solitude only if followed by society, in self-centred development only if social service is its later complement; in spirituality only if nicely balanced by materiality. We should follow Christ's injunction and render unto Caesar the things that are Caesar's, yet not fail to hold fast to the things that are of God. All those things which make, up the best in material life and which the world well covets—property, home, position, marriage, motor-cars, furnishings. and fine clothes—are indeed attractive, but we need not forget our first destination whilst we go off in their quest. Therefore, spiritual retreat is but an episode in my whole life, not a final goal but just a camp by the wayside. I am here in India neither as tourist nor resident, but as a wanderer who might remain fixed for a couple of years or fly off overnight at his whim. In short, I have no settled abode, neither in the wilderness nor in the city. I try to keep my mind cool and my life uncluttered.

Nowadays I have become an idler, useless to society and unprofitable to myself, a do-nothing who merely sits still and endeavours to keep away the waves of invading thought that advance upon him. In short, I possess neither fixed status nor recognized place in the world. I am no longer respectable.

Does it matter?

*   *   *

In a pocket-sized, black-clothed book which a friend in Bombay has just sent me I read at random this sentence which, to me, is a sane and soothing notion:

"For what is a man profited, if he shall gain the whole world, and lose his own soul? or what shall a man give in exchange for his soul?"

That book bears on its title-page the words: *The New Testament.*

It is really only another way of saying that to estimate a man by his wealth or by his output of work is vulgar. It is not alone what he does for the world that most matters, but what he is in himself.

My extract, however, is unfortunate for my friend. She has sent the book with the especial desire that I read a totally different sentence. On the flyleaf she has lightly pencilled this note: "See Acts, Chapter 26, Verse 24."

Accordingly, I turn over the pages and look up her monitory reference. And I now read:

"And as he thus spake for himself, Festus said with a loud voice, Paul, thou art beside thyself; much learning doth make thee mad."

My correspondent apparently disapproves of my activities—or should I write inactivities! I know from a previous letter that she considers I ought to settle down in some large city like Bombay whilst I remain in India and become respectable, that is, meet the middle and upper classes, entertain and be entertained, take hold of some active ambition, hold some sort of a post and stick to it, and, finally, do everything that all conventional people ought to do.

She thinks it would be more sensible, *ergo*, to become a gyrating human being moving to the so-called melody of jazz in an overgrown town. She evidently thinks it is better to look out of one's window on a vista of chimneys, if in Europe, or a vista of flat roofs, if in India, than on the snow-topped peaks and glittering pinnacles which preside over my present abode. She believes that I have isolated myself from reality.

If reality consists of the seething cauldron that is a great city, and of the greeds and fears and hates which boil within it, I could do worse than chain my feet to this untainted Himalayan earth, to pass my days in peaceful contentment, and refuse to drag them back to the world. But fortunately I am not afraid and I shall return to its centreless life. I have executed a strategic retreat from the world, and not abandoned it.

It is not that in her mundane eyes a diviner life has no existence —far from it—but that she likes to keep social wellbeing sainted and set apart.

My correspondent might, of course, denounce my stillnesses as sheer laziness but I think she understands them better than that. I beg her to remember that the virtue which Europeans and Americans make of hard work arises out of the necessities of their climate, just as the virtue which the Oriental makes out of indolence arises out of the warmth of his climate. Look at any energetic representative of the West who has spent twenty years in India. The change is startling. The one-time apostle of hard work has become a practitioner on the path of indolence. The atmosphere has absorbed him, the climate has conquered him, strong muscles and all.

But we Westerners have made a reverenced fetish out of excess of energy; we have turned industriousness into a little god. Whenever I visit the West I have to fit myself with a long diary, the longer its pages the better, for there one question crops up every hour: "What must I do next?" or "Who must I see next?" It is impossible to draw up the chair to the fireside and just sit idle for an hour.

After all, some of us are like the Biblical fishermen, who toiled all night but caught nothing. We try to amass a little money, but succeed simultaneously in amassing many cares. Everything has its price, 'tis true, but few things have their value; we have yet to learn the higher prudence.

Even Shakespeare is on my side. Has he not written:

> "*There's nothing so becomes a man*
> *As modest stillness.*"

I should like to add a gigantic exclamation mark after those words, for the support of England's premier poet and language's gifted lord is support indeed; it is an intoxicating idea but I dare not tamper with his work. True, a knowing critic might rise in ill-suppressed fury and point out that I have arrived at this plausible (and to me, perfect) quotation (or misquotation, he might term it) first by decapitating the sentence and then by chopping off its feet. But I would reply that the whole art of quotation is to wring a few apposite words from their context and reject the rest. What have I done but that?

Yet I fear that the critic would retire annoyed, seething with indignation at my heresies, Shakespearian, spiritual and otherwise.

I could even quote to my correspondent from the book which she holds in such respect a further statement: "Consider the lilies of the field; they toil not, neither do they spin."

The result of my consideration is this incursion into Himalaya! But she will adjure me to descend from these metaphysical clouds and perceive the real world around us.

To tell the truth, I have made no great renunciation in fleeing to my idle retreat. I am not indifferent to social pleasures, but I can do without them. I am not afraid to sit lazily upon a mountain-side and gaze upon the stage below. We must worship at the feet of the goddess of wisdom in utter loneliness, if we would win her. Although I have always enjoyed sipping tea at Florian's in Venice or watching the passing crowd beneath a café awning in France, these places are not necessary to my existence. Nature, however, is. I may leave her for a time, but always I must return, like an erring yet loving husband.

Nor can I resist a final quotation which sticks in my memory like a leech. "Someone should teach that while, in the opinion of society, contemplation is the gravest sin of which any citizen can be guilty, in the opinion of the highest culture it is the proper occupation of man." I am glad to accept Wilde's suggestion and so adopt the tutorial role!

The artist who wants to paint a really fine inspired picture and the musician who aspires to create a symphony which shall bear the authentic mark of genius must go away or shut themselves up behind closed doors until they have finished their work.

At such a time the creative artist who hopes to be something more than a mere mediocrity in his profession permits the world to come in quest of him or himself goes in quest of the world, at his own peril. He must respect the sanctity of his own self no less than that of any house of worship. Solitude preserves and fosters the efforts of his genius; but society destroys them. Genius indeed must labour in spiritual, artistic and physical isolation. It must be selective and take no more from the world than it needs to help its prime purpose. People who lead commonplace lives may laugh at its eccentricities, but they produce nothing extraordinary. In just the same way, when a man hopes to make a supreme endeavour to spiritualize himself, he must go away and shut himself up too. Is he not also an artist, albeit his art shall be intangible yet ineffable in its results?

In just the same way, too, if my own dream calls me here to Himalaya and bids me sit still, surely life may have some use for that also. Am I to assume that other people understand my business better than my Master and my Overself? No, my dear lady, I prefer to be true to myself, and not attempt to counterfeit others. Both you and I should not yield in fear to common custom or public error, but rather obey the highest law of our being. We need not be afraid. We shall lose nothing—no, not one iota. The divine laws will take care of us, if we trust them, and all apparent loss will be but temporary and made good with compound interest. Let us trust the mathematical rightness of the unseen Justice; it shall not betray us.

There remains, lastly, a higher reason for my attitude. Some years ago, whilst plunged in a yoga trance of profound meditation, I received a message, perhaps even a mission, but certainly a work to be done. This message came from four great Beings, angelic figures of an order particularly interested in the spiritual welfare of humanity in the mass, who have come close to this earth sphere from another planet.

In obedience to this message, wherein I was bidden to become for a time a wanderer upon the face of the earth, I flit from place to place as the spirit moves me. I did not care then and I do not care now for public rewards. Fame and renown leave me quite cold and are therefore unwanted; money I require no more of than sufficient to live a decent existence amid decent surroundings, and to meet the exigencies of the travels imposed upon me; pleasure I like to sample in small doses at odd intervals only. Although I accepted the task, I refused its public side, preferring to let others do that part which was likely to bring them public rewards. It is more to my temperament to accomplish the fundamental basis of this task in quiet and secrecy. Literary work is but a side issue with me, and as for reserves, I have always the sense of divine providence backing me; I need no other.

The dear lady has marked the paragraph which she considers pertinent to my case. Such a reference, coming from any other person, might well seem offensive. But she is a friend and takes a friendly licence. Moreover, as the elderly widow of an Army colonel and knowing some of my most intimate and personal affairs, she takes a maternal interest in them. I accept her reference, then, without the slightest offence, indeed with a laugh, for I know she has marked that paragraph out of affection, not contempt.

*　　*　　*

It is curious, nevertheless, what peculiar definitions people place upon the word "sanity". A few months ago I delivered an address before a certain Indian university. Not wishing to stray aside from the studies which had been the mainstay of the students, yet not caring to take the long journey of 160 miles merely to tell them something that did not engage my own deepest interest, I found a happy medium by delivering a lecture on the theme of "The Philosophy of Inspiration". In that way I was able to touch on the subject of inspiration in literature, art, business, invention, life and religion, as well as to provide the students with one or two practical hints on their preparation for a career.

After the newspaper reports of my address had been published, a deputation came to see me to suggest my delivering an address in their own State University. Although a still longer journey was involved, and although I rarely do public speaking, rejecting by habit almost all invitations, I replied that I would agree provided an official invitation were sent me. But when the professors who were friendly to me put forward their resolution at the next meeting of the Academic Council of their University, the Head of the Council used his influence to reject it. Accordingly, the invitation was not sent.

The reason for this opposition was peculiar. The man who opposed my coming was a European, to be precise an Englishman, but in India nowadays all whites are called Europeans by an official order. His chief and only objection was that "a white man who lives among the natives and who spends his time chiefly among Yogis in a hermitage *must* be mad"!

If withdrawal from city to country, from activity to retreat, for occasional and limited periods be an indication of insanity, then I prefer never to become sane again! If seeking metaphysical truth or practising mystical meditation is a sign of disordered intellect, then I pray the gods never to set me right again! If, to this learned but little-minded gentleman, the effort to find and keep inner peace in a peaceless world is incipient insanity, then I am happy to have him label me as mad! But I look upon it as true sanity to try and keep a worthwhile integrity of soul amidst all the distracting forces, the terror and turbulence of modern existence.

My academic opponent no doubt goes respectably to church every Sunday, but would he be willing to walk with Christ to Calvary? I wonder whether he has ever thought that Jesus *meant* what he said? I wonder whether he could possibly realize that a saintly sage of our times, Hindu born though he be, is a truer Christian than most of the mob with a Sunday religion? I wonder whether he could ever grasp the fact that a brown skin is no barrier to entry into the kingdom of heaven, which Jesus held before us as the goal but which so few Christians understand today.

I would make every preacher undergo an apprenticeship to life, and not to professors, before he spoke the first word from the pulpit. I would send him as a young man to live with the poor and the downtrodden before he fitted together those polished periods of his maiden sermon. I would compel him to go out to the lonely mountains and the unfrequented woods and stay there without books or friends to wrestle with his soul in that solitude until he either found God or found that the Church was not his vocation. I would bid him renounce all hope of inspiring others with religion until and unless he had first become inspired himself. If in the sequence his sermons might be less to the liking of conventional audiences and conventional bishops, they would at least be true and sincere, palpitant with the divine breath which ought to enter into every man before he dares to become a minister of God to the godless. This I would require of every preacher and every priest, whether he belong to the church of Christ or the brotherhood of Buddha, whether he admonish his flock in the name of Sri Krishna or in the name of any other prophet.

I am in the fortunate position of owing allegiance to no orthodox religion. When inquisitive persons ask me what is no business of theirs, I reply disconcertingly, and they do not press their enquiries any further.

I have found no mooring for my floating soul in any religious faith, in any philosophy, because I believe in the Spirit which, like the wind, bloweth where it listeth.

People who professedly follow Jesus, but who have never succeeded in understanding or obeying his deepest injunctions, may, in their Pharisaic fervour, naturally resent the intrusion of one who does not outwardly belong to their or any other denomination. A man whose interior vision sets up bar and barrier between him and them, as well as between him and every other creedal group, finds, however, that it also sets him free. If he is strong enough to stand aside from all the orthodox religious and racial groupings surrounding him, and if he is independent enough to court the favour of none nor to fear their frowns, then destiny and choice have indeed combined to give him a unique and delightful liberation. Whilst other men hurl their silent or vocal hatred at each other, whilst race murmurs against race, whilst creeds come into contemptuous collision over trifles, he may regard the foolishness of these quarrelsome folk into whose midst he has been flung as an observer from a distant planet might regard it were he, too, flung here.

Such a man has no contemporary, and does not need to look for one. The orthodox do not welcome such independence, while the heterodox may disdain such "superstitions". It does not matter. Truth, serene and supreme, can wait patiently for her day. She can lose nothing, for she is eternal. Her revelation must come sooner or later, suddenly or slowly.

It is because of this detached position that I can find my friends among all faiths and none, and my enemies in the same wide-thrown groupings too. I live amongst them all as an alien, well knowing where my true native land really is.

No institution interposes itself betwixt me and the sacred beams which fall from the Hidden Sun.

Fate has condemned me to become an interpreter of the Sphinx's language; a task delightful enough so long as one keeps one's interpretations to oneself, but disagreeable indeed as soon as one begins to reveal them to a sceptical world.

But I find a secret comfort in the thought that this penible sojourn of mine is but a temporary one, and that the relenting gods will one day give me swift passage back to my own star, for whose silvery greenish twinkle I search the sky every night with acute nostalgia.

The friend in Bombay, bless her kind but mistaken soul, in attempting to rebuke my addiction to research into matters that lie thickly veiled, however, has done me a real service all unwittingly. She has put into my hands, all bookless as I was when I came into this solitude, the words and life of the wise Gallilean, whose very name carries ever a magic sound to my ears. I shall read these pages right through. It is true that I can never accept the Authorized Version of this book as the accurate record of him, nor as the full one, because much that is worthwhile has been rejected by the compilers and much that is printed has been badly translated, while the record of Jesus' wandering preparatory years between the ages of twelve and thirty is entirely missing. Even the true incidents are not always accurately reported. Nevertheless, even imperfect as it stands, I take the little black book to my heart and shall treasure its gift.

We must look beneath this surface-symbol that men call life, my dear lady, and endeavour to find out what it truly means. Jesus knew. We must not mistake the mere accidents of existence for its fundamentals. He who apes the world at the cost of his interior peace punishes himself.

The words of Jesus have not been entirely lost to the world, as the words of so many other speakers have. Why? Because Jesus spoke out of the deep region of the Overself, whereas the others lectured out of their little intellects. Jesus spoke to his contemporaries but his speech succeeded in reaching all posterity. The others could never get beyond their contemporaries, never find more than an ephemeral life in the daily gazette. They had to speak with some care—care both for public opinion and their pockets. Their excuse was that men must live, that bread is better than a halo. Poor fellows! They did not know that whoever finds the halo will find his bread likewise. Sparrows are fed and why not men with haloes? God is not so powerless that He cannot take care of His own. . . . The speech of Socrates is also still in circulation, because he let the bread take care of itself, which it did. . . . The value of a man's words depends upon his spiritual specific gravity.

The sayings of this god-man Jesus are the most quotable of any that I know. The world of commentators and theologians may quibble over their meanings, as they have quibbled for nineteen hundred years, but a simple soul or a sensitive one will find far less difficulty in understanding them, because they are superbly direct and because Jesus himself was not a theologian. There is nothing in the New Testament which is tortuous or hesitant.

For in this day and age the time has come, as it came once in Palestine, to speak outright, to give plain voice to Truth, and not to mutter half-heard, half-meaningless phrases about it in dark alleys.

*   *   *

Alas, that most of us are spiritual mutes and cannot speak one eternal word!

Alas, too, the cry "Back to Christianity", which I hear in Europe, or "Back to Hinduism", which I hear in India, is a vain one. We have had ample time to try these faiths. If we could not experiment with them properly during the centuries near the lifetimes of their Inspirers, we never shall. Let us not delude ourselves. There is no such thing as a return to the past. The original inspiration of every religion is also its most vital one. Much can be done under its influence which later can only be copied without heart and without fire. The wheels of the clock cannot work reversely, do what we may. The past must now take care of itself. This is precisely what Jesus meant when he said, "Let the dead bury the dead." We must study life in the living present, not in the dead past. The world is still waiting for its Redeemer. The old religions have lost their dynamic. The real Christians were those who were flung as martyrs to the lions.

Let us start our learning of the Truth clear from obstructive vestiges of mummified dogmas.

If the oracles of ancient civilizations are now all but silent, then the oracles of the modern world must speak their word. Inspiration itself does not lie in the grave, even though its earlier instruments do.

If Christ came to Camden Town, as Blake in the beauty of his spiritual understanding supposed he might, no one would recognize him, for the simple reason that our false education would lead us to expect a descent of flaming chariots from the open sky or else a radiant mist-like figure seen as in a dream; whereas he would more likely be found walking quietly along the High Street, with but few marks on his face to distinguish him from other carpenters walking that undistinguished street in an undistinguished neighbourhood.

No one nowadays dreams of calling Jesus mad, yet when he first moved and preached among the babbling crowd of bearded Pharisees the latter murmured scornfully among themselves, "Thou madman!" It was not until later, when they saw that he indeed *meant* what he said and "cast out them that sold and bought in the temple, and overthrew the tables of the money-changers", that they took him seriously. Then, when he had become a menace to their own positions, and to their own grip upon the masses, they "sought how they might destroy him; for they feared him, because all the people was astonished at his doctrine". They were afraid as ever to wake up from their miserable illusions. They preferred prejudice to principle and pride to truth. They would flee the Overself, for they feared it would bring them loss. Foolish wicked people! There was nothing to be lost, but all to be gained.

Alas, "for Jesus himself testified that a prophet hath no honour in his own country."

Therefore "he left Judaea and departed again into Galilee.

And he must needs go through Samaria. . . . Now Jacob's well was there. Jesus, therefore, being wearied with his journey, sat thus on the well. . . . There cometh a woman of Samaria to draw water: Jesus saith unto her, Give me to drink. Then saith the woman unto him, How is it that thou, being a Jew, askest drink of me, which am a woman of Samaria, for the Jews have no dealings with the Samaritans. Jesus answered and said unto her: If thou knewest the gift of God, and who it is that saith to thee, Give me to drink, thou wouldst have asked of him, and he would have given thee living water. The woman saith unto him, Sir, thou hast nothing to draw with, and the well is deep: from whence then hast thou that living water? Jesus answered and said unto her, Whosoever drinketh of this water shall thirst again: But whosoever drinketh of the water that I shall give him shall never thirst; but the water that I shall give him shall be in a well of water springing up into everlasting life. The woman saith unto him, Sir, I perceive that thou art a prophet. Jesus saith unto her, Woman, believe me, the hour cometh, and now is, when the true worshippers shall worship the Father in spirit and in truth: for the Father seeketh such to worship him. God is a Spirit: and they that worship Him must worship in spirit and in truth."

Veni, vidi, vici! The Roman leader's words do not apply to Jesus. He conquered the hearts of a few, it is true, but the mass of Jews remained unregenerate. He himself passed away as obscurely as he had come into their midst, biassed theological historians notwithstanding, so obscurely that hardly a single written reference to him of that time exists today.

Nevertheless:

"In the meanwhile his disciples prayed him, saying, Master, eat.

But he said unto them, I have meat to eat that ye know not of.

Therefore said the disciples one to another, Hath any man brought him anything to eat?

Jesus said unto them, MY MEAT IS TO DO THE WILL OF HIM THAT SENT ME, AND TO FINISH HIS WORK."

Sceptics who find it hard to believe that Jesus lived may be pardoned, but intellectual mystics who would turn all Bibles into mere allegories and all past religious teachers into symbols of the human soul venture too far into speculation. Why should there not have been such great men who discovered their inward godhood? And if they once lived why should their stories not have been written down, however faultily? Christ and Krishna, Buddha and Osiris, are no more myth-like figures than Muhammed, who, being so much nearer to our own time, has his existence accepted without question. The real difficulty lies in the embroidered interpolations to these sacred histories.

The extraordinary quality about Christ is his power of conversion. He walks by the sea of Galilee, finds two fishermen engaged in their daily work, throws out a few words, and straightway induces them to cast a different kind of net amongst men. . . . The son goes out to look for his father's herd of asses, meets the Master, and is changed: henceforth he too shall go out to look for a diviner herd. . . . Saul, journeying along the road to Damascus, is met by the invisible Christ, and falls to the ground at his feet. . . .

Yet even this power of Jesus was not a miraculous one, was not universal. He could not convert the Pharisees; he has not converted them yet—those hard, stiff-necked, formal, overprudent creatures who have existed through all ages and in all lands, not merely among the Jews but among all other races too.

For Jesus could only convert his own. Indeed, he did not seek to do more than that. He had come for them, his children. No man of God can do more than that. Such is the marvellous gift of freedom which God has bestowed on us all—no man's mysterious freedom of will shall be disturbed. We are to turn Homewards of our own accord, not by any pressure or interference.

The Masters of Light, as in Jesus' day, seek those alone who are already seeking them, who in their conscious or unconscious minds are eager to return Home. They know that grapes cannot be gathered off thistles.

CHAPTER NINE

Storm—Precursors of the Monsoon—My Animal Visitors—The Question of Clothes.

SOME unaccountably early precursors of the still distant rainy season make their sudden appearance. Himalaya is exceedingly erratic these days, each day provides plenty of varying samples, both good and bad. Unexpected changes begin in that near horizon where sky meets earth in a white broken line of fleecy cloud and jagged peak and fallen snow.

The only advantage we derive from the fitful rains is the easing of our water problem. Hitherto the essential liquid has had to be carried from the nearest bubbling spring, which is more than a quarter mile away. But now all that needs to be done is to put our bulging brass water-pot outside the door and let the elements kindly fill it. And this is eventually done, so heavy is the rainfall. Yet it is only sporadic and unreliable.

The nights are sometimes bitterly cold, especially to one who has come from the torrid South. For with the fall of day clouds sail like ships over the summits and frequently forgather in the sky, the terrific Tibetan winds come whistling over the snowy range and beat against my bungalow, disagreeable murky mists often make their appearance and blot out the landscape, leaving the building desolate and lone in space after they have rolled around it. Everything then disappears from sight.

But all this is nothing to a Himalayan storm. It is one of the worst I have ever seen for intensity, and yet so impressive as to receive a touch of grandeur. Twice this week we have been stormbound.

It begins with the approach of night. An ominous change occurs to the temperature, which drops and drops. I barricade myself against the invading cold by changing into a woollen shirt and a thick high-collared sweater, and then peer through the door-panel to watch the brooding storm break. Soon peals of terrific thunder break out all along the Himalayan range with the fury of detonating shells, until it seems that the mountains are being undermined, exploded and shattered by violent subterranean forces. Yet I know that the quartz and granite and gneiss which form the core of the Himalayas will well resist the erosions of Nature. But the magnificent and really beautiful displays of lightning which precede the noise provide ample compensation. No mere zigzags of electric light are these, but large circling masses of white phosphorescence that glow weirdly against the surrounding blackness.

A fierce gusty gale shakes the tops of my tall fir trees and makes the branches sough hither and thither as it blows along with the speed of an express train. The blustering winds beat down the valleys and thresh the frailer trees of their leaves. Rain comes down in bucketfuls, large drops that will fall furiously and unabatedly for some hours. To complete the bombardment, the fierce patter of hail-stones, each as big as playing marbles, sounds all over the roof.

These hailstones can be very destructive. Sometimes they even reach the size of walnuts. After a heavy storm I find the little bodies of a few birds near the bungalow, as an earnest of what has been done farther along the ridges, whilst a tall deodar lies struck dead and splintered by lightning.

Early this morning I awaken from sleep to the sound of rattling peals of thunder which echo all over the mountain valleys. The tempest howls furiously outside. And when, later, the cold grey light of a sunless dawn spreads over the land, I look out of my doorway at a bleak inhospitable scene. Impenetrable thick white mists envelop the entire region beyond the first serried rank of fir trees, which stand up at the border of the mists like soldiers on sentry guard. The forest itself has disappeared, the snowy line of crags and pinnacles has vanished as if it had never existed. Here we are, ten thousand feet high in the air, marooned in a sea of milk-white mist. India, Tibet, England—all these seem now but the mere names of mythical countries. This planet Earth, apparently, has dissolved into white space and we are the sole survivors, perched on a scanty foothold in the midst of the ether.

The drenching mists which gather like fleecy wraps all over the landscape, rolling through the valleys, lapping at the steep slopes, and enwreathing the peaks and ridges, finally blotting everything from view, are matched only by the greyish-black sulphurous fogs of wintry England, but the former are far pleasanter. They are, at least, white and clean-looking. But they isolate one so perfectly that life becomes strangely uncanny, infinitely and inexpressibly solitary, enough to satisfy the taste of the most exacting anchorite.

I do not mind these few fitful mists, but the lashing rains and thunderous storms drive me now and again from my gorge-top sanctuary. My meditations have then perforce to be conducted indoors. At such times I can no longer adventure into stillness amid a delightful environment of russet leaves and midget-headed flowers, but have to squat on an oaken blanketed bed, with eyes fixed upon the blank space of a buff-distempered wall. I wonder what my deodar tree thinks of such truancies. What a weakling he must

89

imagine me to be! Afraid of the rain which he bears so bravely and so indifferently!

But for most of the hours the weather makes amends. The rain stops suddenly and a welcome rift of dryness returns. The mists roll away mysteriously, evaporating as quickly as tobacco clouds blown vigorously from a pipe, and a joyous interlude of sunshine comes back. The grey-skinned lizards creep out of crevices in the rocks in order to enjoy the bright beams. Their glass-like eyes look very aged and very wicked. Once again Himalaya raises its stately and stubborn head. In the clarified atmosphere, the sun shines along the entire array of the sparkling snowline, the sky is an attractive deep turquoise blue, and a pleasant warmth is diffused outdoors.

Better, anyway, than being a dejected toiler in the plains, suffering the spring heats.

And then I take up my stick and steal back penitently to the deserted sanctuary, make my weak apologies to the frowning deodar, and spread out the fawn-coloured square of waterproof ground-sheet once again under a calm firmament.

The powerful flight of an eagle overhead reminds me suddenly of those Tibetan teachers who say to their pupils, "Just as an eagle carries off a single sheep out of the flock, so should you carry off a single thought out of the multitudes that present themselves, and concentrate on that."

Butterflies come flitting up out of the forest and alight on the solitary wildflowers, and the peace which enfolds the scene is broken only by the jubilant song of happy birds, cageless and free as they are, which take up the diurnal praise of Himalaya and its forests. My deodar nods momentarily in a light breeze with the grave dignity becoming to a sexagenarian. The speckled crest and saffron neck of a hoopoe bird cross my line of vision.

And in that glad restoration of Nature which makes Himalaya such a constant splendour I discover a diviner footing for my body and a diviner ministration to my mind, for as I sit and let my thoughts melt imperceptibly into the silence the Overself touches me and begins to draw me inside. Then it throws its holy mantle over my blemishes, and I know not what has become of them.

So all men must disengage themselves from the claims of personality.

* * *

My servant comes to me with the plaint that the smashing of my wrist-watch has deprived him of an essential feature of civilized life —knowing what is the time! In consequence he does not know when to start preparing my meals and has to guess his way, with the result that on some occasions he announces lunch only to find himself disconcertingly waved off, while on other occasions I announce my hunger when he has no meal ready yet to satisfy it!

I receive the news with commensurate seriousness for I see that his plaint is a just one. A little pondering and I decide to improvise a rough sundial solely for his benefit. In the forest I select a narrow piece of straight wood which is smoothed and planted firmly in the ground behind the bungalow. Then I wait till the following day when, at sunrise, noon and sunset, I make my first markings by setting up three stones in the ground along the line of the stick's shadow. It is then an easy matter to shift the shadow marks so as to correspond roughly with the desired hours for breakfast, lunch and tea. So long as we have sunny days we shall have our primitive clock in perfect working order, allowing for variations in the length of shadow cast as the season advances.

How time is our tyrant! We have made its measuring and figuring a necessity of our existence. And yet man, in his inmost self, is a timeless being.

* * *

There is little agriculture in this kingdom of Tehri and little space for it. The earth does not yield itself docilely to the cultivator's plough, for nearly everything is either mountainous wild forest or barren rock and stone. Hence the pasturage of goats and cattle, which climb and descend the mountain-sides in a surprisingly nimble manner, is an important occupation for the few inhabitants who tear their scant livelihood from the reluctant bosom of the ranges.

A mountain goatherd who is wandering with his flock of squawking goats in search of pasturage reaches my vicinity. His clothing is ragged, consisting indeed of the usual costume of these men : a round, flat-topped stiff cap, a tight tattered jacket, a loose ancient shirt and a loin-cloth. A stubby growth of black beard fronts his strong jutting chin. His eyes, from long habit, are screwed up in defence against the sun-glare. His skin is the colour of burnished bronze. His arms are folded akimbo upon his chest, a large curved dagger in one hand. His whole face is rugged and weatherbeaten. His naked feet are covered with dust.

I am typewriting letters and sit out in the open air in mellow sunshine whilst I work. The man observes me and stands for about twenty minutes at a respectful distance. At length he breaks his silence and reveals his thoughts, for he approaches closer, touches his brow with both hands closed, and utters a low "Salaam!" and bows profusely. It is then that I notice his right hand crudely bandaged. He says that he lives in a hut some miles away and that his hand has been wounded. Will his honour, the Cherisher of the Poor, give some medicine for the injured hand? Once again he relapses into taciturnity.

Untying the piece of dirty rag which covers his hand I examine the wound. He has evidently been bitten by some fierce beast. A large piece of flesh has been torn away, leaving a terrible sight. It is a dirty jagged bloody mess. The filthiness of its wrapping involves the danger of septic development. The poor fellow does not realize the importance of caring cleanly for a wound on a body which is not too often washed. I wash the mauled hand carefully with some boric solution as a mild disinfectant, cover it well with the dry boric acid powder for the same purpose, apply some green ointment to assist the healing, and then fix clean lint and a new bandage to finish the job. I give him a supply of powder, ointment and bandages with instructions how to use them.

He "salaams" once more and disappears slowly along the ridge with his noisy flock, his face now looking as bright as a schoolboy at games, a hardy, happy little man.

I envy the simplicity of his soul. Hillmen like him live in close association with Nature and develop a sincere if untutored character and one untroubled by intellectual problems. The ancient historians of India tell us that the early people of that country were so honest that they never needed to lock the doors of their houses. Some remnant of this latter custom prevails among these hillmen, and I conclude that something of the same absolute honesty is theirs too.

Their contact with the outside world is but little, and with modernity, less; they have not joined the general scramble for more money and education could not make them much happier than they are. They are surprisingly gentle and surprisingly peaceful. They live the poorest of lives, but keep happy. But despite my envy, I prefer to taste of the tree of knowledge, and pay the requisite price. I cannot undo the past and change places with such a man as the one who has now gone down the lone trail.

These folk have curious proverbs and quaint expressions. The inescapability of fate is described by "God gives, even through the roof of one's house!" The interdependence of humanity is phrased in "No man can shave his own head!" A clever reminder of the transience of life is "Men say that time passes; time says that men pass!" When nothing further can be done in any matter, they shrug their shoulders and say, "No village beyond Mana!" Mana is the last inhabited spot on a pass into Tibet.

* * *

Two large black scorpions have wandered into my bedroom within the week. They are queer unpleasant fellows, not quite so lively at this high altitude as their yellow Egyptian cousins, perhaps, and far less common, but quite capable of administering a vicious sting with their poison tails.

If Nature sends me some varied visitors, destiny to my surprise sends a companion. True I had hoped for complete solitude, but solitude *à deux* may not be altogether bad if the other is a pleasant person, and so the newcomer turns out to be. I can see at a glance that she will respect my hours when I wish to be alone, this lady, and yet sing entertainingly during the hours when I can tolerate company. I could do worse, when my wandering feet shall one day come to rest, than make my permanent home address in the Himalayas with her.

The passing visitor who has stayed as a permanent companion is a warm-breasted little robin which hops sedately around my bungalow and then alights on the nearest bush to take several peeps at me, the while I sit outside in the sunshine and write my letters and enter up my journal—that record of passing scenes and surrounding sights, of a few interviews and many meditations, in which I put my heart under a microscope and report what has come to me, what I have beheld in the shining hours of ecstasy, as some celestial journalist might report them, to keep as a recollection for later years.

It has won a corner of my heart, and for its sake I keep a pocket full of biscuit-crumbs in waiting readiness. When its confidence is assured and it gets over its fear of humanity it accepts my proffered invitation and hops down and approaches nearer and nearer, until I reward its wide-open mouth with a generous measure of its paradisiac food. Each time I see the lovely reddish-gold colouring of its underbreast I feel a trifle happier, a trifle gayer, as though Nature has sent a silent message bidding me be of good cheer. I love my dear robin and I hope it will not leave me. It has its habitat in a newly built nest under the roof of my bungalow, when it is not flitting among the boughs.

But, by way of contrast, there is another inhabitant of this region. He is a vociferous crow which lives on the very top of the forest fir tree overhanging my patch of grassy and stony ridge. With every gusty breeze he is in danger of losing his foothold on the tree-top, to which he insists on clinging; the violent efforts he makes to retain his balance are indeed comical. Once he disappeared for a time longer than his wont, so I went off in quest of the truant. I found him near my sanctuary, amongst a batch of other crows who were gathered in grave assembly, apparently discussing state matters in their croaking voices. He has a hoarse throaty voice which he does not believe in hiding under a bushel; it is like a loud-speaker, with the consequence that every animal, every bird and every insect on the mountain, must know where he is domiciled. He, too, hops around the ground at times with opened beak, although uninvited, in an awkward and amusing series of flops and jumps, pecking jerkily at the crumbs. His large beak, his mournful black feathers, his suspicious yet curious glances as he solemnly watches me tap the typewriter keys, his harsh croaks, will all print themselves on my memory for after years. If the robin is the pretty little singing-girl of my court, then the crow is the unofficial fool and unconscious jester.

Just before dusk every evening, and with the oncoming end of the violet sunset, a whistling thrush appears upon the stony patch which does duty as a stage for my bird companions and treats me to an excellent performance. It whistles as well as any schoolboy equipped with an instrument, and certainly far more musically.

Again, in contrast to the crow's harsh croak is the gentle, soft cooing of a pair of turtle-doves, with brown mottled plumage, who come quite close to me and watch my movements with great curiosity. I watch them too, did they but know it, for I am interested to see how loving they are towards one another, never going out of each other's sight, nor permitting much more than a few yards ever to come between them.

A fourth companion I never see, but hear. It is a cicad. The insect inhabits the crow's tree, albeit much lower down, and its shrill chirp whirrs at fixed intervals like a rattle.

Strangest of my comrades is a tame housefly. Its favourite roost is on one of my thumb-nails. There it is content to pass its happy half hours in playful exploration. At suitable intervals I place some sugar in my hand and the fly clings to the food, no matter how I twist and turn my hand when writing. When I tire of supporting it on my thumbnail I transfer it to the other hand, where it remains perfectly contented.

An unwelcome visitor is the horse-fly, a huge and vicious fly of incredible size. I discover its existence one day when it pokes its pointed barb through my shirt and administers a sharp sting which remains to irritate the skin for a long time. But I do not think any horse-fly will venture to do that a second time!

Grasshoppers, too, dance comically around the place.

There are other visitors here, belonging to the animal and insect world, both pleasant and unpleasant, both tame and wild, but they come only occasionally and pass on like the strangers they are. Most unexpected, however, is the call I receive one afternoon when eating lunch. I hear stealthy footsteps behind me, creeping closer and closer, moving with the cat-like tread of a thief. Wondering whether a panther or leopard is about to spring, provoked into probing this mystery, I switch round suddenly and see—a mountain goat!

It is a cream-coloured hungry creature which has wandered away from its herd and has been attracted through my open door by the savoury odour of the food.

At nightfall, when I sit occasionally at the forest's verge, under the perfect sphere of a full moon set in an indigo-blue sky, strange cries come to me out of the depths. The savage population is astir. The night invites wild animals to begin their roaming. Above it all the nightjar, that noisy bird, screeches overhead in the darkness. Fireflies flicker between the trees, weaving weird patterns of phosphorescent light in the blackness.

*　　*　　*

I sit down to meals in the same old clothes with which I potter around the peak-top. I do not trouble to change into a starched uncomfortable shirt for dinner. It may be that I have lost my sense of dignity and decency in this wild place, I do not know. Anyway, I feel so utterly free, so deliciously abandoned to Nature, so remote from the formal restrictions which men and women place on one another in society, that I cannot bother myself with all the manners requisite to civilized life. Such is the treason which Nature has subtly instilled into me.

It is true that I continue the daily scrape. I must shave. A beard, however, would be quite fitting to a hermit, but I fear to go as far as that.

There was an Englishman, a Forest Range Officer, whom I knew not so long ago. His service for three years was in a sparsely populated part of the Punjab, where a meeting with another European or with an educated Indian was a rare event of his lonely existence. Nevertheless he did not hesitate to put on his black dinner-jacket suit and white stiff collar every evening without exception, when sitting down to dinner, as though he were at a formal party. Only his servant was present to witness this sartorial preparation for the nocturnal meal. He told me that he could not enjoy his food if he had failed to change his dress; I believed him and admired him.

Yet it is a moot question whether a man should grow careless about his personal appearance because he is living amid no other society than sombre trees and silent peaks, occasional illiterate tribesmen and twittering birds. I presume a coat, collar and tie are really necessary in city life, but they are not so necessary here. Why should a man continue the habit of worrying about the hang of his tie here, where all his environment bids him be free as Nature is free?

In Himalaya uncreased trousers are most natural, almost inevitable, for one cannot carry heavy press-irons around these mountains; in Hertford Street, Mayfair, they are unnatural, an error of taste. There is the difference, however, that whereas Himalaya is more interested in the wearer, Hertford Street is more interested in the trousers!

Yet I can understand how a man's aesthetic taste may induce him, for his own satisfaction, to rebut this liberating influence and even persuade him to take as much care over his personal appearance in such primal solitudes as in the buzzing crowd of a fashionable drawing-room. 'Tis all a matter of taste and temperament. Let a man do as he pleases, when he enters these wide doorless domains of mountain and forest. Let him be happy in his own individual way, and not necessarily in the way which others would impose upon him.

Brusque, bearded Carlyle has given us in his peculiar panting style a philosophy of clothes and shown us how, in their glass, we may read the man. Half the tailors' advertisements tell us of the importance of wearing the right habiliments. Fashion and Fastidiousness are the dictatorial rulers of the world. Only the millionaire and the sage can afford to wear shabby suits or the wrong dress. Not needing society's good opinion, the world has to accept them anyhow. But they are the rare oddities, whom we meet once in a while. The others must keep their ties straight or their pride will fall to the earth, devastated by the censorious frowns and shallow judgement of the fashionable.

CHAPTER TEN

Another Visit by a Yogi—His Adventurous Journey from Kashmir to Mount Kailas—His Wanderings in Western Tibet—How his Master Lived Naked Amid the Snow—Explanations of the Feat.

I WATCH the winding trail of rock-ledge cut along the mountain-side until the late afternoon light reveals a tall orange-robed figure turning a hairpin bend and moving quickly in my direction. I await him patiently upon the verandah of my bungalow, for it is the figure of an expected visitor.

Two days ago a letter came from him, bringing with it the pleasant and surprising announcement that he would divert his route and spend a few days with me.

He is the Yogi Pranavananda.

He is also the man with whom I had planned to go to Tibet on pilgrimage to Mount Kailas. He had been very disappointed at my failure to obtain governmental permission for my journey. When he realized that the Government's refusal was final, he decided to make the journey alone. For him entry was free and unbarred, because the Tibetans permit Hindu holy men to visit Kailas as pilgrims, although they are not allowed to stay there for any length of time.

He crosses the stony patch of ground upon which the bungalow has been built, and we look at each other. I raise my upturned palms and close them in salutation, bowing slightly. He does the same.

His stature is commanding, his eyes large and gleaming, his face heavily bearded, while his hair hangs in long thick waves down to his shoulders. He is well wrapped in several folds of long, thick orange-dyed robes, over which he wears a loose fawn-coloured waterproof coat.

The Yogi takes a proffered seat. His grave face looks very impressive. We talk for two hours and then retire for meditation. After that I have my supper. Pranavananda eats no evening meal but drinks some goat milk and takes a little fruit.

We sit up late, for there is much we have to discuss.

My companion loves Mount Kailas and Lake Manasrowar. A photograph which he once took of that sacred region has hung in my room since my arrival. He has been there twice; first in 1928, when he took the western and longest route, from Kashmir and through Gartok and then back to Kashmir; and again in 1935, when he took the southern, shortest, safest, and least troublesome route from Almora.

After his visit to me he will return to British India, and set out again for Almora, whence he will proceed to Kailas for the third time. But on this occasion he will go not merely as a visitor, but to pass a whole year as a resident of a Buddhist monastery, most probably the great monastery of Truphuklho (also called Jaridhipu, Tuthulphuk and Tsuntulphu). There he will pass his time in meditation and study. He will be the only Hindu Yogi living in Western Tibet, and the Tibetans have given him this permission because they hold him in such great regard.

I realize ruefully that amongst my papers is a heavily sealed envelope addressed to the Head Lama of Truphuklho Monastery, containing a letter requesting him to permit me to reside there and pursue my own studies and meditations. This letter of introduction was written by a Tibetan officer, for the monastery lies on the southern bank of the Lake Manasrowar, and therefore under the benign gaze of Mount Kailas. But now, alas! the beautifully-rhythmic flourishing Tibetan characters of the handwriting on this envelope will remain unread by Lamaist eyes.

Pranavananda will be cut off from any direct communication with India for nearly two-thirds of the year, for the heavy autumn snows will close the passes over the Himalayas and isolate Western Tibet. I express some concern as to how he will bear the terrible cold, because he has never before had to endure the Tibetan winter, but he seems quite confident and optimistic.

Before we retire to sleep we both gaze at the photograph which hangs unframed against the buff-distempered wall: Kailas, sheathed in a white rime of frozen snow and ice. His eyes are filled with love and admiration and reverence. There is no doubt that Kailas means more to him than any other place on earth, more even than his own native land.

"I have found contentment through my life of world-renunciation and Yoga practice," he murmurs, and strokes his flowing beard. "I am never unhappy. Yet once I felt a deep sadness and heavy depression—a melancholy I have never known since I gave up worldly life thirteen years ago. And that occasion was when I had to leave the Kailas region last year and return to India before the route over the Himalayas became snowbound and impassable. I suffered its icy climate, its scarcity of food and fuel and the lack of even the most primitive comforts, but all these privations meant nothing to me and did not disturb my mind; it was only the agony of parting from this wonderful place which had the power to cloud my feelings and distress my soul. Oh, Kailas is most bewitching, its beauty is overpowering, and, from a spiritual point of view, it possesses a subtle magnetic vibration of a supremely high order.

"I have been on pilgrimage to most of India's holy places but none of them has such a high spiritual vibration as I have found around this Tibetan peak and lake. Local legends say that the Buddhas still dwell in their invisible, subtle bodies upon its gorgeous silvery summit, and I can well believe it. And I do not know a more fascinating or more inspiring scene than sunset upon the bluish-green waters of Manasrowar. It looks like a huge emerald set between two majestic mountains—Kailas on the north and Gurla Mandhatha on the south. The resplendent rays of the waning sun add a mystic charm to a lake which is already mysteriously charming in itself. The spiritual vibrations emanating from it enrapture me and lull the mind into sublime serenity; often it has transported me into involuntary ecstasies. The best type of Buddhist monks in Tibet are to be found in the monasteries around these holy shores, and several among them strive day and night to attain the eternal silence of Nirvana. Could you have come with me this time it would have made me happier still. But we must accept destiny; perhaps next year it will relent and the permit will be granted to you; then I shall return to India and, if you are free, we shall go together."

He touches his palms in salutation and is gone for the night.

Next day we wander into the forest and move along happily under the spreading branches of sombre firs, treading a yielding carpet of decaying fir-needles. A few wild Himalayan primroses, with their serrated petals, give some occasional brighter colour. A sudden gust of wind sweeps across the valleys, and the trees wave their dark-green arms above the ground. Each of these firs looks like a giant Christmas tree. Perhaps this forest is the elusive home of Santa Claus? Perhaps I shall come face to face with him here one day? I shall dearly love to meet the white-bearded old gentleman and ask him a few questions, for he haunted my childhood days and gave rise to visions of his big bag of gifts that, alas, never materialized.

We find a clean shady spot and sit down. How wonderfully restful for the eyes to be out of the glaring yellow light of the plains! We chat and chat. Soon we turn to our favourite theme and the Yogi becomes autobiographical. I induce him to recount the story of his first visit to Kailas. Pranavananda strokes his thick black beard in reflective silence, then finds voice.

*   *   *

"Eight years have passed since I set out, with a companion, a brother disciple. Our teacher, the holy Swami Jnanananda, had

99

already gone on pilgrimage to Kailas and his vivid descriptions of the journey and its goal whetted our own appetites and influenced us to undertake this difficult and dangerous journey. We travelled first to the State of Kashmir, and in the capital city of Srinagar we collected some clothing and equipment for life in Tibet, that land of Arctic snows.

"Then we moved across the lovely valley of Kashmir, and over the mountain-ridges that enclose it, following the Sind river to Kargil and thence to the town of Leh. The road led us across the famous Zoji-La Pass, the approach to which being a dangerously slippery narrow ledge cut in the rock and curving around corners of the mountain-sides. We had to cross snow-bridges and snow-beds. At times the way was very steep and even treacherous, for avalanches slip and fall down on the path, sweeping to death those who are unfortunate enough to be in the way. These avalanches leave the path covered with slippery ice and at some places we had to jump over crevasses. Near Lamayuru the trail descended into what is said to be the world's deepest gorge. Its bottom is lost in gloom.

"We reached Leh after some time and there visited a Buddhist monastery, where we saw an immense statue of the Maitreya, the Messiah of the Buddhists, who will appear to save the world in two thousand years, according to their belief. Although it was a seated figure it was so tall that its shoulders passed through the ceiling; its head being in another storey of the building!

"Leh is an interesting little town for it stands at the junction of four great caravan roads. One leads to Central Asia and Yarkand, another to Tibet and China, and the others lead by different routes to India.

"We were now in Ladakh, or Little Tibet. This country was once part of Tibet proper but was invaded and conquered by the Kashmiris in the middle of last century. It is therefore still a province of Kashmir, but retains all its Tibetan characteristics.

"We pushed on in a south-easterly direction until we came to Hemis, where we found the largest monastery of Ladakh. It is famous for its devil-dances. In these dances a group of lamas wear large and frightful masks over their heads, each coloured to represent a devil or some terrifying horned beast of the other world. They dance with tinkling bells on their feet. The monastery itself is built on the face of a grey cliff in a narrow ravine, but the Head Lama has a solitary and special seat for meditation placed on a distant rock high above the building.

"No sooner were we across the Tibetan frontier than we began to suffer from the cold, although it was still a good season of the year. Freezing icy winds blew over us from the glaciers. Our hands and ears became benumbed. We found ourselves unable to hold the reins of our horses; it was only after some days that we became able to accomplish this feat. We tried to warm our hands over a fire of burning shrubs, but by the time that one side got warm the other side was again frozen. You may imagine our sufferings, for we were Hindus, accustomed to terrific heat, I being born in the South at Rajahmundry and educated in a college at Lahore—both places being among the hottest in India. I was curious to know how the temperatures of Tibet compared with those of India and so I took a thermometer with me on this jounrey. I found that the average figure between the frontier and Kailas was not far from freezing point.

"However, we persisted with our adventure, for to us it was a holy pilgrimage and once begun was not to be given up except through death. We had great difficulties on the way owing to our ignorance of the language, and sometimes could not obtain change of horses and had to walk over the icy ground. At other times the difficulty was in procuring food of any sort. In many of the villages we found that the people did not and could not take a bath even once a year, so cold was it.

"At the trading mart of Gynamina a guide we had engaged deserted us on hearing news of a big caravan of merchants which had been attacked and robbed by bandits of all its goods and personal belongings, down to the very clothes of the unfortunate traders. Armed bandits are fairly common in Western Tibet and make travelling unsafe. The robbery had occurred upon the road which we were due to take. Without a guide we could not proceed. However God did not fail to protect us. A merchant turned up later who befriended us with food and lent us his own personal servant as a guide.

"Yet no sooner was that trouble at an end when further distress awaited us. False rumours were spread throughout the place that we were two spies in the service of the British, and that the robes of holy men which we wore were merely a disguise. The Tibetans held us up, watched us closely and spied upon us in the effort to discover our supposed true identity. Thenceforth I had to hide the camera which I carried and use it only in secret. Somehow we managed to refute their suspicions, sufficiently at any rate to enable us to get away.

"One Tibetan habit which I tried to acquire but failed was that of tea-drinking. The tea is boiled for an hour and mi xed with rancid butter and salt. The first time I drank it I became ill only a half hour later.

"A curious fact was that the prickly shrubs, which in many places were the only fuel we could find, burned quite well although they were fresh and green—as well as if they had been old and dry.

"At Darchen we met with a hospitable Tibetan householder who lived with his family in a single tent. He offered us shelter and food for a few days. When I awoke the first morning at about dawn I noticed his youngest daughter, who was only about three and a half years old, and who had slept through the terrible cold of night-time, when the temperature had sunk ten degrees below freezing-point, with only a single skin covering her half-clothed form. As soon as the little child saw that I was awake she leapt like an arrow from her bed upon the floor and flew outside the door of the tent. There she hurled herself upon a pile of snow that lay upon the ground and lay almost prone upon it. At the time she watched me closely. After a while she returned to her bed and covered herself with the skin-blanket once more, until I made a movement as if to rise and get up from my own bed. At once she flew outside the tent and flung herself upon the snow-pile for the second time. I could not understand the reason of this curious behaviour, and through my guide I made enquiries of the parent.

"He told me that snow falls heavily during the night and buries his dog, which sleeps outside in order to guard his tent. Only the animal's nose and eyes are left uncovered. The dog does not attempt to move all night, because that would cause its sleeping-place to become wet, so it remains quiet under its snow blanket until daytime. These Tibetan dogs are large and ferocious mastiffs, and so powerful that they tear men to pieces, like wolves. He explained that the little girl realized that my life would be in danger should I attempt to go outside the tent on arising, for the dog would treat me as a stranger to be attacked. Hence she had watched me since the first break of dawn, and at my first signs of movement had leapt out to hold the dog which lay hidden beneath the snow and which I would not have seen, and thus prevent any injury to me. She could not speak and explain the danger, because she did not know my language. I marvelled at the wisdom and goodness of this little mite of a child, and I regarded this as being inherited, because her father was a highly spiritual man. He had begged me to give him some lessons in the art of *pranayama* (breath-control used as a means of concentrating the mind) and I taught him some of our Hindu methods.

"In the ancient monastery of Silling we found one hundred and eight monks, whose ages ranged from as young as seven up to grey-beards of over seventy. It possessed a primitive printing-press which was worked by an old lama. Instead of using movable types, he engraved the whole page upon wooden blocks, and in this way each book was slowly and laboriously produced. A boy lama was working as his apprentice, to succeed the old man when he died. The finished books were well-made and exceedingly attractive. They were printed on Lhasa-made paper of three qualities: common, superior, and royal superfine. Books produced in the last edition had very thick strong paper and all the letters were printed in gold.

"When we were nearing Taklakot we were overtaken by night and lost our way in the darkness. As we wandered helplessly a stalwart Tibetan rushed at us with a big dagger in his hand. He knocked my fellow disciple to the ground and then thrust the edge of his dagger against my neck, shouting at the same time, 'Who are you?' I answered gravely, feeling my last moment had come, 'We are poor *sadhus* (Hindu holy men). We do not fear your dagger or your threats.' Thereupon our attacker burst into peals of roaring laughter. When he calmed down he said that he would not hurt us. He explained that meeting us unexpectedly, he decided to play a practical joke upon us! Tibetan sense of humour is very peculiar!

"At the foot of a mountain six miles from Lake Manasrowar we reached the beautiful monastery of Punri. The walls were painted white and the tops were decorated with brilliant red borders. We slept there for the night and in the morning a young Lama conducted us to the library. Every monastery in Tibet possesses its own ancient Sanskrit library. Books are sometimes included, brought there more than a thousand years ago by Buddhist monks fleeing from persecution in India. In the Punri library there were magnificent images of sacred Buddhist personages placed on raised platforms amongst the old books. Many valuable paintings done in Chinese style upon silken scrolls hung upon the walls.

"Our guide led us to a recess in the walls which was heavily curtained upon both sides and sheltered by a gorgeous silken canopy. As all the windows of the library hall were hung with silk veilings, there was only a dim light in the place, except for two tiny butter-fed lamps which burned before this recess, and it took us a minute or two to realize that a figure placed upon a raised platform inside the recess was not a mere statue like the other figures, but a living man. And quite a young man. In fact, we were told that he was only sixteen years old and that he was the Head Lama or Abbot of the entire monastery highly honoured by both senior and junior monks, and deeply respected by the common folk. As you know, the Grand Lama of Tibet as well as the Head Lamas of important monasteries are selected by Councils who search for the reincarnation of the deceased Lama. They are found as infants and then carefully educated for their high office. In the case of this young Abbot of Punri Monastery, he had had a number of articles belonging to the dead Abbot placed before him by the Council. They were well mixed with other objects purposely added. Without hesitation he recognized and picked out correctly all those things which belonged to the departed, and rejected the others.

"He sat absolutely motionless before us, with his right foot placed upon the left thigh, and the left foot placed upon his right thigh. One hand was placed upon the right knee, but the other lay flat in his lap with palms upturned and the thumb raised.

"I was highly impressed by his looks. He had an intelligent and serene face, a light ivory-coloured complexion, and a mild compassionate expression. Really, he looked like a young living Buddha. I quickly feel the spiritual atmosphere around any person. In his presence I experienced such a sense of reverence that I felt constrained to prostrate myself before him in profound respect—an act I had not hitherto done in Tibet because among the hosts of monks and Lamas I had not met one who deserved the veneration which I give only to my own personal teacher. The Head Lama acknowledged the devotion shown him by making his first movement and stretching out his right hand to touch my bowed head in blessing After that he took a richly engraved brass plate from his side and gave me a handful of dried apricots—a gesture which carried the same sacred significance as in India. I left feeling greatly exalted, for he was the most spiritually powerful, the most Buddha-like of all the Lamas I met in Tibet.

"At last, after all our sufferings from unbelievable cold and adventures in a strange country, weak, hungry and benumbed, we reached Lake Manasrowar. My shoes had been worn out on the rocky trails, and I walked with blistered feet along the snowy paths. My long-felt yearnings for a sight of the holy hill-bordered lake were satisfied. It was evening when we arrived and we put up in a very small *gompa* or monastic hermitage situated on a pyramidal hill. At ten o'clock at night I opened the window next to my bed and looked out. I was fortunate, for a full moon lit up the whole lake. A cold wind was blowing and the surface of the dark-blue waters was broken up into high waves. The moonbeams glittered upon the waves, but the middle of the lake was calm, reflecting both the stars and the moon. Red-beaked, white swans glided over the surface. The water dashed against the white, treeless sandy shore, producing pleasant and melodious sounds at rhythmic intervals. Then a cluster of thick black clouds appeared and threw shadows over Manasrowar. Such was the spiritual vibration in the atmosphere that my heart leapt with joy. The mind unconsciously shook off all other thoughts and slowly but steadily attained one-pointedness. My consciousness plunged into a mystic lake of bliss. My happiness was indescribable.

"The last stage of my journey brought me to Mount Kailas, famous throughout Asia. My first view of it was of a white-wrapped dome standing between two other peaks that almost touched its sides. The ice which covered it shone like polished silver. That is why we Hindus call it 'The Silver Mountain'. Our *Puranas* (sacred books) say that the god Shiva lives in meditation posture upon its white summit, while the Tibetans believe Buddha to be there. Of course, I do not believe that he is there in his physical body, but I do believe that his spiritual presence is there. The vibrations are unique and surround the mountain with an invisible field of enrapturing divinity as a magnet is surrounded by an invisible field of magnetism. And it is because the atmosphere causes one to become involuntarily meditative that it is superior to any other atmosphere I know. That is why I am now going to spend a year in one of the Buddhist monasteries of that region.

"I made the traditional thirty-mile walk around Kailas and the fifty-mile walk around Manasrowar, pacing slowly and with my mind intent on holy things. My pilgrimage was at an end. I will not weary you with the details of my return journey to Kashmir. I returned safely and, seven years later, repeated my visit to Kailas but took the much shorter route from Almora, which I intend to take again."

The Yogi's story is finished.

We return home through the forest in silence, and move with slow deliberate steps.

* * *

During the few days of his visit he gives sundry little glimpses of Tibetan life. In Ladakh he had encountered the same superstition which Sir Francis Younghusband had found on his military expedition to Lhasa. The Ladakhi people told him that their country had been annexed to Kashmir after the Maharajah had sent General Zoravah Singh to invade Tibet in 1848. They asserted that the leader of the Kashmiri troops possessed supernatural powers so that no ordinary leaden bullet could penetrate his body. His forces crossed Western Tibet to a point not far from Lake Manasrowar. The Chinese Emperor sent a large army to help the Tibetans and it victoriously defeated the Kashmiris by sheer weight of numbers, but the only way they could kill Zoravah Singh was to shoot him with a golden bullet instead of a lead one! He was afterwards hacked to pieces.

Possibly due to his commanding presence and his absolute sincerity and spirituality, the Tibetans regard Pranavananda with much respect. They now believe him to be the best of Hindu Yogis to have visited their country and so have accorded him this privilege

of living there. He will be, within a month or two, the only Indian
Yogi living in a Tibetan Buddhist monastery, except for his friend
Rahula, who resides at intervals in Lhasa. Rahula, however, is a
Buddhist monk born in the Indian province of Bihar and educated
in the temple-schools of Ceylon; he is not a Hindu Yogi.

I met the monk Rahula some years ago. I thought it curious that
he should have a Tibetan cast of countenance although wholly
Indian in ancestry. When dressed and muffled up he looks indistinguishable from a Lama. He showed me a large, costly and rare
collection of ancient silk paintings, oblong in shape, which had been
taken down from monastery walls and presented to him by various
Head Lamas. The Tibetans like and trust him and he has the
privilege of residing in Lhasa's chief monastery whenever he wishes.
He brought back in triumph from one of his journeys another gift
consisting of a huge library of rare palm-leaf Buddhist Sanskrit
volumes which had totally disappeared from India for a thousand
years through destruction by anti-Buddhist invaders or fanatical
Brahmins. From these Tibetan translations he intended to prepare
copies of the missing Sanskrit originals. He needed no fewer than
twenty pack-mules to carry his gifts back to India.

Buddhism has almost disappeared from the land of its birth, and
Rahula hoped to save the low flame from total extinction.

One afternoon, whilst we sit near the bank of a valley stream,
Yogi Pranavananda begins to talk of his teacher, the Swami
Jnanananda:

"My Master belongs to a wealthy family living in Andhra, the
north-east part of Madras Presidency. At about the age of seventeen
he had a dream in which a Great Soul appeared to him and asked
him to leave his home, but this request aroused a struggle in his soul
and he did not obey immediately. Again the Great Soul came to him
in a second dream, repeating his request, but this time the inner conflict was sharper than ever, between his desire to obey the Great
Soul and his devotion to his wife. Again he hesitated, lacking the
courage to break all family ties. However, the Great Soul came to
him yet again, touched him in a dream, and this time gave him the
strength to obey. Thus he left his home and, renouncing the world,
disappeared in search of truth. He travelled to the north and the
west in quest of a real teacher. Some years later, when he found his
Master, the latter simply said, 'The spiritual goal is already in your
lap,' he saw how highly advanced was the young man. And so it
proved, for soon after my revered Master entered the highest state of
spiritual trance from which he emerged a new man.

"However, he wanted to make his realization perfect, steady and
unbroken, so for that purpose he came to the Tehri State and went to

live in solitude at Gangotri in 1923. Whilst there he had an experience which demonstrated the power of his spiritual achievement. He came face to face with a big tiger which made no attempt to harm him but just sat on its hind legs and stared at him for some time and then disappeared into the jungle near by.

"He remained in the neighbourhood throughout an entire winter, when no other soul would have dared to stay because the snow, seven feet high, buries the whole place. No food of any sort could be obtained there during the winter season, but the Tehri State authorities arranged with the nearest local officials to send food supplies at intervals. But the astonishing thing is that Swami Jnanananda insisted on remaining almost absolutely naked throughout the period of his stay, except for a very narrow loin-cloth. Jnanananda lived in an exposed cave, without door and without fire. When he was asked how he could remain naked in such terrible cold, he said: 'In front of my cave at Gangotri I would sit on a slab of stone for meditation and enter into Samadhi. I became accustomed to the inclemencies of the weather without any difficulty. One day I was urged to throw away all my clothes suddenly without any apparent reason. I felt some power urging me from inside. That power and the name of the Lord rendered me quite indifferent to the cold which I did not feel.' Imagine him living in that wild deserted region, surrounded by snow and ice alone, with great avalanches sweeping down from the high peaks from time to time and liable to fall upon him. His only company was the silent Himalayas themselves and such wild animals as chanced to pass that way, and a few simple hill-folk. Today, if you ask the hillman who used to bring his food about the Swami, you will discover how he grew to love this great soul, for his eyes light up as he speaks and his heart melts with joy——"

Suddenly, Pranavananda stops talking. His eyes half-close, he breathes agitatedly and stertorously. I think he is going to have a fit. But no, soon he quietens down and passes by gentle stages into a trance. His body remains serene and unmoving, save for the slight rise and fall of his shoulders as he breathes silently.

And then I become aware of a vital change in the atmosphere. That mysterious stillness which heralds the coming of a higher state of consciousness or of a higher being invades the air. I realize at once that something important has happened so I swing half-round to face the Yogi directly, as I sit on the ground, interlock my legs in meditation posture, and attempt to adjust myself mentally to whatever is to come.

Across the inner eye, the mind's eye, the clairvoyant pineal gland—the name means nothing to me—there flashes the face of a bespectacled, bearded and broad-nosed man. An amiable smile plays around his lips. A pregnant glance at me and, immediately after, a message.

I understand.

It is the Swami Jnanananda. By the mysterious power possessed by men of his class, he has projected his mind, his soul, his subtle body—again the name means nothing to me—to his disciple and overshadows him. For the moment the two are spiritually one, their hearts interblent. This process of self-transference may puzzle the world, but it means the same thing, in a minor degree, as Jesus meant when he said, "I and my Father are one." This is the true significance of discipleship, its inward secret. Not for nothing do the Hindu Yogi traditions declare self-surrender to the Master to be an essential qualification, but the foolish have always materialized this and misunderstood it. All that a real Master requires of his disciple is the inner identification with himself, not the surrender of material goods. The latter is the hallmark of charlatanry. The former is the short path which cuts out all the long and laborious disciplines imposed by other paths.

For half an hour we both sit in complete silence, the "overshadowed" disciple and I. I endeavour to harmonize myself with the loftier vibrations which now pervade the place. The master talks to me, without words and without speech, and I make myself as sensitive, as receptive, to his message as I can. The outer world may see nothing but two men sitting still and facing each other, the one with eyes almost closed and the other with eyes wide open. But I "see" a sublime presence, whose visitation temporarily lifts me above my petty personal self.

Ultimately my companion comes slowly back to his normal condition, turns his head and then touches his eyes with a handkerchief. We continue to sit, although no longer facing each other, both hushed into muteness. When, later, we rise and walk along the valley, we talk of other matters, but not of this. It is not easy food for conversation, this experience, and we let it dissolve away unspoken.

Back in the bungalow, I ponder over the short life-sketch of his teacher which my friend has given me. I picture him taking his seat at Gangotri for meditation with, perhaps, a deerskin laid upon a bank of ice, snow falling around and half-burying him, and piercingly cold winds howling over the pass from Tibet. How has he resisted the terrible hardship of life in such a benumbing solitude? How has he endured the whole of a bitter Himalayan winter at the high altitude of Gangotri, eleven thousand feet at the temple level, but overlooked by the snow-clad peak which is twenty thousand feet high? How has he lived through it all, nude and fireless, to emerge safe and sound from his self-imposed ordeal?[1] The body obeys certain well-defined natural laws and any other man attempting to exist stark naked under similar conditions would inevitably perish. Yet Jnanananda seems to have suspended the operation of these laws at his own sweet will.

What is the explanation?

I find some hint of it, from memory, partly in two ancient Hindu volumes and partly in the statement of a Tibetan ascetic whom I met at Buddha-Gaya years ago.

One of the volumes is the *Hatha Yoga Pradipika*, a Sanskrit text-book for the use of those who are practising the Way of Body Control. It describes a hard and difficult physical system of self-discipline, involving tremendous efforts of will, and then promises those who follow it the power to resist all changes of temperature. The other book is the famous *Bhagavad Gita*, a manual of both Yoga and philosophy, which counsels the practitioner to withdraw his mind so completely into his deeper spiritual centre as to be oblivious of bodily feelings. "Be beyond the pairs of opposites, heat and cold," are its words.

From the Tibetan I learned that among the advanced ascetics of the Lama kingdom there are quite a number who specialize in generating, by certain physical exercises and mental practices, an internal heat, a subtle fiery force which they call *tomo*. In these exercises deep breathing is coupled with efforts of the will and imagination. First a secret invocation is chanted to receive the requisite magical power, and then the power of visualization is drawn upon and a subjective image of fire is produced. Then the flames are drawn up, to the accompaniment of deep breaths, from their supposed seat near the sex organ and sent to the head. The theory of these ascetics is that this imagined fire warms the generative sex fluid, which is then distributed along the arteries and nerves all over the body by other practices. Finally the ascetic passes into a trance in which he remains for some time with his mind fixed on the fire-mirage which he has created. My Tibetan informant claimed that this practice entirely drives off all sensation of cold from the body, and enables the man to feel a pleasant warmth pervading it although he be living in the depth of Tibet's hard rigorous winter. In fact, he added, some ascetics deliberately sit in freezing water when practising their exercises.

The clock must tick and the pages of the calendar must be turned. Yogi Pranavananda wraps his orange robe a little tighter

---

[1] The Tehri State Medical Officer, Dr. D. N. Nautyal, M.B., B.S., examined Swami Jnanananda after his return and found that his pulse-beat is now permanently set about thirty degrees below normal, I am informed by a State official.

around his body for the long journey that lies ahead of him. His muffled form must cross the sixteen thousand feet high Lipu Lekh Pass over the Himalayas before it becomes snowbound and impassable, if he is to enter Tibet's lofty tableland this year. Our delightful travel talks must come to an end. Our silent mutual lapses into the greater Silence must cease.

I shall not see his self-reliant fearless face nor hear his strong vehement voice again for at least another year, perhaps more. Yet I tell him that I shall feel, whilst he is living in the delectable spiritual atmosphere which surrounds Mount Kailas and Lake Manasrowar, that the inner link between us will profit me, and that some souvenir of the atmosphere will be sent occasionally along the invisible telegraph lines of that link.

He nods his bearded head.

"Yes, and I shall send you, through a trader, some pebbles of rock gathered on Mount Kailas itself. They will be more than a memento; tread on them and you will tread on Kailas ground, and thus defy the Government prohibition!"

CHAPTER ELEVEN

On Philosophy and Fun—Reflections on Mr. Charles Chaplin—His Silent Art and Genius—The Necessity of Modernizing Yoga—The Inadvisability of Asceticism—Some Truths about Sex and Yoga.

IF one of my more serious friends were to intrude during this period of my Himalayan hermitage and enter my room, he might lift more than one eyebrow in surprise at a certain object which hangs upon the buff-distempered wall above the mantelshelf. He might take the thing as an outward and visible sign, not of grace, oh no! but of the inevitable degeneration which sets in when people live without healthy active contact with society. He might even suggest that I am prematurely entering into an early dotage. And he might turn his highbrow head aside with a pronounced sniff of contempt.

The object which would cause such supercilious conduct is, I am almost ashamed to confess, a portrait of a certain film comedian, one Charlie Chaplin, and nothing more. The picture is no full-length artistic figure painted in fresh-looking oil-colours and framed in richly scrolled gilt wood. No, it is just a common print, a line drawing impressed in cheap ink on ordinary grey newsprint paper. It is, in fact, I am again almost ashamed to confess, merely a scrap torn the other week from an advertisement of a cinema theatre.

Not that there are any cinema theatres built on the steep slopes of my Himalayan domain (I wish there were!) In the whole of Tehri-Garhwal State, as in the tiny European countries of Lichtenstein and San Marino, no pictorial shadows flicker out the tragedies and passions and comedies of human existence upon white screens; no audience gathers in the twentieth-century temple of worship to do reverence to blonde Hollywood heroines and their romantic self-assured heroes; and no mountain goatherd pays his hard-earned annas to hear that incredible magic of the West, the talkies.

But a friend who labours editorially on a certain newspaper takes pity on my fancied loneliness and sends me a supply of his journals through the post. Although always a little out of date with their news, through the exigencies of a postal service that must climb up and down the narrow mountain trails of Himalaya, these reminders of the existence of an outside world are always welcome. And it is to one of these papers that I am deeply indebted for this frameless portrait of the unique, the inimitable, the naïvely charming yet ever-pathetic figure of Charlie.

It is true that the scrap of paper is neighboured by more dignified pictures, but that is no excuse for its own existence. For on its right there is a magazine photo of a wonderful cloud scene, while on its left hangs a real photograph of white-mantled Mount Kailas, which was given me by Yogi Pranavananda when our projected pilgrimage together was frustrated. But Mr. Charles Chaplin incongruously occupies the centre of the scene, thus revealing my lack of taste for all the world to see.

If my highbrow visitor were to make more audible comment upon my taste than a sniff, and ask why I have hung the thing upon my living-room wall, I should have to search for an answer. Whether he would be satisfied with my explanation I do not know, but I certainly possess strong reasons for the act in my own mind.

Why do I regard the bowler-hatted, baggy-trousered little Cockney with all the adoration of an unphilosophical cinema fan? My first answer would be extremely simple. Mr. Charles Chaplin makes me laugh. This primal activity of his put him into my heart twenty years ago, when he took the world by storm. I do not regret having kept him there all this time. He lives there quite comfortably, even though the long-bearded figure of Philosophy occupies the adjacent space. I have plenty of room for both, thank heaven. I have never allowed any of my excursions into life's gravest topics to push the grey-haired clown out of the guest-room which he occupies. During all my wanderings in the mystic courts of heaven I have yet to notice any prohibitory announcement upon the walls proclaiming that laughter is forbidden.

After all, it is better to jest and joke about this ephemeral life of ours than to imitate the undertaker. Life without its sprinkling of humour is like soup without salt—it lacks savour. We must laugh if life is to be made endurable. "If Nature had not made us a little frivolous, we should be most wretched," declared one of the wittiest of Frenchmen, and added, "It is because one can be frivolous that the majority do not hang themselves!" Voltaire was not unduly exaggerating. Life is mostly tolerable when we laugh at it.

My second answer would be that Chaplin arouses my sympathy. When this timid nervous figure shambles along the road, apparently suffering from a permanent inferiority complex, I feel sorry for him. I see millions of other shy men typified in his person, men whom the accident of birth has unfitted for the awful struggle of competitive existence and who consequently shuffle through life as pathetically as Chaplin shuffles through his pictures. I feel sorry for them all. Their helplessness, their misfortunes, their bewilderment in the face of social cruelties and social callousness, find a focus in the screen character of this man with a bewildered look in his eyes. We find ourselves in our cinema heroes, it is said, and maybe I recall in him the same besetting sense of inferiority with which I had to battle before I realized that the world was not worth taking at its own valuation.

Thirdly, I might point out that Chaplin and I possess a great deal in common. Our professions, for instance! He, as a comedian, tries to show people a way of escape from worldly realities. His particular way of escape is laughter. I, as a superficial unacademic philosopher, try to show people a way of escape from worldly reality, too. My particular way is mental quiet!

Humour is a mysterious quality which the gods have given to fallen mankind as a soporific substitute for the divine exaltation it has lost. It provides an excellent way of liberating oneself from the dismal effect of misfortunes, from drab environments, from unpleasant realities and persons, but above all from one's personal ego. The man who can laugh at himself has to that extent acquired some degree of impersonality. The spiritual philosopher aims at precisely the same effects. He too seeks to liberate himself from all these things. His method alone differs. He merely quietens thought, for he knows that a thing cannot hurt until it is allowed to intrude among his thoughts.

In any event, I would not give my scornful visitor more reasons than these three. If I, in common with many millions of other people, regard Chaplin with real affection, I need not be ashamed of sticking his portrait on the wall.

His popularity is something phenomenal. His name carries with it the international interest of a high politician's. I do not know how many millions of people look forward to his pictures as I do (my wanderings have made me miss more than one alas!) When he visited Paris the French went mad about him, while a Cabinet Minister publicly pinned a decoration of honour on his coat! In the larger cities of Asia he is as renowned and as beloved as in the automobile-filled cities of the United States. The Russians hold him enthusiastically in as high esteem as they do any of their Communist Commissars. For he speaks a universal language, which men of white, brown, yellow and black skins understand almost equally well—the language of humour and of pathos.

His little toothbrush moustache, his comical cane, his big shapeless boots and his funny clothes are world-renowned. His clowning is priceless. Those inimitable postures, those gestures of melancholy resignation, that forlorn, battered, tramp-like figure, that naïve, child-like character—all endear him to us. That astonishing awkward gait of his comes from the realm of inspiration. He learnt it from an old London horse-cabman, whose bad feet

H

necessitated his wearing boots of an abnormal size and caused him to move along the street in a ridiculous manner.

His dignified gravity mingles with ludicrous childishness. The merriment, the laughter, the foolery, arise out of the simple situations which he invents and which are far removed from the stale and ancient formulæ of unsuspectingly falling down street manholes and having sticky custard puddings flung pat upon one's face. This tramp with shiny, creaseless trousers yet with whimsical self-respect is often solemn yet never dull. The artistry, the construction, the production, the direction, the detail of his films are all perfect. One can see here that Chaplin is far more exacting about his own work than the critics themselves. He is not merely an artist alone but a man tortured by the quest of perfection which haunts true genius.

The dumb show of pantomime is more telling in his hands than all the verbal expressions of other actors. After all, primitive men understood each other by means of sign and gesture for many ages before they learned how to talk in sounds and words. Silent acting is thus among the most ancient of the arts. Chaplin's unmoving lips are more eloquent than speech and if ever he begins to talk on the screen I fear for the result. His dumb show is far better than his conversation could ever be. Let us hope that this frail figure in its tight-fitting ludicrous frock coat will never break its muteness, which is more attractive than the bright sallies of others, yet I am afraid the talkies are too irresistible and will conquer him yet.

May heaven help him to preserve his silence, for financially it will be his best move. The Asiatic and the African, who now comprehend his pantomimic gestures, will fail to comprehend his words once he begins to talk: that will bring dissatisfaction into their minds, and with that the beginning of their hero's downfall. His motto, artistically, should ever be the old tag: "Silence is golden, speech is silvern."

It is strange and symbolic that the year of his birth saw also the birth of Edison's Kinetoscope, which was the forerunner of the modern motion picture camera.

Chaplin's rise to fame was almost as miraculous as his acting. A single turn of fortune's mysterious wheel brought him, a little flushed and dazed, before two continents within a few months. From being an obscure actor's son, he became the Chief Clown to this planet. The lessons he learnt during the days of sordid poverty reveal themselves in those little incidents of the screen stories which make him beloved by the poorer classes everywhere, and which fill their hearts with laughter and moisten their eyes with tears. They pass through the inescapable tribulations of life a little happier for having seen his pictures. And if the latter do not generally end with the "happy ever after" note, but rather with the Buddhist's philosophic appraisal of mundane existence as being well-blent with sorrow, thus betraying the profound pessimism in Chaplin's inner being, those poor people know well that the former is but a false note struck by fiction-writers rather than realists. The little shadow-figure of the funny pranks, who greets every major misfortune with a whimsical raising of his shoulders, helps them towards a light-hearted fatalism as exquisite as are his hands.

So every cinema theatre may fulfil its mission as a place wherein to spend a couple of hours happily, free from the oppressions of care and the burdens of cogitation, released from the doubts and difficulties which cling like unwanted barnacles to the ship of modern existence.

* * *

I once stayed at a Continental country house where, not long before, Chaplin had himself been a guest. His signed portrait stood on the drawing-room piano. After I tried to pour out my tribute to his genius, my hostess admitted his gifts but retorted with the accusation, "But he is a Bolshevik!"

It appeared that his conversations revealed his deep interest in the subject of economics, as well as in the immense revolution which has been wrought out in the vicinity of Moscow's Kremlin. As a matter of fact, I do not think she was quite correct, for her personal fears of the Bolshevik forces which menaced her country caused her to see flaring red when the actual colour was only a mild pink. Chaplin is too much of an individualist and too great an artist to be fit prey for the doctrines of State Socialism. The evidences of his individuality, his strength and his uniqueness, are shown by the fact that whereas almost the whole moving picture world has submitted to the supremacy of talkies, he stands away alone and keeps the flag of speechless films still fluttering.

But whatever his political views, whatever his economic views may be, his simple unpretentious manners, his sensitive modest disposition in private life tell us plainly that he has not been spoilt by success upon the fevered heights of Hollywood, as so many other actors often are.

* * *

Alas, that life without love is incomplete! Man and woman need one another. We are not disposed to enter the chill arena of celibacy.

Unfortunate in marriage though he has been, the fault lay

neither in him nor in his wives. When two decent people, who might have got on well enough with other persons, are yoked in matrimony without understanding whether they are suited to each other, the painful discovery of their disparity usually brings out what is worst in the characters of both. Free them, and they become decent once more.

I have thought more than once about the reasons given by Chaplin's first wife on behalf of her suit for divorce. He was a man of strange moods, she complained, who wandered down to the seashore and stayed there alone for hours; he was a silent man, indulging in overmuch thought; he was a solitary who frequently tramped away from society into the Californian hills.

They were married, but not mated. Men marry in haste for women to repent at their leisure! Mrs. Chaplin, poor creature, was too young in body and soul to understand that if Charles' genius was to survive, he had to do these frowned-upon things, he had to practise solitary self-communion. If divorce had not come, his work would have suffered and Chaplin, like several other geniuses, would have had to live on the memory of his past greatness, on his past reputation.

His withdrawn moods and his taciturn silences were the price of his genius.

When the bond of matrimony becomes a heavy clanking prison chain it is sometimes the hour to pack one's boxes and depart; at other times the hour to learn the difficult yet divine lesson of personal renunciation.

Genius walks into marriage at its own peril.

Thomas Burke, the novelist, once observed that, "Chaplin is the loneliest, saddest man I ever knew."

Why? The reason is not far to seek. Charles Chaplin is an unconscious spiritual hermit, a potential Yogi.

He should be up here in the mighty Himalayas with me! What a wonderful time we would have in silent spiritual communion! What beautiful moments watching the sun smite the peaks into apricot yellow at day-fall! What unscreened, unphotographed adventures, seeking and finally discovering the true spiritual self! But my reflections upon him must come to an end. And so, just as at the end of his films, he shrugs his shoulders pathetically, twirls his familiar cane, and shuffles off into solitude—a wistful lovable oddity amongst the human species!

*　　　*　　　*

It strikes me, on further reflection of this delicate matter today, that if I invite Mr. Chaplin to become a Yogi, the first thing which is likely to happen is that I shall be much misunderstood, such are the varying conceptions and misconceptions of that elastic term. I have not the slightest notion of persuading the sad humorist of Hollywood to cast away his Western habiliments and don a yellow-coloured robe, to wrap a turban round his head and to wear a pair of open sandals upon his feet. On the contrary, I should prefer, possibly insist, that he make the morning parade upon this rocky ridge-top in the full ceremonial dress of the screen. It would afford me much pleasure to introduce him to my deodar properly attired in his short frock-coat, ancient bowler and big boots.

I fear that he has to form his conception of Yogis from the oratorical Swamis, or self-sent Indian religious teachers who have made their appearance in the United States of America, lured by dreams of an easy conquest of adoring disciples. Strangely enough, most of them have themselves been conquered, for the temptations of the novel and freer life of the West were not provided for in their philosophy. There are some honourable exceptions, of course. But the rest form a funny crowd. When I heard a certain advanced Yogi teacher at Rishikesh, the city of holy men, near the foot of the Himalayas, turn with horror from the suggestion of an American doctor with whom I visited him, that he take some Western pupils, denouncing them with the words, "Westerners will make a trade of Yoga," I felt nonplussed at his unjustness, for I knew that spiritual sincerity is not a monopoly of India. Now, however, many of his compatriots who have exported themselves to the transatlantic El Dorado, along with their self-provided titles of Yogi and Swami, have shown that the East has nothing to learn from the wicked Westerners in this matter, having, indeed, forestalled them.

I hope Mr. Chaplin will not judge me by the dress, person and doctrines of these gentry. I do not want him to make their goal his goal, nor to renounce his hard-bought Western wisdom for the sake of acquiring the distorted echoes of ancient truths which today pass current, even among the majority of the Indians themselves, as the Eastern wisdom. Truth is an extremely elusive lady. She resists the wooing of Occidentals and the caressing of Orientals alike. She may be captured, nevertheless, but her price is her own secret.

The tamer compromises which almost all present-day holy men have had to make with the ancient prescribed diets and disciplines indicate significantly the insufficiencies of those ways in our own time. Why not go the whole distance and adapt yourself completely to the era in which you live?

The old prescription for a dwelling-place was a cave, a forest, a mountain, an unsequestered river or a jungle. All excellent places—for a time. Such spots provide the ideal solitude and quietness for a man who seeks to practise meditation. Let him resort to them by all means, if circumstances set him free to do so. But if he tarries there too long he may get tuberculosis, as one Yogi I know got it, or contract rheumatism, as another one has contracted it; or worse, he may become their unconscious victim. For only in the seething crowds of cities may he test the cloistered virtue of what he has gained during his solitude. Only in the busy life of congregated towns, with their innumerable trials and temptations, may he discover whether the seeming gold of his spiritual attainment is acid-proof. Nature is the mother of every man aspiring towards truth, peace and happiness, yes, and will help him, but the child which wants to stay for ever in the safety of its mother's lap will never become a real adult.

I think a man will be a better Yogi if he uses the wild and lonely places of Nature as temporary retreats alone, and not as permanent habitations. Use solitude but do not abuse it. The principle of the pneumatic mining drill, which is plunged into the ground until it penetrates some distance and is then withdrawn for a while, only to be re-plunged into the earth to a still greater distance, is a good principle for spiritually aspiring people too. Let them retire from active life for periods of retreat, periods which can vary from one day, one week, one month up to a few years even, but let them then return to the world which they have deserted and plunge into active existence as the next phase of their being. And they should stay until they feel that the world is becoming too much for them again; then spiritual retreat should be sought once again. Such a life is a balanced one, and obeys the ordered rhythms of the universal creation itself. The social life will then express the spiritual life, the inner will influence the outer and both will be better for the change. The co-ordination of spirit and matter can hurt no one.

Those who vegetate for a lifetime in monasteries and hermitages are doing what is perhaps best for them, or they would not continue to stay there, but sometimes it is the worst for them. In several cases their fancied spiritual growth would disappear like pollen blown by the wind were they to put themselves to the test of city life. The more intuitional and the more intellectual amongst them would be wiser to seek an integral freedom by using the world from time to time as springboards on which to try their diving capacity.

We should appreciate the wonderful habitations which man has constructed no less than the beautiful regions which Nature has called forth out of the primal Chaos. It is not by abandoning false environments that we make our highest progress, but by abandoning false thoughts. The real place where all our troubles start is in the mind.

Whether it be a Park Avenue apartment in New York or a solitary tent in the wild Central Asian desert, I am ready to take either as my temporary home, if needs be. I can enjoy both, yet leave either of them without a qualm, for I know well where my true home lies. It is not here. It is in the Overself.

So, Mr. Chaplin, whilst the old hermits tended to go to unnecessary extremes we shall do somewhat better for ourselves, preferring comfort and convenience. We can do Yoga more efficiently with all the latest modern comforts than with all the oldest discomforts, just as artists can do better work in painting and literature when well-fed and free from financial harassments than when they have to subsist on bread and cheese alone and be harried by creditors. For we too are to be artists in our practice of mental quiet.

*   *   *

Another point on which there will be much misconception about my call to you to become a Yogi is that of sex. They will tell you, these Swamis, that it is essential to become absolutely chaste, to renounce all women as being in unconscious league with the devil. They will tell you not to marry if you are single, or to leave your wife if you are married, or to live with her as brother and sister if you cannot cast her aside so lightly. That is their Yoga, the path they have elected to follow. Let them follow it by all means, as it evidently suits them. But do not let them impose it upon you, with the ancient dogma that there is no other way to the kingdom of heaven save that of strict celibacy. It is not for all of us to do violence to Nature and ourselves. It is not necessary for everyone who aspires to the spiritual life to become the victims of such narrow doctrines. It is not the fiat of the Deity that all shall torture themselves by unsuccessful efforts to drive off the besetting attentions of what is, after all, a purely natural function. Sex is not a separate thing nor an evil one, added as an afterthought by the creative forces in order to ensnare us. The notion is as atrocious as it is absurd. No, it is a part of the organic totality of the human microcosm, and it is to be regarded with no less reverence than we give to any other part of our being.

The obedience to ascetic moral precepts and monastic disciplines is essential to those who need them, but all do not need them.

But even those who have not attained this condition of open communication with the Overself are not bound to adhere to complete asceticism. There is more than one way to divinity, a fact which the preachers of rigid asceticism frequently ignore simply because they know nothing about it.

What a man does require is decency and self-restraint; he needs to remember that the body has its own hygiene which must be observed for health's sake, but he does not require conflict and self-immolation.

Many of the ascetic rules were given to former ages, when social conditions were very much different from what they are today. What is the use of demanding that everyone should obey injunctions which were specially intended for centuries now in their grave? The old epochs are disappearing into the abyss; do what we may, we shall not be able to drag them back.

It does not concern the body so much as it concerns the inhabitant of the body—the soul. We shall find it not through fussing about our physical organs but through conquering that which ultimately rules them—the mind.

The whole question of asceticism, misunderstood at all times as it has been, can only be disposed of on a personal basis after all. It depends, more than most people realize, partly on the peculiar traits of each individual's temperament, and partly on the type of life-experience which he has had.

There are those whom Nature and destiny and Deity have given a vocation for complete asceticism and world-renunciation. My ideas are not for them and it would be as wrong, as unwise and as sinful for me to attempt to impose such ideas upon them as it is for the ascetics to attempt to impose their own upon me. Such persons should profoundly respect the inborn way which is theirs. Let them be true to their inner voice, and thus they shall achieve their best. For such the monastery or the hermitage, the forest or the mountain, must be a permanent home; complete chastity and inexorable celibacy a lifelong acceptance; and worldly affairs kept at arm's length. I respect, nay, deeply revere such men, when I meet them and find them sincere.

But they are necessarily the few. The rest, who ape and imitate these great souls, do so to their own danger. For the snares of self-deception and the pitfalls of reaction lie in ambush for them.

The old man whom I used to see rolling himself in the dust every day around the eight-mile circuit of Arunachala Hill became for me a powerful symbol. I saw in him the representative of ideas and principles which are today being carried away by the undertaker. He may be, in fact he is, an exceedingly pious and devout old gentleman; his worship of this sacred spot attests to that. But all that he gains may be gained with less discomfort and more simplicity by sitting down quietly anywhere on the hillside and receptively letting its high spiritual vibrations find access to his mind. It may be a silent and unostentatious method, but it will be more effective, less bothersome and wiser.

For somewhat similar reasons the rules for the practice of Yoga are not easily obeyed in the present age. They have been handed down for thousands of years from an age which differed in many things from our own, and whose face and soul were alien to ours. The sensible thing to do is to adapt and re-adapt such rules to suit our altered times. The old must give place to the new. Had the advocates of Yoga shown a more flexible spirit in the past their science would not have become the abnormality, the curiosity that it seems today, nor would it have disappeared almost completely from the world, as it has likewise done today. These ascetics float over our heads in a sort of spiritual stratosphere, and seem to hold out no help, no hope, to the weaker mortals that we are.

Asceticism is not attractive to the modern man. My belief is that it is also not essential. The outward life and inward spirit can and must be reconciled. He may learn to practise an inward asceticism which will not interfere overmuch with his outer life but which will very definitely interfere with his heart and mind. Then, whatever changes he ought to make in his active existence, he will make freely from inner dictation, from inward authority, and not by blindly obeying an external discipline.

I have learnt, if I have learnt anything at all, that renunciation is really an attitude of mind; that the mere physical gesture of renunciation is futile where it is not accompanied to some degree by the corresponding inner outlook; and that, Nature herself being in no hurry, the attempt to achieve perfection and outwit normal physical functions by heroic methods of voluntary abstinence is sometimes unwise and frequently futile. Instead of counselling men to abandon existing habits of action, I would counsel them to abandon existing habits of thinking. Walled round by ancient habits of thought, as they are, it is better to overthrow those walls than to spend their energies in fruitless alterations of what they are doing within those walls. All actions, in the ultimate, are the outcome of thought. They are the result either of our realization of truth or of our unconscious mental struggles thereto.

And this brings me to a further misconception of the Yoga science, Mr. Chaplin. They will tell you, also, that solitude is to be sought because we must give our whole time to the practice of meditation. Those who can do that are doing an excellent thing. Let them do it.

But the mind is not to be conquered so easily as that. I have seen quite a number of our modern Yoga aspirants, both in the East and

West, and I doubt whether more than five per cent could keep up such practice the whole day through. Those who attempt it, however, inevitably end by suffering from discontent with themselves. Their unsuccessful efforts produce natural inner conflicts, and the goal of peace is not much nearer. Nature, in the end, drives them finally back to a more balanced existence.

How much wiser would they have been, how much unnecessary self-torture would they have saved, if they had started from the first with a sane rhythm, with a daily programme that allowed so much time for meditation and so much for active life! The moral is that meditation is only a means to an end—not, as so many think, a goal in itself. We need not mistake the road for the destination. There is a whole lot more which I could say about meditation, about the ancient ways in which it is practised and the modern methods which must supplant them, but I shall desist.

They will tell you, perhaps, that the arts are snares and the intellect is a trap. True, they can be, but they need not be. They are dangers to narrow men, like themselves, but we can turn them into friends: we can use our cultural gifts and enjoy the gifts of others, and the world will be the better for it.

The real truth is that there is no final virtue in any place *per se*, nor any superiority in inactive solitary life as compared with active social life. Whoever vaunts one at the expense of the other thereby betrays how little a distance his eyelids have been opened by the Great Light of the Universe. But when men, who take the teacher's robe upon their shoulders, proclaim the old paths to heaven as being the only paths, and the old ways as being true for all time, I must control the urge to refute their narrowness and await the appropriate time when the inner voice bids me speak. And then I shall reveal how mean a conception they have formed of the broad tolerance, the all-embracing charity, the universal unfolding of the Supreme Father, Who is the life and support of all beings without exception.

There is divine light, there is comforting salvation for us all, no matter who we are or what we do, whether we are old sinners or whether we are new saints, for men hard at work in business offices as for those who are mere dreamers, spinners of gossamer webs, and wholly irrespective of our interest in Yoga, religion, philosophy. One day the realization of this truth will ensoul all adult humanity. And then the subtle patterns of Divinity shall be outworked on this wobbly old earth of ours.

CHAPTER TWELVE

A Sacred Influx in the Stillness—Mountain-climbing Expeditions and Their Significance.

ONCE again the days flit across my mountain home like light-winged butterflies. I do not forget, I cannot forget, the ethereal aim which has brought me here. Above all else lies this inexorable necessity of attaining and retaining for a while an increasing degree of spiritual, mental and physical stillness.

In a multitude of places upon this sorry planet a multitude of men are running hither and thither or jumping this way and that, in an endeavour to develop a more athletic body by such constant activities.

I, on the contrary, am pinning this body down to a dead stop, in an endeavour to free myself from all intimations of physical sensation.

Shall I exaggerate and say that the man who does nothing at all engages in the highest form of activity; that the man who is always busy really does nothing at all: that in fact the supreme mission of man for which he was sent down to this world is precisely to do nothing? But, alas, few will understand this thought!

We desire concrete justification of man's right to exist in the form of work, but nothing else that is great in Nature asks us for it. The sun does not work, yet it accomplishes the law of its being better than any man ever does. It merely shows itself and at once all the thousand activities of the earth begin to hum of their own accord. Let us be like suns, and learn how the highest form of the art of doing nothing will bring all Nature running to our feet and ready to become energetically engaged in every kind of activity on our behalf.

In a multitude of other places a multitude of other men are agitating the molecules of their heated brains in intellectual reflections upon a hundred subjects. I, on the contrary, take symbolic ice from yonder summits and apply it for a time to my head, in the hope of freezing away all manifestations of reflective action. And in all the five continents of the world other men are cajoling their Creator with offerings, rites, self-tortures, aspirations, incantations, prayers, and ceremonies. I, in final insurrection against all these mummeries, keep my heart as quiet as a placid pool and await the

Creator's revelation with the proud patience of one who knows he is eternal.

There is no hurry in my effortless efforts. Failure is and shall be meaningless to me. I do all acts now under a sense of the cyclic nature of things, and under a sense of the immortality that is in the midst of our mortal existence. The wheel of life turns in its course, as the wheel of the universe turns through creations and dissolutions, and my attainment must unfailingly come to me in the end. There is no being and no obstacle strong enough to keep me from that. No creature, whether human, sub-human or super-human, whether evil or not, can stop the water of my life from ultimately rising and returning to the level of its divine source. That return may not be accomplished for many years or for many lives to come, for I cannot predict the hour or the day when this sacred influx will take place, but I can wait. The sense of inescapable eternity envelops me now like a cloud. I live, move and breathe within that cloud.

But how do I know that success is so certain? Wherefrom emanates this unquestioned optimism that roots itself so deeply and so strongly in my heart?

I myself can but answer that I hardly know. It is there and I accept it. I do not question the sun which homes itself in the sky. I cannot question this confident instinct which homes itself in my heart.

Some reinforcement has come to it in the past, true, but had it not already existed no external contact could have made it live so powerfully as it does now. When, on the Thames bank one summer evening, my spirit was drawn unexpectedly out of its earthly case as a sword is drawn out of its scabbard, and I was taken into the realm of inter-stellar space, that contact was then given and imparted an immense strengthening of the already-born instinct. The message of the gods' implacable will to effect man's divine restoration was delivered to me, and from that memorable presence of the Sacred Four I returned with a string of words impressed upon my mind whose purport sometimes frightens me and sometimes exalts me. But whatever the result, I place my unreserved trust in the eternal nature of those forces which hold the world within their grasp, and consequently hold my individual life too. Knowing the glorious end, the glorious if unfulfilled destiny of mankind, I can wait calmly. I, too, as a human being, must share it with the others. All the defeats are but temporary. The miseries which walk in the train of mundane life do not touch the Overself, which will one day reclaim Its own, for all else is subordinate to It.

With such confidence, then, a man may sit on his mountain-top and let life hasten by him. With such inbreathing of the air of eternity, he may afford to bide his time and know how to wait without complaint. Life is invested with unalterable benign principles. Let me accept them, then.

Hope is the herald of all Truth. We begin to sense the coming of our overdue revelation by a blind unconscious questing eagerness to receive it.

* * *

One more evening on the leaf-strewn sanctuary is markedly fruitful. The inward presence has been waiting unweariedly for me. The air vibrates with loveliness for I begin to bathe in the beautiful element of Truth. The mind quietly settles down into its own centre with hardly an effort. The tide of blessed serenity begins to inundate the heart. Peace, divine and delectable, rolls over my head wave after wave. Breathing sinks away into the gentlest of movements, so gentle as to be almost unnoticed.

The procession of eternity passes by. All the petty irritations and egoistic twists, the deep-scarred bitternesses and rebellious cynicisms and trivial cares, fall for a time out of my character as dead brown leaves falling from sapless darkening trees in autumn. How can they continue to exist in such a grand rarefied atmosphere as now overwhelms me with such well-defined strength? How can these futile pain-bringing elements continue to afflict me when another self, the Overself, now arises in all its sublimity and makes me its temporary victim, seizing mind, heart and body in its grip as a cat seizes a mouse with its white teeth?

Ah, but the victim is all too-willing! For he is utterly helpless. He is penetrated through and through with the subtle aroma of those words: "Not my will, but Thine, O Lord, be done." Herein lies the primal felicity. We must needs love the Absolute Good when we perceive it.

Helpless, and yet what joyful freedom! The bonds of the personal ego are flung aside by the unseen hand, and with their going goes all care, all anxiety, all concern for the past errors and future uncertainties. The Overself, in announcing its presence, announces also that It comes as liberator. It commands—and everything mean, petty and cramping shrinks back and disappears. It glances— and flowing sea of love, adoration, humility, surges up to Its feet.

How soothing is the sense of Its benign enfolding presence! All inner conflict is stilled. The blood no longer wars with the brain; nor passion with thought. When our minds have been totally subdued by logic, we are lost. The divine transcends logic.

Himalaya has opened the golden windows of heaven for me and I must bless the day that I entered its quiet realm.

With the hushed fall of eventide, the stillness within and without grows more and more intense. To this humbler degree, I know now the spiritual meaning of Christ's words : *I and my Father are one.*

Take your prodigal child, then, O Overself, take him captive! How sweet is life when one penetrates its hidden depths! Our greatest need is not for a wider and more diffuse existence, but for a profounder one. Such an experience helps one to understand why men cling so desperately to life, even in the face of acute bodily suffering and terrible torture of mind and spirit. For their very clinging is but a faint percolation into our world of that intense ecstatic satisfying peace which dwells in life's secret heart. They hold to life because they sense unconsciously that it is a boon worth having. Could they but trace physical life back to its original source they would possess themselves of this boon. For the ephemeral existence of a few score years holds only a distant reflection of the real hidden life-current.

'Tis but a small arc of the entire circle of being.

*   *   *

A message comes from Darjeeling with the news that Ruttledge has at last been forced to abandon his expedition to climb Mount Everest. The world's best-known peak and loftiest pinnacle will not yield. Himalaya's highest aspiration outsoars mankind's reach. Ruttledge's party has crept to within a few thousand feet of the summit but the weather has now beaten him. To remain any longer near the shoulder of that storm-whipped, world-surveying giant will be certain suicide.

Everest remains, the most sought-for diamond in this massive girdle thrown by Nature around India's northern face.

Ruttledge and his companions will descend with well-earned glory, however. They have done all they could, it was impossible to do more. After all, a period of only about six weeks out of the entire year was at his disposal for the effort. The cold is too unbearable before May, and the monsoon too insupportable after mid-June. Tremendous blizzards which screech across the mountain's face like howling monsters will soon hurl every human being in their path to death; vast snowfalls which swiftly blanket the slope to an incredible thickness will soon bury every corpse. Honourable retreat is the only wise thing to do in the face of such hardships and difficulties, when the forces of Nature reveal how violent they may become.

The credit for rendering the climbing of Mount Everest a practical proposition belongs to my respected friend, Sir Francis Younghusband. Himself born in the Himalayan region and belonging to an old British military family which has been associated with India for generations, his interest in and love of these white-mantled mountains is phenomenal. As far back as 1887 he crossed the unknown and unexplored Mustagh Pass from the Central Asian side, after performing an amazingly lonely and dangerous journey of three thousand miles through the entire length of China and thence by way of the infinite desolation of the Gobi Desert, where he and his camel could only travel at night. In much of this vast landscape there was no hint of the existence of man, no single sign of his activities. And it was near the Mustagh that he suddenly came face to face with the second highest mountain in the world, the renowned K2, which is only seven hundred feet lower than Everest.

The thrill of that unique vision planted a seed which germinated more than thirty years later when, as President of the Royal Geographical Society, Sir Francis formed the Mount Everest Committee.

The first task of the latter was to remove the political difficulties which had till then barred all approach to Everest, for the Nepalese and Tibetans were unwilling to permit their frontiers to be crossed by any expedition for this purpose. Even Lord Curzon, so accustomed to have his own way, could not obtain this permission when he was Viceroy of India. Everest is a sacred peak to them, although far less sacred than Kailas. No Western foot will ever be allowed to stand on the summit of Mount Kailas whilst religion keeps even a quarter of its present force in Tibet.

The Committee, however, succeeded where Curzon failed. Its next business was to finance and organize the necessary preparations. Five expeditions have assailed the mountain under its auspices during different years, and if all have failed, the failures are the most glorious in mountaineering history.

But if Everest refuses to submit to profane feet, some of the other if lesser giants have fallen to human endeavour. Frank Smythe took an audacious party a few years ago up to the top of Kamet, an altitude of twenty-five thousand feet. Their feet sank in soft snow, they had to clamber over perilous rocks and they had to cut footholds in solid ice. One slip was enough to send them over precipices to the bottom. Lieutenant Oliver ascended the sloping flanks of Trisul and reached the summit, a height of twenty-three thousand feet, in 1933, during a summer leave from the Army, panting, utterly exhausted but triumphant. Eric Shipton has struggled through and up the inhospitable awful gorges of Nanda Devi into the immense unexplored natural basin which the mountain hides. Dr. Paul Bauer has twice tried to scale Kanchenjunga, but at 25,600 feet, with the summit in sight, he could find no further foothold on those mountainous walls of ice and snow and was in momentary danger of impending avalanches. He had to turn back. Merkl's German group attempted Nanga Parbat two years ago. Half of them lost their lives, Merkl himself dying of cold in an ice-cave 23,000 feet high after being terribly frost-bitten on those accumulated cones of snow.

Here, too, in the Tehri-Garhwal region of the Central Himalayas, came Palis and his comrades in 1933. They must have passed my forest bungalow on their route to Gangotri and probably spent the night here. At Gangotri they found a cluster of peaks, chiefly of the 20,000 feet size, awaiting them. They climbed an 18,000 feet mountain first, descended over to the Kedarnath group and ascended a 20,000 feet summit. Then they attacked Satopanth, an altitude of 22,000 feet, and succeeded again. Their exhausted bodies needed rest, so they returned to Harsil near Gangotri for a few days. They set out again, climbed a glacier into the rugged Nela Pass and descended to the Spiti Valley on the Tibetan border. From here they fought their way through mists, blizzard, and wind to the accompaniment of violent thunder up the dominating peak of Leo Pargial until its 22,000 feet had been surmounted.

Very few other Himalayan heights have been conquered and the record of successes is still extremely brief. Mummery went up Nanga Parbat, yet how far nobody knew, for he was never heard of again. The Duke of Abruzzi found K2 unclimbable. But man must struggle upward, physically no less than spiritually, and his powers of invention may yet find means of defying Nature and do to the Asiatic Himalayas what he has already done to their shorter cousins, the European Alps.

The adventure of braving the world's worst glaciers and steepest slopes and highest altitudes demands, however, an exceptional bodily fitness and power of endurance which many do not possess. The small amount of oxygen in the air at these altitudes renders every breath an effort and every step an exertion. The pressure of the atmosphere alters and severe prostrating headaches attack the unacclimatized intruders. Hearts must be perfectly sound, lungs must be large and strong, limbs must be hardy or a man had better remain where I remain now, at a little less than 10,000 feet on the Himalayan altimeter, unless he wants to play roulette with death.

The biting cold and the cutting winds and the constant storms render these icebound regions above the snowline painfully purgatorial. Stung into helpless irritability by the arctic temperature, numbed into morbid depression by the sluggish circulation of blood in the body, experiencing respiratory distress to the point of needing three or four breaths between each step, haunted by the ever-present danger of a slip over a ghastly precipice down to certain death, and affected by internal sickness through changes in the working of the kidneys, men can only dare to climb the proud peaks of Himalaya if they are made out of heroic optimistic stuff, quite apart from having to possess the necessary qualifications of physical soundness and comparative youth.

There is, indeed, a spiritual value plus a spiritual significance in these repeated challenges to Himalaya. Anyone who voluntarily sets out to explore its face and permits no limit of height to daunt him must surely possess qualities which belong also to the novitiate of a diviner life. He is ready to part with his dearest property, his right to exist, in the risk of his high enterprise. So must a spiritual aspirant be ready to go where the inner voice bids him go, even to torture and martyrdom, as several have gone, and let life slip out of the flesh too. He must cut loose from all conventional land-marks and start the fearless climb up unpathed slopes, creating his own path as he climbs. So must the truth-seeking aspirant cut loose from the conventional dogmas of religion and philosophy and walk with eyes open, thinking out each further step for himself, finding his own way into the truth-world which abides within himself. And finally the mountaineer must love solitude, simplicity, tranquillity and the scenic beauty of Nature or these unfrequent heights would not attract him at all. So must the aspirant love the same four things if he would one day receive the sublime gift which the soul of Nature keeps for him.

And what is the inner significance of these Himalayan ex-peditions? Is it not that aspiration sings through the hearts of all worthy men like an under-motif in music? Is it not, too, that pilgrim-age abides in our nature and that stagnant self-satisfaction is a sin?

The sparkling pinnacles which jut up above the flat face of our planet and glitter high in the Himalayan sky above deep clouds must typify for us the race of superior men who shall be the crest-wave of evolution. Nietzsche's dream of Supermen shall surely be realized, albeit not in his crude and cruel picturing. A solitary few even now exist. They shall be both goal and guide. In the illum-ined Sage and the powerful Adept there is a present picture of our future attainment.

Florentine Dante put his Earthly Paradise upon the top of a mountain, just as the Japanese painters set the abode of their gods high upon the lovely snow-clad peak of Fujiyama, the highest of Japan's many towering heights and a now extinct volcano—the Mount Kailas of Japan, visited by pilgrims from every corner of the country who return to their respective villages inspired with deep reverence by its physical beauty and spiritual significance.

Beyond and above us all, mountaineers or plainsmen, shines the silvery glory of the white summit raised by the Creator for our climbing. It is eternal, and it will silently call us through the æons. We, too, must be Everest climbers. Shall we be cowards and keep to the comfort of our homes? Or shall we take staff in hand, put determination into our hearts, and set forth on what is, after all, the most wonderful expedition which this world can offer us?

CHAPTER THIRTEEN

An Encounter with a Panther—The Problem of Nature's Cruelty.

RAMBLING through the forest this afternoon, when only about fifteen minutes distant on the homeward journey to my bungalow, I am reminded of a thing one is often likely to forget amid the resplendent beauties of this region—the fact that wild animals abound in this isolated kingdom. My gaze wanders aimlessly forwards towards my right hand when an unusual glint of colour in the afternoon sunlight stops me. Half hidden in a leafy tree I perceive a panther in an extraordinary situation. It lies along the fork between two horizontal boughs at a distance of about a dozen yards from the ground. The rounded head rests between the forepaws and the spotted furry coat is stretched out almost full length.

The beast is sound asleep.

The mid-day sun, pouring its vertical rays upon the earth, has kindled a sultry heat which has caught the creature in a lethargic mood and sent it off into somnolence. No other explanation can I find for its exceptionally exposed position. Its presence up the tree is also explicable without difficulty. The ravines close by have plenty of panther lairs in their keeping. Generally the beasts come out at night, their eyes having become supernormally sharp through constant activity in the dark. This particular animal has wandered out at an unusual hour. Of all the forest animals, the panther is the quietest; walking very slowly and stealthily, its soft paws make no sound. Evidently to avoid disturbing a prey prematurely, it has climbed this tree and perched itself among the branches, where it may watch the surrounding area more intently and yet remain hidden from an intended victim on which, at the psychological moment, it will pounce.

My own position is unusual too. I am tired and want to get home as quickly as possible. Yet, if I advance forward I must pass the tree whereon the panther is sleeping and probably awaken it. I am in no mind to turn backwards, much less to tarry where I am. My armament for defence consists only of a short light bamboo cane which I have picked up *en route*. It is about as useful in the circumstances as a matchstick.

There is nothing left to do but to advance, so I step gingerly forward almost on tiptoe. My caution proves useless. In the silent forest even the slightest noise is magnified. One is alert to the rustle of a falling leaf. The panther awakes just when I am about to pass its leafy lair.

This time there is nothing to do but stand stock still and await events. The creature raises its cat-like head, then its beautiful furry body stands upright, and it peers questioningly at me with evil-looking yellow-green fiery eyes. I return its gaze just as questioningly.

My pulse thumps away a good deal faster than normal. I am not a brave he-man, with an overplus of physical courage and robust vigour. All I can command is a little inward stillness. So I call up my reserves of that under-valued quality, which, somehow, brings me perhaps the same result as courage.

Perceiving that I have detected it, the panther's expression changes into one of rage. It opens its jaws slightly in irritation and the bared teeth show defiance. The ears are turned back close to the head. Then with an angry snarl which sounds like a hoarse human cough, the muscular body rises arch-like and leaps headlong to the farther side of the tree and lands with a heavy crash in the tangled growth of underwood. My last glimpse is of a long, black-tipped twitching tail and then the panther disappears into the forest.

There are other animals in Tehri State which neither love nor are loved by man. The black bear is common enough, whilst the leopard roams hither and thither, the wild boar leaves its ravages, whilst the tiger has now confined itself to certain tracts. But as a rule they keep themselves quiet by daytime and stir forth only with the coming of darkness. Then one hears occasionally queer sounds, ominous growls, whilst lying in bed at night, evidence of some prowling creature which has deserted its lair in the forest or ravine and is investigating the possibilities of this region. Once I flash my torchlight upon the face of a small bear which comes grunting round my bungalow and peeps through the glass panel of the rear bedroom door.

On the mountain slopes there are large herds of wild stags, wild spotted deer, and of that curious creature, the goat-antelope—simple, innocent, shy and likeable creatures which are well behaved until forced to fight for their lives with the wilder species. Then their powerful antlers come into play and sometimes they render good account of themselves. A single panther will pursue a herd of wild deer who moan their fright until the last moment, when the necessity of defence calls up fresh courage.

The barking-deer is here, too—a beautiful, slender-legged animal.

The black Himalayan bear is an unpleasant creature to meet suddenly. Its temper at the moment is generally the deciding factor as to whether it will attack a man or not. It has a reputation for being utterly vicious, spiteful and destructive.

A curious story one hears in these parts is of a young hunter who had seen a bear in a forest-clothed slope above him. He fired his gun and wounded the beast slightly. Growling with rage and pain, it rushed down the mountain-side at incredible speed, seized the unfortunate man and flung him down a precipice into the chasm below. He was killed.

Life, in its primal attributes, did not bring such terrors as these savage beasts have brought with them for the agonizing of two kingdoms of man and creature. I know that the materialistic evolutionists tell us of a time when man lived a bestial cave-dwelling existence and when gigantic animals roamed the planet with ferocious intent. That something of the kind did prevail one need not go further than the nearest museum to discover, for the fossil remains speak eloquently. But our theorists unfortunately do not go back far enough. Having retraced man's history and this globe's fortunes to such a distant epoch, they become exhausted and stop. Yet the long tale did not begin there. It is like a reporter from another planet arriving here in the midst of the last war, and then returning to his own people to tell them that the inhabitants of this earth are exclusively devoted to mutual destruction. Had he come a couple of years earlier his report would have been differently fashioned.

I cannot produce any fossils to support my contention and I cannot find any appurtenances left by the earliest men as their testamentary remains. I can take no one for a walk upon the solid ground of tangible evidence. The planet of today is not the planet of yesterday and the tremendous shifts of its surface and the vast changes in its structure which time has brought about have swept away the trifling records of æons which are now so distant that they really do not matter. Mother Earth is not concerned with preserving every testimony of her ancient history in order to provide a few scientists with materials over which their intellects may churn away in fresh theorizing. She herself is well aware of what she has done, and if puny men think otherwise that is their affair and not hers.

But if I come with arms empty of fact when I come forward with my declaration that Nature's first intent was not to begin the universe by a reign of terror, of which the spider who lusts after the fly is an apt symbol, but rather the reverse, I possess sufficient intimations of her original benevolence to satisfy my own criticisms, which at one time were perhaps more devastating than those of the scientists whose guesses I had absorbed in my innocence. Those intimations, however, did not come to me through any source which the modern world treats with respect, and it would be a futile waste of time to talk of them to the exacting audience of today. Let it suffice to state that there is a certain condition of being, similar to that which exists in a semi-trance, and that in this condition normally invisible forces may speak to man. In that way I have learnt a little of the unwritten history of our race.

What has emerged in this way retraces the picture of a primal age when the Good, in no narrow sense, was entirely dominant, and when matter was in submission to spirit. The humanity of that time lived by the light of a divine instinct and did not need to dally with the hesitations of cunning and intellect in order to understand what were its best interests. The exploitation of the weaker peoples by stronger ones did not exist and could not exist; for all men *felt* in their hearts the common Father whom they worshipped as their own, universally.

The animals of that age did not fear man and had no reason to fear him. Nor did they fear one another. Nature provided abundantly for their needs in a harmless way. The depredation of one species upon another was not only unnecessary but likewise unknown.

*　　*　　*

If, as I say, I have no facts and no fossils to produce so as to convince those whom I have no desire to convince, I have indeed a question. Every intelligent man—that is, intelligent through the experience of life and not pseudo-intelligent through the books of schools—must say at some time or other, with Napoleon, when he gazed out of the palace window one night at a star-studded sky: "Do not ask me to believe that all this vast creation possesses no Author!"

If, further, he admits the likelihood of this Author's, this God's, existence, he will have to face the problem of suffering and evil; why God allows them in our midst. Acknowledging the existence of these miseries, he will have to admit that God has deliberately introduced them into His creation or that they have arisen of their own accord without His express intention. The only way to burke this issue is to assert, upon the evidence of the mixed character of the world, and of the simultaneous presence of deplorable sorrows and delightful pleasures, that God created this universe whilst in a state of inebriation!

This problem is without doubt the oldest, the most hoary-headed, with which the thinkers of both antiquity and modernity have had to grapple. All have failed to solve it. I do not propose to trouble myself with it either.

But the only messages of God to man which are readily available to us are embodied in the great religions which have appeared from time to time. We may not accept them as such, but it is unlikely that they were mere smoke without fire. It is not at all irrational to suppose that some daring souls have adventured into higher regions, surpassing mankind's common reach, and returned with news of the Creator. All such religions speak of God as being a God, at the least, well-disposed, at the most, loving and compassionate towards us.

If every religious leader, if every sage and prophet of the past who has declared this to be true is utterly deceived or deceiving, sanity demands an abandonment of all that is decent in life, a turning towards ruthless savage selfishness and a cynical surrender of all hopes for the future of this muddled and muddling race of ours. We must then accept the doctrine of Oswald Spengler, German apos'e of pessimism and force, that man is himself a beast of prey.

Fortunately most intelligent men do not think so. They do not worship reason to the utter exclusion of feeling, as do our modern intellectual coxcombs. Where they turn away from a religion like Christianity, they do not quite turn away from Christ. Where they desert their decaying Hinduism, they still hold to some kind of reverence for its former saints. And so the thought of God's benevolence is yet a hope and faith with many.

All these people, however, with their education, accept the scientific story of evolution from barbarity to civilization. This story is not a complete novel but only a serial story. The scientists, as I have said, so far have got hold only of the last few instalments. If and when they receive the earlier portions, they will be compelled to revise their judgments.

This notion that Nature started by being "red in tooth and claw", creating the most bestial men and the most ferocious animals first, has been fashionable and popular amongst educated people for nearly three quarters of a century.

My question is now ready and it is addressed to these people. If you believe in a benevolent God, how can you believe that He *began* His work of creation in such a foul manner?

Is it not more rational to believe, on the contrary, that God began in accordance with His nature in the best possible manner, by creating the noblest men and finest animals? Is it not more rational to believe that this was His first intention and that degeneration into barbarity, when it came, set in through these men and animals falling of their own volition and not by God's desire?

The Bible story of the fall of man is only partly an allegory, but nevertheless it is a true one.

We need to distinguish between a fall and a push. God never pushed his creation down into a worse condition. Nor did He create a set of automatons which would work like puppets on a string. The fact that we fell is sufficient evidence that we were given enough freedom to fall.

Yet if all the assembled religious teachers of the entire universe and all the gathered prophetic luminaries of the firmament of history were to tell me that our Creator was wicked, cruel and barbaric, I should disbelieve them. Even if the whole of the human race were to tell me that, I should turn away unconvinced.

For my final proof that they were mistaken would depend upon my own inner experience. Not even by clairvoyant perception of former phases of universal life would I rebut them, but by something infinitely more profound, more precious and, to me, more irrefutable.

Slowly and haltingly, humbly and with oft-slipping feet, I nevertheless find myself creeping into the courts of the Lord with the passing years. And the closer I creep towards the divine Presence, the more I feel myself surrounded by a compassion whose breadth is limitless, and the more I find myself supported by a love whose nature is endless.

But my thoughts, however luminous and however factual they may seem to my visionary mind, will seem but idle and rambling speculations to the clever learned omniscient men of modernity.

CHAPTER FOURTEEN

A Visit of a Nepalese Prince—A Queer Experience with a Fakir and a Spirit—We Explore a Beautiful River Valley—An Adventure with a Mad Elephant—Buddhism in Nepal—Krishna and Buddha Compared.

WHEN we last met I told Prince Mussooree Shum Shere Jung Bahadur Rana, of Nepal, of my intention to go into the recesses of the Himalaya Mountains upon a spiritual and inward adventure. My bright friend lightly responded with the wish that he could escape the whirl of pleasure and duty for a brief time and accompany me thither, as if such a trip were a half-hour matter. To which I jokingly replied: "Anyway, Prince Mussooree, come and have a cup of tea with me there one day." And thus we both laughed off this trifle.

I hear nothing further of the Prince until today, when, totally unannounced and quite unexpectedly, he arrives! Accompanied by a couple of servants and ambling up the trail on a handsome brown horse, he appears in my solitary domain.

"So you have come for that cup of tea!" I remark, when the first astonishment of this sudden incursion departs and yields to the hospitable emotion with which every man should greet a friend.

But the Prince denies my natural inference and declares that he has little partiality for tea; he will drink anything else but not tea. Unfortunately it is impossible for me to offer him, in this refuge from civilization, anything else—except water. Excellent, he declares, he will drink water! However, the rigid traditions of his caste demand that his own servant provide the drink out of the supply they carry.

And whilst he sips the colourless fluid I muse over the phenomenon of a man who goes into the mountains to play the hermit, who expects not a single visitor but succeeds in having quite a few. Under the law of averages I may hope to have another ten visitors during the balance of my sojourn here! Thus it is amply proved that in this twentieth century nobody can become a Robinson Crusoe. Whether he maroon himself on an unfrequented Pacific Island or perch himself on a wild mountain top, the world will track him down and invade his solitude. If there is no other means of approach, aeroplanes will nose their way into his retreat!

Nevertheless I am not a churl. I am grateful for these visits. Fate has been kind enough to send none but those who are welcome indeed. My visitors have stimulated my own intellect and given me

137

the pleasure of spiritual communion. Indeed, we must have some kind of inward relationship, some kindred tie, unseen and intangible, for what else could have brought them upon the weary journey over the rugged mountain slopes into this isolated region? They have prevented me from becoming entirely self-wrapped. Best of all, they come with affection in their hearts. What finer gift can a stranger or a friend bear to any man?

Prince Mussooree is about thirty-three. He possesses a good-looking Mongolian-featured face, with flat nose, yellowish skin and slightly elongated eyes; he is quite short, no taller than myself, but this is a feature which we share in good company, however, for Colonel Lawrence, of Arabia, was at first rejected for service at the outbreak of the last war on account of his not being sufficiently tall, whilst Napoleon's lack of inches earned him the famous title of "Little Corporal". Yet he has the strong powerful voice which is typical of the mountain folk of Nepal. He is a good-natured, good-humoured person, yet capable, when roused, of that fiery, fearless outburst which is also typical of the people of Nepal.

He is a nephew of His Highness the Maharajah of Nepal and possesses a patriotic devotion to that little-known land which is almost fanatical. When, a few years ago, there was a risk of war with Tibet over some petty frontier incident, a risk which was averted only at the last moment, he exclaimed, "So much the better for the Tibetans!" And he would often point proudly to the fact that the sturdy little Gurkhas are the best fighting material in the British-Indian Army, and that they have their own officers.

Whilst an early evening meal is being prepared we leave the whitewashed, fir-fringed bungalow and go for a walk. I take my visitor up the steep slope to my treasured sanctuary. He wanders around, admiring the magnificent views of narrow precipitous valleys and rugged, uninhabited heights. When he has seen enough, I lead him to my meditation spot, where we sit down. The immense natural amphitheatre which stretches out below our feet draws an exclamation of admiring surprise from his lips.

"This is perfect for your purpose! You have chosen well!" We chat of bygone events until, towards the end, our talk veers round to my own subject. The Prince tells me of some of his own experiments in Yoga during his earlier days. He too has been educated along Western lines, but no superimposed scientific training will drive out the beliefs in the supernatural forces of life which dwell in the blood of every thoughtful Oriental.

"My great attraction has been Hatha Yoga, what you call the Way of Body-Control. I had a teacher, of course, and still keep in occasional touch with him, but I mastered a number of things by sheer instinct before I ever met him. My theory is that I had already practised Hatha Yoga in former births. I began with physical postures which form the basis of this system and found, to my surprise, that these seemingly difficult contortions of the body came easily enough to me. Even now, after being out of practice for some years, I can do about half a dozen of them."

"Could you do them here?"

"By all means."

And the Prince demonstrates a few of the Physical-Yoga attitudes which are familiar enough to me. First he gets into Peacock posture, socalled because the finished attitude strikingly resembles the outline of a peacock's body. Then he adopts the Grasshopper posture. His third posture is the Embryo posture (the child in the womb); the fourth posture, Sarvangasana, he performs exactly as it was performed by Brama, the Hatha Yogi whose life and attainments I described in *A Search in Secret India*. The Prince's final effort is the Bow posture.

I have to admit that the Prince's body offers an excellent testimonial to the efficacy of the Yoga of Body-Control, because, although only now 33, he looks as young as a lad of nineteen. His health is perfect; he diets himself strictly, eating no more than one meal a day and often even doing with less than that. He strongly believes that most people over-eat and thus wear out the bodily organs with unnecessary work.

He mentions Basti, a curious practice of the ancient Hatha Yogis. It is their way of cleaning the colon by flushing it with water, after going waist-deep into a river. "It is still being done," he tells me.

"I do not know of a single European who is able to perform that hygienic habit," I reply, "although some of us have taken to imitating it by artificial methods; we call it the 'internal bath'."

"My own son, who is only twelve years old, practises Basti perfectly by the ancient way," he adds.

We return to the bungalow under a sunset sky, where blue and cerise pale down into fainter and fainter colourings. How I love these pauses between daytime and nightfall, when Nature takes up her palette and tints the Himalayan world with her glorious hues!

At night I look up at the sky. The beautiful Southern Cross is almost on the point of setting. Gemini, third of the zodiacal constellations and mute symbol of the fraternal affection of Castor and Pollux, jewels the north-western rim. Vega, a bluish-white point of light towards the eastern horizon, seems the brightest of the stars.

*　　　*　　　*

Next morning we follow a narrow ribbon-like path which winds across the face of a ridge. A brown crag which towers high into the air at the valley end is our objective. In the background we see the jagged mass of snowy mountains, soaring upward through banks of cloud, a long line which shimmers in the pre-noon light. The glaciers show themselves as clear white streaks running down to the foot of the range.

This region through which we march offers plenty of game. Wild animals haunt the Tehri-Garhwal forests and mountains. From time to time I hear some wild creature's howl breaking the forest's uncanny stillness when I lay awake at night, and then realize what a tempting field of operation the State of Tehri would be for me were I a game-hunter.

We ascend a sloping ridge along a trail of broken bits of rock and loose stones, which are swept down from the mountain-sides by the high winds which sometimes attain cyclonic force. We skirt around ravines and then make our way along the face of a high bluff. We climb to the top of another ridge and later dip downwards a little towards a grove of deodars. In one place we have literally to cling to roots and stones with both fingers and feet, such is its steepness. When we have walked or climbed for some miles, heavy mists come rapidly on the scene, blotting out most of the landscape and threatening rain. We are compelled to halt.

Fortunately for us the mists clear later. As they lift and float away below our feet into the valleys below, they disclose the mass of tangled ranges once more and the scene is magically changed. We make our way along the high, tree-girt ridges.

Our conversation turns to talk of the Prince's own country while we ramble onwards. Interesting odds and ends of fact about Nepal emerge from his lips, interesting because the ruling authorities of his land keep it still a land of mystery and permit very few persons of Western birth to cross its frontiers, although they do not go so far as Tibet in their exclusiveness. Nevertheless it is a closed land—closed doubtless by mistrust of the Europeans. Moreover, the mountains of Nepal are already separated from India by the Terai Jungle—that hot, rank, malarious and deadly tract at their foot.

"In these post-war days part of Europe has taken to dictatorship as the most effective form of governing a country," I remark, "and I believe that your people have adopted that form too."

Prince Mussooree replies:

"Yes, what Nepal did more than half a century ago Europe is doing today! My uncle, His Highness the Maharajah, wields the widest powers over the people and is virtually a dictator. He rules in the fullest sense of the term. But his rule is benevolent and his desire is to use his power for the benefit of all his subjects. For instance, two years ago we had a tremendous earthquake in Nepal which shook and split the land from end to end of its five-hundred mile length. Our capital town of Katmandu was almost completely shattered to pieces. His Highness went to live in a temporary shelter. He stayed there for a long time. When the public and his relatives repeatedly begged him to rebuild his palace he replied, 'Not until my people are comfortably rehoused will I allow a single stone to be laid for my own home.'

"His Highness, incidentally, is a daredevil rider on horseback and will make his horse gallop furiously down the steepest slopes of the Himalayas. Even our best cavalry officers cannot keep up with his riding."

A little later I learn that:

"The Sherpa tribesmen, who help us so largely in the various Mount Everest climbing expeditions, live in Nepal near the Kanglachen Pass. Their courage and endurance have made possible the results already achieved in these enterprises, and without them your British mountaineers could never reach the heights attained."

When we reach the top of the crag we sit down and surrender ourselves to contemplation of the panorama which unfolds itself. I then rest for a half-hour in silent meditation and the Prince joins in this speechless friendship. I sense the peace that coils itself around us both in spirals. I squat beside him and let my mind disengage itself from its moorings and slip gently back into the holy Source whence it derives its life. Without difficulty it abandons itself to the interior existence, where all is perfect, where all is calm, where all is heavenly. I do not realize how short a time thus passes, for time indeed has taken itself off as an unwelcome entity. I know only that I have thrown off the rags of personal vanity and intellectual pride, that I have been suddenly humbled, and that I sit wearing the robes of ineffable reverence before the great power of Nature that has manifested itself with such overwhelming grandeur. Take back thy truant child, O Great Mother, I cry silently, and let him henceforth depend upon thy guidance and thy love alone. In her high presence the true relationship betwixt man and his Maker discloses itself anew, and there is a hush as poignant and as gentle as the hush of eventide.

When we arise and begin the return journey, a quiet smile of understanding passes between us, but there is no verbal reference to what we have felt.

This evening I hear an extraordinary story from Prince Mussooree about an experience which came to him several years ago.

"In your book *A Search in Secret Egypt* you have described a

Cairo magician who claimed to have under his control the jinns, or non-human spirit beings. Once I met a similar man, and the events which followed were so startling that I cannot, however, dismiss them as some trick of imagination nor can I believe in all that my own eyes saw. I wonder whether you would agree in putting them down to the jinns also. Really, it is a case for a 'jinnologist', if such a type of researcher exists!

"A fakir visited me and asked me to join with him in an experiment involving these jinns. He belonged to the Himalayan people called Garhwalis. I did not care for that sort of experiment, however, and refused to have anything to do with it. But for several days he continued to press me, although still without success. Finally, he said that he would insist on carrying it out whether I consented or not. His explanation was that he had been associated with a jinn for many years. It had been in his service throughout that time. Now, however, he wished to renounce magic, or sorcery, as you might call it, and take to the higher path of a spiritual Yoga. To accomplish this he would have to give up the jinn and separate from it. The jinn replied that it would never agree to leave him unless he got it transferred to a suitable master. The fakir therefore went in quest of such a person who could relieve him of the jinn. For some reason which I never knew he picked on me. But I continued to tell him that I would have nothing to do with such sorcery.

"One night about two o'clock I seemed to awake with a terrible start. A feeling of suffocation overwhelmed me as though the bedroom were full of smoke and flames. Actually I was in a state midway between sleeping and waking. Then a voice, apparently within my ear, said, 'You shall pay for your obstinacy!' The choking sensation got worse and I felt that my last moments on earth had come. Fortunately I had the presence of mind to remember my Master, who was a great Hindu Yogi living in the Kangra Mountains. I prayed silently to him and begged for his protection. My Master's power eventually manifested, a sense of reassurance returned to me, the smoke seemed to clear away and the feeling of being suffocated gradually disappeared.

"Next day the strange fakir visited my house again. His very first words were: 'Do you know why you had that experience of suffocation last night? I shall tell you. My jinn was so angry with you for refusing to become its master that it tried to punish you. But your own Yogi-Master interfered and saved you. I am sorry it attacked you and wish I could have prevented it. Unfortunately, I have now lost much of my own control over the spirit and I was almost helpless. That day I attempted to transfer the jinn to your service without your knowledge. Had I succeeded it would have helped your material affairs to an extent which you can hardly guess. But something went wrong with the magical ceremony which I performed. I left out one of the essential precautions, either through carelessness or forgetfulness. The result was that I could not control the jinn any more. Now that it has failed owing to the protection of your Master, the jinn has turned an evil attention towards me. It declares that it will kill me before the next new moon. I live in fear that I shall pass away from this world soon.'" The Prince stops his narrative to catch his breath.

"Such was the weird story I heard from the fakir," continued Prince Mussooree a minute later. "To me the whole thing seemed too utterly fantastic. With my modern education I was sceptical and could not credit his explanation. I preferrred to believe that I had been the victim of an ordinary nightmare. But wait...."

"Pardon me, but are you sure you had not told the fakir about the experience before he attempted to explain it?"

The Prince is most emphatic.

"Not a single word. Not even to anyone else. The man knew all about it before his arrival. It was astounding. But listen to the sequel. I know that this will sound like a tale from the enchanted days of the *Arabian Nights*, but you have had enough experience of the Orient by now to know that these incredible marvels may have been and perhaps still are possible."

My companion pauses; a grave expression flits over his face.

"Very soon afterwards the fakir was attacked by that dread disease of galloping consumption. Eighteen days later he was dead. His end came exactly one day before the new moon—just as the jinn had threatened!"

*   *   *

Another slow-footed day passes. Another turn of this restless rotating globe of ours. Another pleasant excursion with my Nepalese friend.

We descend a forest-covered gorge to a depth of a hundred and fifty feet or so and then, holding to the tree-trunks, make a horizontal deviation along a trail through the tangled undergrowth for some distance.

We proceed along the path for about half a mile. Then we make an abrupt turn to the left, and start a precipitous descent down the thickly-wooded sides of a deep gorge. The trees are chiefly sombre firs, with occasional clumps of sturdy oaks and a sprinkling of flowering rhododendrons here and there. Our journey begins to take on the colouring of a hasty flight from some wild beast, owing to the sharp gradient affording us no firm foothold and compelling us to move involuntarily so fast that it might be said we slide down all the way, steadied at dangerous places by our pointed Alpine sticks. In this manner we cover about two thousand five hundred feet in record time and reach the bottom of the gorge after a wild passage among bushes, trees, thorns, stumps, rocks, stones and loose earth. With our arrival there we gain our first reward for all this trouble at such a rapid rate.

One of the loveliest little scenes reveals itself. We find ourselves in the bed of a river which has dried up from twenty-five feet in width to a narrow torrent but a couple of yards wide. Huge rocks and tumbled boulders surround us on every side. Gorgeous flame-coloured rhododendron flowers are spangled against the dark-green bushes and trees which stretch along the river sides like an avenue. The water itself dashes madly along at a fierce pace, tumbling over low waterfalls here or skirting round tremendous boulders there or musically gurgling between multitudes of clean-washed stones and pebbles which glisten with every hue and tint in the bright shafts of sunlight. High above us tower the tall walls of the gorge into a limpid azure-blue sky flecked with delicate formations of milk-white clouds.

We cross the swift-running stream and sit down upon a boulder to drink in this beauty. The water laps at our feet. I watch the sunbeams play about the stones. The fascination of finding Nature in her wildest and grandest form in this region never passes, for there is a magnetic lure about our environment which is indescribable. Well does the ancient Sanskrit poet say: "In a hundred ages of gods I could not tell you of all the glories of the Himalayas." I do not think that the scenic splendours of this fifteen-hundred mile mountain world can be overwritten. Whatever one says of it will never be exaggeration.

Prince Mussooree soon decides to take a ramble along the river-bed. We jump from boulder to boulder across the running water with the help of our sticks or crunch the pebbly ground beneath our shoes as we make our way for about a mile between the walls of the gorge, which increase in precipitousness as we proceed, until they become quite perpendicular and completely unclimbable. These huge walls of granite look like a gigantic Gothic cathedral whose towers and buttresses have been riven in two by an earth-quake. Now and then we stop and chat and listen to the musical tinkling noise of the rushing stream as it splashes quickly over the rocks in its onward course. In a month or so the latter will be con-verted into a broad, torrential river by the monsoon rains, and a ramble such as this will then be impossible.

We return from our ramble tired but contented. We start for

home. The steep wall of the gorge confronts us and the arduous climb up two thousand five hundred feet becomes a breath-taking exertion, which we endeavour to lighten by cracking occasional jokes upon sundry unconnected subjects. We struggle upwards somehow.

On our way we pass through the forest, and stop to admire the scene, which is wild yet exquisite. I know that this forest is a favoured haunt of bears and warn the Prince, for the hour is late. He laughs at the danger.

"We have lots of bears in Nepal. Some districts are so infested with them that the women peasants carry pitchforks and large curved knives used for grass-cutting with which to defend themselves against their attacks. With the fork in the left hand they endeavour to keep the animal at bay, whilst they hack at it with the knife in their right hand.

"Our hill people say that if you encounter a bear unexpectedly and are unarmed, the wisest thing to do is to throw yourself prone with your face to the ground and pretend to be dead. The bear will then sniff around you and go away. I have not tried this myself, but I hope it is true! Incidentally, have you ever heard a wounded bear cry? We shot one some time ago, but failed to kill it. It wept like a human being. Incredibly like one!

"There is even something human about the sound of a horse whinnying with intense fright. Once my brother, I, and a servant were proceeding along a trail in the Nepalese Himalayas which was just like the one at the top of this gorge—a narrow, rugged cutting in the rock face. My brother was a little tired of riding and dismounted, leading his horse by the rein whilst he walked on foot. In turning a corner with a hairpin bend the horse slipped over the edge of the trail. Its hindquarters fell down the precipice, but with its two forefeet it managed to cling to the edge. My brother got hold of its head and we two other men ran to assist him. Most of the horse's weight was hanging over the gorge, and despite the best efforts of the three of us we could not succeed in lifting it back to safety. The poor creature realized its danger and began to whinny piteously. We did our utmost to save it, but the weight was too excessive, whilst our own foothold was too precarious. The horse's howls increased as its strength gave out. Its cries of fear and anguish became almost human. Finally it slipped from our grasp and fell into the deep chasm below, moaning all the time until it reached the bottom, where it was smashed to pulp.

"One of my servants has told me about a chance meeting with an extraordinary tribe of animal-men who exist in a wild region of the interior of Nepal. They hide themselves well and always endeavour to avoid human beings. Their bodies are entirely covered with shaggy hair; they are smaller in size than men and women of our race; whilst their faces seem to be a cross between the likeness of a chimpanzee and a human being. Our native historical traditions have long spoken of this queer race, but it is nowadays very difficult to track down any specimens.

"Still talking of animals, I must tell you how I once ran a race with an elephant! Several of us formed a party to go out big game hunting. We were mounted on elephants, and whilst crossing a river one of the mounts dashed out of the water, tried to shake its rider off its back on to its tusks, and to kill him. No argument is of any avail with a maddened elephant, so its frightened rider fled to another mount and was taken on its back for protection. We got away as quickly as we could and left the rebel creature to itself. Unfortunately we had to pass through the same spot later in the day during our return journey in order to reach our camp. There we found the mad elephant waiting for us! It dashed at our party and caught hold of the leg of one man by winding its trunk around it. In a moment he was dragged off the back of his mount and waved about in the air as though he were a flag. The man, thinking he was going to be dashed to death, shrieked aloud with terror, so loudly, in fact, that even the mad animal seemed to become a little frightened and let go its hold of its victim. The man fell to the ground but remained uninjured. He immediately dashed between the feet of another elephant and got away to safety. Baulked of its prey, the infuriated creature became angrier than ever and charged into our party, dashing directly towards me. Here was a clear case for illustrating your proverb that discretion is often the better part of valour! I leapt down from the back of my mount to the ground and fled away into the jungle thickets. The mad elephant rushed after me, its trunk waving furiously in the air. I ran as I had never ran before. The perspiration streamed down me. At one moment I felt its hot breath against my neck. Knowing that I could have no possible defence against it, I put all my strength and all my reserves of wind into escape. I literally flew over the ground and escaped."

I return to the night meal with appetite whetted by the keen mountain air and realize, with Roman Cicero, that hunger is indeed the best sauce. The food is then always attractive, whilst even ordinary tinned fare seems fresh and flavoursome.

The three days which follow see a fresh journey to other points of this region. Thus throughout the Prince's timely visit I become better acquainted with my own neighbourhood and obtain a little needed exercise for my body. We travel along narrow mountain-side ledges with precipices below, which form the only paths available, or climb peaks which are scarped and striated masses of subdued brown rock, or descend through thick forests into deep ravines. Overhead, vultures wing their straight flight across the ever-changing sky. These vultures soar very high and then glide for phenomenal distances with outstretched motionless wings. Not once do they flap their wings in a few miles or more, but move steadily forward on their horizontal routes at high speeds. One beholds them amazed and wonders how it is done.

Many parts of these tangled ridges which lie all around us are too rocky to possess vegetation, while others are dense with green growths and clothed with forests upon every side. Yet even the brown drabness of the barren rocks is broken here and there by solitary wild mountain flowers, nearly all with heads and petals so tiny as to appear like units of a Japanese miniature garden. Dainty white marguerites and yellow, pink and white daisies peep into the air upon the slenderest of stems; occasional forget-me-nots grow in the crevices between stones and make me stop to gaze at their haunting colourings; a single miniature marigold flaunts its yellow beauty amongst the green moss on the inner side of a rock-cut trail; a species of the Himalayan wild raspberry bush unavailingly yet often tempts us with its unripe vermilion fruit; pink-veined wood anemones stud the forest floors; exquisitely small-petalled violets are here, too, and even the English yellow primrose finds a fitful existence.

At the prelude to dusk, when the green peaks become purple shadowed, the bare tracks are flushed with rose, and when the dying sun turns the snow ranges into gold-tipped crests a heightened peace becomes the reigning king of Himalaya. In this serene, town-free silence, where no car syren hoots, no tram clangs, no omnibus rattles and no human crowd rushes, the days disappear into yesterdays with a gentle imperceptible effortless ease. Here, and as far as the distant line where earth and sky meet, if anywhere, a man can know what contentment means and enjoy a true tranquillity.

*　　*　　*

Another bright afternoon arrives. The mid-day sun pours its vertical rays upon the earth. The drone of questing bees resounds through the air. Jackdaws, tiny wagtails, tom-tits and other birds hop and chirrup about among the moss-covered monarchs of the forest. Except for these delightful sounds of Nature, there is an enchanted stillness in the atmosphere. One cannot believe that life is anything but good and kind and quiet. Yet, far away to the north, Europe rages with strain and tension and fear; a similar distance to the east civil war splits the Chinese republic into a broken vessel; while somewhere in the west the death-rattle sounds in the throat of the Ethiopian royal house.

In the crowded centres of civilization, microscopic men are running hither and thither, inflated with their self-importance and quarrelling over the crust of a planet which, in the last analysis, does not belong to them. Here, a score or more of high peaks squat perfectly still with their heads uplifted above the planet, as though unconscious of their kingship, power and grandeur.

We sit in the shade of the bungalow verandah, Prince Mussooree Shum Shere Jung Bahadur Rana and I, ensconced in spacious cane-backed armchairs and both replete with that contentment which comes immediately after an enjoyed and enjoyable lunch.

Whether it is the surrounding peace or the mere entry of a stray thought that sets the other man talking of Buddha I do not know. Anyway, he says: "Nepal has contributed something more than good troops to the world. Do you know that the great Gautama Buddha was intimately associated with Nepal? He was born within its border. To three hundred million Asiatics the lovely little five-acre wood of Rummindei, in Nepal, is sacred as his birthplace. A great monolith set up by the Emperor Asoka nearly 2,200 years ago to commemorate the spot still stands there with its lettering as clearly cut as ever.

"And when, through the opposition and even persecution of Muhammedan invaders or of rigidly orthodox Brahmin priests, Buddhism was destroyed in India more than a thousand years after its foundation, many of the monks and scholars who would not give up their ancestral religion fled into the mountain fastnesses of Nepal, where they were safe. That is why we have today thousands of rare and ancient manuscripts and palm-leaf books, statues, carvings and antiquities, in our monasteries and temples, brought by these refugees. That is why, too, the religion of modern Nepal is a curious mixture of Buddhism and Hinduism. A Nepalese is not conscious of any antagonism between the two faiths and will often worship in a Hindu temple one day and a Buddhist temple the next. My own faith is Hindu, as you know, yet I feel much respect for the other belief.

"Do you know, too, that although the last strongholds of Buddhism along the North Indian border today are Nepal, Tibet and Sikkim, it once flourished here in Tehri-Garhwal State? At a spot now called Barahat, about twenty-five miles as the crow flies from this place, there is, among the ruins of ancient temples and other buildings, a great brazen trident of immense antiquity which bears an inscription recording the visits of Nepalese Buddhist

Rajahs who came there on pilgrimage as late as the twelfth century. Huien T'Sang, the Chinese Buddhist pilgrim-traveller, says this region was called in his time the kingdom of Brahmapura, and that Buddhism existed here alongside of the older faith."

We fall to chatting of the two religions, Buddhism and Hinduism, their striking similarities yet strange contrasts. I tell the Prince that as an intellectual European I feel a kinship with Buddha which I cannot feel so easily with Krishna, because the former was a thinking man who became a god whilst the latter was a born god who sometimes behaved like a man. Buddha kept himself spotless and immaculate with women only after he had experienced and lived through the temptations they offer the normal man, whereas Krishna made love to many girls. Buddha had not renounced a world about which he knew absolutely nothing, as so many monks have done. For him to have achieved such purity in the face of the opportunities for sensual indulgence which his princehood gave him was to make him worthy of the highest respect, but for Krishna to have succumbed to human feelings was not so admirable. It may be that childish myths have been built around his story, and the gaudy lithographs of this flirtatious deity and his adventures with which the Hindus often decorate their walls may be totally unhistorical. It might be wiser, then, to keep these tales in the background. However, I tell him, too, that as a man who has won through to a religious devotion, albeit late in life, I find the teaching of Krishna superbly elevating: his encouragement to the young disciple Arjuna to place his entire life fearlessly and unreservedly in the hands of a Higher Power is likewise encouragement to every other man. Whereas Buddha becomes too coldly rational, too dependent on human effort alone, too independent of the high help which God bestows on the surrendering soul.

It is only in his dialogues with Arjuna that Krishna becomes superb, more lovable and more adorable even than Buddha, for there he preaches no harsh leaping asceticism, as did Buddha, but calls to the human disciple from where he stands.

And then I invite Prince Mussooree indoors and open a long box to show him a treasured Buddhist work of art, the lately acquired gift from one who shall be nameless. It is something which shall henceforth accompany me around the world; a wooden roller two and a half feet wide wrapped in a faded yellow silk dust-jacket and tied with two narrow laquer-red silk bands. With slow careful hands I untie the bands and unroll the casing, thus revealing a large brilliantly coloured picture painted upon an oblong banner of blue and yellow silk. Stretched upon the bottom roller and a narrow wooden lath at the top, this beautiful representation shines out when I hang it from a nail in the wall like a polished sapphire in a plain metal setting.

My companion examines the picture closely.

"It is a genuine Tibetan monastery hanging!" he exclaims, and then turns it partly over to inspect the back. Seven vertical rows of scarlet ink writing in Tibetan characters confirm his statement.

Although the wrapper and background of the picture are dark with age, the painted portion is bright and fresh with gay colourings as though it had left the artist's hand but a year or two ago. It represents thirty-eight small portraits of the Buddha pleasingly arranged in seven straight lines from top to bottom. In each of these the Light of Asia sits in his conventional attitude with interlocked feet, but the hands are given a different arrangement of gesture throughout. These thirty-eight variants of hand-posing are symbolical in meaning and bear profound significance, whilst the writing on the back is placed to correspond exactly with the miniatures; thus by holding the whole painting up to the light, these words read like key captions fitting each picture. They are not so, in reality, but mainly repetitions of the phrase OM-AH-HUM, as uttered by the lips of each figure, a mystic Buddhist phrase symbolizing many sacred and solemn meanings.

The centre of the whole piece is occupied by a much larger portrait of Buddha, still with feet intertwined in the famous Lotus posture; his left hand rests with palm upward and thumb upraised in his lap, whilst the right hand droops to the ground with outstretched fingers. He is the thirty-ninth Buddha, who carries for me a personal significance.

We gaze long upon my treasure. Those statuette-like figures of the wise Gautama seem to bear with them a serene blessing, a sense of utter peace. How artistic is the rhythm of the whole ensemble, how exquisitely beautiful in pose and form! I must confess that the sculptured effigies or brazen idols of Krishna, which are so countless in Hindustan, usually leave me cold. His dancing grotesque figure arouses no enthusiasm, bestows no benediction. And yet there is no shadow of doubt that the message of Krishna was as divine as that of Christ, and both as informed with wisdom as that of Buddha. It may be that my modern outlook, searching for a Greek simplicity of form and questioning like Socrates in the market-place, finds more intellectual directness in the homely words of the Buddha than in the inspired revelation of Krishna. Yet Buddha unfortunately took existence too seriously. He might have taken a leaf out of the book of certain Hindu philosophers and seen it all as a dream, mere fussy agitation, a churning of the waves that leaves the ocean very much as it was before. Had Buddha known how to laugh at life, Asia's religious history would have been different.

But I must rewrap my trans-Himalayan treasure and put it tenderly away for the while.

Then the Nepalese prince prepares his farewell. I thank him for the delightful surprise of intellectual stimulus which has come to me so unexpectedly through him, after so many weeks of soliloquizing among the trees, the rocks and the ravines. He leaps into the saddle of his horse and, with a final wave of his hand, disappears among the firs down the tree-shaded trail below my bungalow, holding himself stoutly against a high wind. His lithe vigorous figure has joined the small procession of those who have come and gone, as the stars come out with the night and depart with the dawn. The world to which he belongs has reclaimed its own, but something which that world does not perceive and cannot perceive roots in his heart and grows in secret like a delicate plant which is destined to bear a fine blossom.

CHAPTER FIFTEEN

My Nightly Vigils in the Open—Reflections on the Stars—The Truth about Astrology—The Mystery of Sirius—Are the Planets Peopled?—The Symbolism of the Sun—The Deodar Tree Speaks—Farewell to My Bungalow.

THE days do not move so rapidly when one is completely alone again. I spend odd slow-turning hours examining the richly-varied plants or curious slabs of striated rock. I gaze studiously at the forest animals whom one meets or sights from time to time, creatures who roam care-free and unhunted. I become a watcher of the skies, carefully following the voyages of wandering mists. I listen to the thunderous downpour of rain which accompanies the periodic storms, as I used to listen in my more civilized days to the symphonic notes of a city orchestra.

Sometimes I rise and prowl around like a panther at unearthly hours, for I feel no necessity to obey the ordered programme of clock-watching which makes up modern existence. Seated on the top of a boulder, surrounded by the eerie night-world of ten, eleven, twelve, one or two o'clock in the morning, I comb the constellations from that of the Ram to that of the Fishes with my gaze.

The mystery of these twinkling lights, so ignored and so unheeded by comfortably sleeping house-dwellers, begins to affect me. I return again and again to my nocturnal contemplations of them. They look like sparks struck off the anvil of eternity. I cannot study them with the technical expertness of a professional astronomer who peers through his high-powered telescope, nor with the anxious interest of an old-time navigator who made nightly observations to them for finding his latitude. But I can sit and speculate about their nature and perhaps, through sheer intensity of reverie, attain a slight clairvoyant contact with them.

Here are millions of living glowing worlds arrayed above my head. The man who cannot see that a Higher Power guides and directs their ordered rhythmic activity must be intellectually blind. The Universe lives, and is not dead. But this is not to say that a God in the form of a glorified gigantic man guides and directs them. The intelligence and force which actuate the stars are inherent with them, and constitute their soul, in precisely the same manner that intelligence and force are inherent within the body of man and constitute his soul too. God is not external to His creation; the stars are not marionettes which He pulls upon a string; and man is not a mere puppet to be worked with detachment from a distance.

Meanwhile our clocks tick away to the motion of our planets and our own earth circles unfailingly around its Lord.

I look from one part of the sky to another. There in the north is the Dragon which shines near the Pole with a brilliance unseen by the low-dwelling people of the plains. Adopted by the Chinese as their national emblem thousands of years ago, fit pictograph for the world's oldest existing civilization, it is the most picturesque of the northern constellations. Sprawling across the north-western rim of the heavens is the Great Bear. In the centre of the whole sky is Arcturus, "the Watcher of the Bear"—a flush of orange colouring. Low in the south-west lies the constellation of the Centaur, the half-man and half-horse. And like a tautened bow, the Milky Way sweeps along the eastern horizon until it terminates in the Southern Triangle, equally aglow with a light which the dwellers under clouded northern skies never know.

The clearly defined Scorpio group, like an elongated letter S, is in the south, with the gleaming radiance of a companion, the planet Jupiter, in contrast on its right. In its midst I detect a smallish-looking red star, whose apparent size, however, is deceptive, for Antares must be one of the biggest in the entire firmament; just the same are we deceived by the sun's magnitude in contrast to several stars which are really larger but appear smaller.

And then there arises out of the depths of memory the words of an old astrologer, who has now vanished from our own star, and his charts, calculations and ephemerides with him. "Antares sits in your horoscope in close conjunction with the planet Saturn," he said slowly, "and that means early blindness."

His statement was true and its verification came long before I met him. One morning the lids of my eyes became fast shut, the world vanished from my gaze. I became blind and remained so for months. Sun, stars and streets no longer existed for me. I might have been a spirit for all the use this earth was to me. But what I lost then became balanced by what I found—an inner world where ghosts became realities. Little did I guess that two books I would write later would one day be printed in Braille-embossed type for the benefit of the blind poor!

Do I then believe in the truth of astrology? Perhaps I do, but I do not believe in astrologers. For they possess only a bazaar-jumble of half-facts, revealed verities, sheer superstitions, sound principles and unsound interpolations. There is enough in astrology to give every candid investigator some surprises and there is also enough to delude him greatly once his faith has been caught. The whole thing is incomplete, semi-scientific. For every accurate prediction about which a fuss is made, there exist a couple of dozen totally wrong ones. The Indian system is probably more complete than that which is used in the West today, and differs from it in important details. Yet both possess important lacunae, secrets that were lost with the ancient world, and therefore both become quite unreliable as guides, although hitting the mark now and again between their numerous mistakes. But who is omniscient enough to indicate beforehand where they are correct in prediction and where they are wrong? There is no certitude in them. The wise man will therefore walk warily when he uses them or, better, turn completely aside and place his faith, not in faulty astrologers but in the faultless Overself. There may be a myriad influences out in interstellar space, but there is one that is supreme within himself.

He will then cease to worry whether Mars has entered into malefic relation with the Sun in his horoscope, as it has in mine, or whether Saturn will ever lift its millstone from his neck. Nor will he become unduly jubilant because a trine to Jupiter has promised him some money in five years' time, or an opposition to Venus a divorce in three! He will understand that a wise indifference is better than a slavish submission to all these fears and hopes, for through it, as through a gate, he may pass to peace.

He knows that the predictions of the most famous astrologer may be utterly wrong and if acted upon may lead to ruin, whereas the guidance of the divine Overself will always be perfect and can lead only to more serenity, more wisdom and more happiness.

*   *   *

Another time my eyes come to rest on Sirius, brightest of morning stars, which pierces a velvet-blue sky on the very edge of the horizon. For me and for the watcher in an observatory, the Dog-Star is the grandest of all stars in the heavens. The astronomer, however, registers only the physical expression of the superlative magnitude of its steely blue brightness; I register its surprising brilliance too, plus a purely psychic impression.

The Egyptians thought so highly of this beautiful star that they called it "The Divine Sothis (Sirius), the Queen of Heaven". Its midsummer rising marks the beginning of the annual inundation of the river Nile, which irrigates the entire length of the land and brings food to millions. They gave it in their scripts and carvings a similar hieroglyph to that of their greatest monument—the figure of a triangle. There is another striking correspondence between star and Pyramid. The priest-astronomers took it as their basis of measuring the epochs of universal history. They watched its successive risings at a particular place during the few minutes before its light vanished into the coming light of dawn, and noted its position relative to the earth and sun when its rising coincided with the summer solstice. They knew, by observation and calculation, how long it would be before that position would be repeated, naming the period the Cycle of Sothis. This epoch was no less than 1461 years. Thus Sirius' rising immediately before daybreak on midsummer morning became the starting point for the chief Egyptian calendar, forming the Grand Epoch of its secular cycle. Now the number of casing-stones on the base around the four sides of the Great Pyramid was exactly 1461, precisely the same as the number of star years in the Sothiac cycle!

The other and traditional name of Sirius is the Dog-Star. Yet the first symbol for Sirius among the learned men of Egypt was not a dog but a giraffe. This long-necked animal possesses no vocal organ and hence makes no sound; it is undoubtedly the quietest of all creatures of its size. Moreover, it can see both ways without turning head or eyes. Hence it is a perfect symbol of the four gods who guard the evolution of mankind in Sphinx-like silence. The star Sirius is definitely connected with these superhuman beings, the Silent Watchers, and the wise men of ancient Egypt knew of this connection.

Sirius does not belong to the multitudinous company of our own starry system: it is a mere stranger who is momentarily close to us but in distant time will flicker off into the depths of space. The Egyptians were not alone in their knowledge of and reverence for Sirius. Most of the ancient races knew and reverenced this glorious star too.

But spiritually it is a still greater stranger. The beings who people it are infinitely superior in every way to the creatures who people Earth. In intelligence, in character, in creative power and in spirituality we are as slugs crawling at their feet. The Sirians possess powers and faculties which we shall have to wait a few ages yet to acquire. They have detected our existence already, when we do not even know and often do not even believe that the star-worlds are inhabited.

Evolution, involution and devolution have not ceased with that petty proud creature which lords this planet under the title of man. His name comes from the Sanskrit root, *manas*—to think! I cannot count the immense number of years since he first made an appearance upon this stage, but it is perfectly obvious that he has begun to

155

use this faculty of thought only lately, and that he has still much more distance to travel before he uses it fully. If any Gulliver of a Sirian were cast ashore on this Lilliput of an Earth, he would find not less astonishing things to write home about than did his famous prototype of the fable.

Those who imagine that because our own planet bears its load of frail humanity, no other planet may therefore bear one too, betray an ant-like narrowness of vision. Just as the brown earth, whose molecules compose part of the crust of the lobe, revolves through space only to provide habitation for ants, as the ants themselves are firmly convinced, so this spacious universe reposes grandly in the ether with all its living inhabitants concentrated in a single relatively microscopic speck called the Earth, our human ants are likewise firmly convinced. It would be difficult to choose between their delusion and Bernard Shaw's theory, that this planet is the lunatic asylum for the whole solar system!

We have measured the precession of the equinoxes to the thinnest shade of a degree; we have calculated the time of the eclipses to the very second; but we have not yet detected a single one of those intelligent personalities who exist in other parts of this universe. But if we do not know them, some of them know us, some of them pity us and a few even serve us. One such servant was/is the Christ. Men may strike out whichever of these two verbs they fancy, whilst those who deny Him may delete both; the truth will never be imperilled by their petty arrogance of opinion.

And so I return to my nightly contemplation of the star-clusters and of the planets which revolve around the sun, yielding myself to the nightly wonder which wells up unbidden at their sight. If God did not really exist I should worship the sun; if the sun did not exist I should worship Nature, could I but see it then; and if Nature did not exist I should worship the stars. I could not and would not worship the moon, that cold ghostly ghastly sphere!

One sees a goodly number of falling and shooting stars in this tropic hemisphere. What tremendous event dislocates the universal machinery when a comet cuts a vivid path across the night sky!

I arise one night to glimpse the last stars scattered in the sky and to watch the oncoming of dawn. The moon's face, white-powdered like a woman's, keeps its vigil upon my own vigil. My boulder-seat is bathed in the mellow radiance shed by these groups that twinkle against their dark background. I cannot compute the speed at which their light is travelling in order to reach these Himalayan pimples on the skin of our own star. Certainly a hundred thousand miles per second would be an under-estimate. Nor can I measure the tremendous distance of some stars from the earth.

Certainly a billion miles would likewise be an under-estimate. Nor can I count the infinite galaxy of nebulae, worlds, suns, moons, satellites, asteroids and planets which fill this complex universe. Certainly, again, one billion would be an under-estimate.

Who can gaze thoughtfully at this amazing creation throned in unfathomable space without experiencing at least the beginnings of awe and, at most, the humility of knee-bent veneration? My spirit slips away, loses itself in the recondite mystery of it all. . . .

It seems so remote, so etheral, so austere. How puny, how insignificant, the troubles of a man when confronted by those multitudes of aloof impersonal lustrous eyes!

The clock must turn and once again I must resume my vigil. I watch the sentinel lights fade gently out of the sky, as once I watched them fade over the head of Egypt's Sphinx. Soon dawn arrives with its hues of pearly greys succeeded by steely blues, grows apace and admits the sun to our darkened world. The atmosphere is clear and brightens rapidly, so I turn my head to view Himalaya's pride, with its snow and silence, amid the red aurora.

The early sun has tipped the white snows with fiery plumes of burnished gold. The fretted line of frozen summits shines resplendently against the changing background of the turquoise sky. The pinnacles of unmelting ice keep once more their daily tryst with the flaming bringer of light. The rays of quivering colour steal through the valleys and among the high peaks, staining them all to a rich rose. Powdered snow streams to the sky from these peak-tops.

My final reflections desert the vanished stars and turn to the oncoming sun. In almost every early religion it appears as a divine symbol, the sign of God in the heavens for all men to witness. Its diurnal appearance and disappearance typified to the ancients the universe's own death and reincarnation, too. Both sun and Nature were really undying, they knew. And with the sun they often coupled the lotus. Both Indian and Egyptian, Aztec and Atlantean, took this as their sacred flower. This lovely flower shuts its petals at eve and opens them again in the morning; once again symbolizing the death and rebirth of the life-force. The ancients never tired of picturing it upon their temple walls and papyrus scripts.

The parallel between sun and lotus runs even deeper. The sun shines impartially into the foulest dirtiest places; so too does the lotus oft rear its beautiful head out of slimy pools and rank mud.

We may read in this precisely what the ancients read: that the divine Overself in man exists unstained while he descends into the most abysmal depths of Matter.

And now the whole Himalayan region is alight and fully on

view. I make my devout morning prostration before Light, the primal manifestation of God in the physical world, and then return.

* * *

if the clock must turn, so too must the sheets of the calendar. Time travels on in the old way, even here in Himalaya, and the weeks with it. The monsoon season is about due in this part of the country. Parched India awaits this pitiless flood of water which the heavens collect for nine months in order to let loose upon it in three. Too protracted a monsoon may destroy crops and ruin peasants, yet too light a one may have precisely the same effect. The failure of one monsoon may create sheer starvation in thousands of villages. How anxiously the watchers on the coast have awaited the massed armies of invading black, angry-looking clouds which foreshadow this Janus-headed, delightful and dreadful monsoon! Some parts of India are already under its dominion, I know; the Eastern Himalayas have received their gargantuan baptism, whilst I daily await the dismal fate of the Central Himalayas. The first foretaste I have had has not been too pleasant.

The coming of the monsoon will change the general tenor of my life. The major part of my stay in these mountains will henceforth perforce have to be spent indoors. I shall soon become the resigned captive of tremendous rains, tempestuous winds and raging storms. There will be some brief interludes, of course, when a shy sun will peep through the clouds for an hour or two as though to reassure the world of its existence and then disappear again. The rains will recommence their torrential downpouring and virtually keep me prisoner in my room day and night. A wall of water shall constitute the barrier between me and freedom.

How opportune, then, is the chance which comes to me now, through the courtesy of the Tehri-Garhwal State authorities, to move away into the interior of the State and occupy better quarters in a large house near the summer Palace of Pratapnagar! How kind of destiny to arrange better shelter for me just at the very moment when it is needed! For if I have to spend the summer indoors as a monsoon captive, it will be well to be comfortably housed, untroubled by extreme weather conditions and unworried by the difficulties of procuring further food supplies.

There will be no change in my mode of life otherwise. I shall continue all my meditations as before. There will be no change in my liberty and solitude. My solitude, if anything, will be more complete, for not a single visitor will dare to cross the mountains to Pratapnagar during the rains merely to see me. I shall therefore be more inaccessible than ever.

Pratapnagar Palace is perched on a lofty mountain ridge in a region as solitary as my present abode. It is little used, for there are more conveniently situated palaces farther south in Tehri township and in Narendranagar. I am assured that the surrounding country is exceedingly beautiful, but, alas, my rambles must perforce come to an end with the coming of the monsoon. They will have to be continued in the mind, amongst the peaks of high ideas and the valleys of mild meditations. In any case I have a growing disinclination to go out of doors. According to Yogic standards I have had more than enough exercise to suit the period of my stay. I want to explore the outer world less, to keep quiet, and to explore the inner world more. Thus, during the monsoon, my new house at Pratapnagar with its superior accommodation will be better for this purpose than the bleak forest bungalow which I am now occupying.

So now, not long after sunrise, I must go to bid a last farewell to the deodar, for so long my admonitory guardian and kindly if aristocratic mentor. My conversations with it must come to an end. My meditations underneath its drooping needled branches shall reach their finale.

With stick in hand I climb the rugged height whose tree-girt top holds my sanctuary. It is not pleasant, this valedictory task of mine, and I do not know how the deodar will take my unexpected desertion.

When at last I emerge from the thorny undergrowth and scattered stones of the slope and cross the open space of the sanctuary, I halt to catch my breath. One swift glance at the deodar, one accusing frown upon its mossy face, one melancholy sigh of its low-sagging soughing branches, and I realize that it reads my thoughts. Why is its face so sad? It knows. I hang my head in shame.

I squat down on the leaves in the old familiar spot, still averting my gaze from the tree. I feel the blood flushing my cheeks. Then I too become sad. The wrench of parting affects me.

But eventually I look up. Forgive me, dear deodar! This is life, you know. Acquaintance, friendship, farewell. The caravan must wind on across the desert of worldly existence, its halts are but for a night. Yet it is sweeter to have built up what shall be, for me, a beautiful memory than not.

Dear, friendly deodar! Such is the transitoriness of life. We need but to part; we come to friendship and love only to lose both again. Yet our spirits shall not part; they can wing their way through space, drawn to each other by love.

There is a curious brooding hush in the air.

And then a butterfly, so surprisingly common and so beautiful an insect in this high region, flits around my head and alights upon the fern which droops beard-like from the deodar. Youth and beauty thus come into striking contrast and juxtaposition with age and decorum. The gorgeously winged creature, much larger than its European relatives, attaches herself (surely this daintily-clad, delicately groomed visitor can only be a high-born lady?) to the plant, gathers her exquisite highly-coloured raiment around her, and settles down into a fixed position. Has she come to grace my graceless departure?

The overpowering stillness gathers around us, folds and enfolds the entire scene.

I notice the dewdrops which still hang, like tears, from the needle-tips of the old deodar's branches, which sag low as though weeping. Yes, I too feel like weeping.

Have you any message for me, O deodar?

The intense silence, the unperturbed peace, holds us for a minute more. At last it is broken, not by any sound, though, but by a thought-whisper which floats through the atmosphere into my brain.

"You came to me out of a world which I do not know and do not understand. Sooner or later, I knew that you would be recaptured by it. Why should I wish to detain you? Have I not learned how to live alone? Have I not found in my own solitude the strength to endure all things—even the buffetings of snarling winds and the rage of destructive lightnings? Where did I get this power of endurance from? I drew it forth out of my own heart, where at first it lay asleep. Now I fear none and nothing—not even death, which cannot be far away. I have learned to depend on no help, except my own. That, my younger friend, is my answer to you. Be self-reliant. Wheresoever you go, remain a hermit inwardly. Then your world can never weaken you. Do not leave your stillness here after you find it. Take it back with you into that distant life whose agitation rarely reaches me, hold to it as your most treasured possession, and then, unafraid, you may let all storms blow past you. Remember always that you derive your being from heaven. My own peace I give to you."

These are the last words I ever hear from the deodar. For with the ceasing of its telepathic whisper I pass insensibly into a deeper condition. The peace outside seeps into me. I rapidly become like a man hypnotized and fall into a semi-trance. I cannot stir a finger, much less a limb, and remain rooted like a tree to the ground.

No effort to meditate has come from my part, no endeavour to control the wanderings of thought has arisen. I just slip into this enchanted state as easily and as resistlessly as a hospital patient slips into sleep under the grip of a powerful anæsthetic. I am as helpless as a drugged man, but with this difference, that I am perfectly conscious of my physical surroundings. I feel that my mind is being propelled inwards, irresistibly and powerfully drawn by some magnetic force within.

What have you done to me, O deodar!

All thoughts are stilled like a lamp in a windless place. My mind is as quiet as the still ravine below me.

I can neither shut nor open my half-closed eyelids, nor exert myself sufficiently to get out of this half-trance, nor do I wish to do that, so pleasurable is the sensation.

It is a serene and beautiful experience, an ecstatic reverie so intense as really to be indescribable. I discover anew that our existence is embosomed in divinity. All words merely hint, suggest, touch the fringe of its garment. To describe accurately one must write like a scientist and analyse exhaustively; the analytic scientific process merely converts the glowing fire of beauty into dismal ashes; yet perhaps even the ashes may be welcome in a world where such ethereal beauty is remote and rare.

Within the circle of inward quiescence, my happiness is made perfect and complete.

How long I remain thus I do not properly know, although I know it is less than half an hour. The Overself, alas, takes its egress from the mind as well as its ingress. Only the superman can stay for ever within its sublime grasp. I rise, reluctant.

It is the end. I creep over the cliff-side and cautiously descend to the trunk of the deodar, clinging with both hands to stones and roots. I strip a tiny piece of bark and climb back to the top. It shall be my souvenir, my lingering remembrance of the silent dominion of Himalaya.

A last look at the sanctuary, set in its panorama of soaring peaks and silent valleys, and I turn my heel.

At the bungalow I find the coolie-porters awaiting me, the baggage ready to be loaded on their backs. Also a strong-limbed grey horse, with wide bulging forehead, large knees and hocks, and a fine sheen on its coat. There is nothing else for which to wait.

I mount into the saddle, fix my feet into the stirrups, pick up the reins and start off on the journey among the mountains to my new abode.

CHAPTER SIXTEEN

I Set Out Again on Horseback—Gorgeous Panorama in Tehri State—My Journey Along the Ridge-tops and Mountain Trails—Through the Forests in the Darkness—I Arrive at Pratapnagar.

IT would really be incorrect to say that one rides a horse across the Himalayas; one merely sits in the saddle and lets the animal amble slowly on at its own leisurely pace. To ride along these steep narrow paths cut in the mountain-face at any proper pace would be to ride abruptly off the outer edge of the ridge into pathless space and dis-embodied existence. Besides this extremely obvious danger, there are some minor difficulties in the way of indulging in a canter or two, let alone a gallop, such as high gradients and low declines, frequent corners like hairpin bends and rugged stony surfaces of the tracks which sometimes billow up and down like the waves of the ocean.

For about three-quarters of a mile I pursue my way through the forest and then emerge into the open. I can now see the winding path run upwards like a grey ribbon along the ridge to the top of a peak, then disappear over the other side, then reappear again and dip deeply downwards and make a serpentine detour around the three sides of a narrow glen and finally turn around a corner for ever.

My coolies are already lost to view somewhere in the forest and I shall not meet them again until the next day. The journey to Pratap-nagar requires two days, if it is to be done with any degree of comfort, but I intend to accomplish the whole distance in one day and be done with it, even if it means arriving after midnight.

In this sparsely populated country, where one might travel for miles and not see a single person, it is fortunate that I cannot possibly lose my way, even though I am not mapless. There are no cross-roads to puzzle one, no side paths to distract and no sign-posts to be examined. One must either go forward or retreat back-ward; there is no other choice, unless indeed it be to go downward into the bottom of a ravine!

I ride on right through the morning, noting with relief that the early mists have cleared off completely and that the sky betokens a perfectly fine day. The long toilsome ascent up the peak comes to an end and the horse ceases to pant. At this point on the journey the view of both the surrounding and distant landscape is wonderfully widespread and well-defined against the horizon. I see a vast stretch of the Himalayan barrier from the low-lying plains of India on the right to the savage line where Tibet adjoins Tehri-Garhwal State on the left. Nearly all the rainbow-colours are here, from the snow-white of a moonstone to the violet of a spinel ruby, and from the dark blue of a lapis lazuli to the olive green of a chrysoberyl. Everything is radiant in the vertical rays of the midday sun which pours heavily upon us both. We move over the broken rubble and loosened earth and fallen rocky slabs which mingle to make the path and proceed downward a little more quickly.

At the end of five hours' riding I have had enough of the saddle and dismount. I find myself in a sunburnt region of barren heights and purple rocks and chalky stones which remind me curiously of the arid Valley of the Tombs of the Dead in Upper Egypt. So far I have met only two other travellers, a man returning on foot from a pilgrimage to Gangotri, who looks footsore, weary, slightly ill, but determined, and a half-clothed peasant mountaineer who crouches respectfully on one side as I pass. With the first man I have a few words in greeting before we part. The second is most obviously a simple soul who, despite his arrant poverty, can teach some of our shrewder townsfolk a few lessons in honesty and integrity.

I sit down on a smooth-topped slab of rock beside the trail and open my vacuum flask for the inevitable drink of tea. In the small saddle-bag I find some solid food, which I share dutifully with the horse. For a few minutes I stretch my limbs upon the rock and then, refreshed, spring into the saddle again and we trot off once more.

On and on we go through a constantly changing variety of scenery, up hill and down dale, along summits and around peaks, amid rocky escarpments and woodland dells, in and out of gorges, valleys and ravines, creeping always along the edge or face of precipices. Tier upon tier of the mountain ridges, which cut up the whole of this kingdom, rise beyond, their heads uplifted like rows of waves. Everything blends and mingles to make up the Himalayan landscape. It is a magnificent sensation, this, of being alone with Nature in her wildest grandeur, almost intoxicating in the elevation which it gives to one's thoughts, hopes and ambitions. For one seems to draw a power out of these strong granite mountains, a magnetism which tones up the will and renders less insuperable the barriers which handicap every man's life. And this is as it should be, for Nature herself must and does possess an aura, a mental atmosphere no less than man. Whoever is at all sensitive feels it, absorbs it, and is consequently influenced by it. I write that statement not as a poet, but as a scientist. Where can one find a more powerful manifestation of this aura, I reflect, than in the Himalayas, one of Nature's supreme attempts to express herself upon a cyclopean scale? Most of the gods and many of the godlings were not associated with this place for nothing.

I pass through a dense deodar forest, which sets me thinking of that deserted friend in the sanctuary. Shall we ever meet again?

The sunlight falls through the foliage and stipples the ground with light here and there. Banners of moss hang from the trees, which stand up like tall masts. Here and there the gnarled spreading boughs of a mighty oak tree, a sylvan king, change the uniformity of the scene.

I keep along the flank of a valley and then turn into another wildly rugged and dreary region. The ascents and descents are here sometimes so steep that I prefer to get off the horse occasionally, rather than tumble with it off the cliff-side.

The miles are steadily slipping behind me, meanwhile. I am confident that the journey will be finished before midnight, although my confidence is really a matter of guesswork because I am totally ignorant of the conditions which yet await me on the way.

At last, when the sun has begun to decline and both steed and rider are exceedingly hungry, thirsty and tired, I decide to take a second and final rest. The sight of an unpolluted bubbling brook emerging from the tiered rocks of the cliff-wall on my left hand is the real precipitant of this decision. The horse greedily sticks its nose into the puddle of pale-blue water on the ground below the brook and swallows an immense quantity. I, too, take a couple of cupfuls of the clear sparkling liquid, which has a most refreshing coolness. Then I open the saddlebag and remove all the solid food for a final meal, which I share again with the animal, whose obedience and intelligence have pleased me greatly.

*   *   *

It is pleasant to rest on the fragrant, flower-starred earth once again rather than on horseback, however. I watch the sun splashing the world with an apricot-yellow light. The sky is beginning to change in parts from deep blue to delicate rose with the setting of the sun.

Somewhere in the neighbourhood a cuckoo faithfully pipes out its sweet daily call. A response seems to come with the delightful song of a skylark. I bend down and touch a wildflower, a blue harebell, which grows in a cranny among the rocks, and inhale its clean fresh scent. In the most unlikely places one finds these wild plants clinging for life to stony crevices among the mountain fastnesses. Even wine-red rhododendrons and yellow primroses bloom amid the snows. It is extraordinary at what high altitudes flowers can flourish in the Himalayas.

I appreciate all the grandeur and beauty which surround me and offer humble thanks for them. The solitude is absolute and possesses an extraordinary soothing quality. Himalaya is so restful that a work-weary business magnate might well change his itineraries for once and seek it out, if he seeks a cure for his worn-out nerves. It is good and necessary to get away from people at times, to put ten thousand feet of mountain height between one and their fidgety restless bodies. Such days of flight are not wasted, even for the busiest of executives; they bring a new viewpoint, a better perspective, an additional inspiration. Nature may sometimes be as good as any efficiency expert to help a tired director sift and simplify his problems of management, manufacturing and salesmanship. She too has a report to submit. Only—hers comes not upon elaborately-typed sheets of foolscap; it comes with the illuminating flash of intuition that upwells from one knows not where, when one makes the penitent return to her secluded and silent abodes.

Once again I start out on the next phase, which now takes the shape of a steep ascent. Most of its surface is littered with loose pebbles and chunks of broken rock. The horse sets its feet down more cautiously and seems to have a dread of slipping on this irregular ground during its arduous efforts to attain the top of the slope.

Signs of the severe earthquakes which have repeatedly struck at the whole of this region are not wanting. Evidential fissures show themselves to the observant eye.

One evening but a week ago I felt a shock of moderate intensity which lasted about thirty seconds vibrate my body violently during meditation.

We reach the rim of a huge natural basin in whose placid circular depths there repose a few tiny villages. On the opposite side a hamlet clings like a nest to the side of a less steep mountain. The buildings look like miniature dolls' houses.

From valley to height and then to snowy top the whole landscap is bathed in rose and pink light succeeded by ruby and orange, and then in the last purple glow of sunset. Here and there the ground is starred with midget wildflowers. A flock of small black goats bleats behind me and I back the horse to the inner edge of the path to let it pass. The herdsman is evidently driving them homewards from some neighbouring patch of pasturage lower down the mountainside. He is bare-legged almost to the tops of his thighs, and wears a loose hanging shirt covered by a tattered grey jacket. A flat-topped round black hat rests sideways on his head, like the cap of a Scotch soldier or Gurkha warrior. His picturesque tawny face is good-natured and he greets me respectfully when he comes up abreast.

I let his herd go ahead of me because I espy a small hamlet only a hundred yards or so away, and I want to watch it being driven into shelter for the oncoming evening. Within a few minutes I reach the collection of half a dozen houses and a few barns built upon a narrow clearing. One house is perched somewhat precariously upon the very cliff-side itself. The bleating goats are packed off out of sight, while all the inhabitants of the hamlet come out to greet me. I rein in and buy a large cupful of curds from one of them. These mountain folk are extremely fond of this appetizing drink. They ask me whither I am bound, and when I tell them Pratapnagar they advise me to hurry as there is a tremendous dip and an equally tremendous climb before me yet.

The advice is timely. The sunbeams are becoming feebler. I spur the horse on to a quicker pace. A ride of a mile and a half along the top of the ridge brings me to the deep valley of which I have been warned. The path twists down through emerald-green grass-covered slopes to the very bottom—a matter of several thousand feet. There I behold a shining milky-grey riband stretched right along the whole valley as far as the eye can see. It is a river, which I identify from my map as the Bhagirathi The stream flows down from a 13,000-feet glacier beyond Gangotri, close to the Tibetan border, and is really the headstream of the Ganges, for it joins another river before it finally issues from the Himalayas and the combined waters are then named the Ganges. I shall have to cross it in order to make the other side; the long narrow bridge which spans it from bank to bank is just faintly visible as a thin black line.

"The Ganges falls from the foot of Vishnu like the slender thread of a lotus flower," says an ancient poet.

Beyond the water rises a precipitous ridge, studded with forests, which rise many thousands of feet into the air. Somewhere on the very top of the ridge there is a white gleam in the slanting sun-rays which I decide must be Pratapnagar Palace, near which is the house that shall be my next home.

This final lap of my journey will be the hardest, whilst the long toilsome climb beyond the river will be impossible for my exhausted horse. Fortunately, a change of mounts awaits me at the bridge, I know.

We make the descent in record time for the path is fairly smooth although it twists often. Two or three times I have to get on my feet and trot beside the horse at very dangerous gradients, but generally I take risks now that I have not taken before. Such is the lure of home-coming!

We reach the valley bottom without mishap and at the bridge-head a waiting groom comes forward to greet me. He takes over my perspiring panting mount and hands me in exchange a sturdy-looking chocolate brown horse, which looks neat, fresh and powerful.

I dawdle, saddle-weary, on the simply constructed bridge for a few moments and watch the white-foaming, flowing current pass beneath me. Bhotia traders, half-Indian, half-Tibetan, come down across this point from the higher passes with goods from Tibet, generally salt and borax, and take back grain and cloth. Many bells are tied to their pack-animals, which are often sheep and goats, each being loaded with little double panniers. Fifty yards higher up there flashes a steep waterfall, where the stream roars and sprays like a cascade as it enters into combat with massive rocks and then dashes victoriously through their ranks. The noise of its fall to a lower level. sounds like the hurrahs of an invading army seizing a fallen capital.

Before it plunges over the rapids the Bhagirathi flows through a narrow canyon-like gorge whose steep grass-grown granite walls confront me like a pair of enormous fortresses. They are grim and relentless despite their green colouring, and no human feet could ever scale their impressive perpendicular faces.

What masses of drifting snows and melting glaciers have mingled to make these frosty waters that run beneath my feet? What titanic cargoes of avalanches, ice and minerals have disappeared, to be carried into their depths? For the swift torrent of the Ganges has yet to flow onwards across the entire breadth of this Indian sub-continent into the seven mouths of the Hoogly, a distance of more than a thousand miles, and to broaden until its banks are very wide apart. Who can feed the gargantuan thirst of the plains if not inexhaustible Himalaya?

It will be long, if ever, before I forget the dancing streams of this region.

I turn my heel on the swirl and roar of the river and mount the waiting horse. I direct its head towards the forbidding height which awaits us and move on once more in quest of another transient home.

The path here is a little broader, with a fissured precipitous rocky wall on the left and the river below on the right for the first part of its length. Its surface too is superior. Then it becomes steeper, forcing the horse to move with slow and laborious steps despite its strength. Whenever we reach a bend the animal stops unbidden and puffs for a minute before proceeding. However, the gradient becomes steeper still until, at one point where the path-makers seem to have relented, it becomes a zigzag streak upon the mountain face, thus rendering the ascent less trying at the cost of doubling the distance to be travelled.

Multitudes of pebbles and rock fragments line the way. Most of them are tinted a beautiful violet colour. Thick forest vegetation begins to appear again on the route. Hanging trees clothe the slope. Branches occasionally nod downwards over the path, forcing me to brush their leaves aside. A few firs fleck the brown height with green, but oak and pine are the predominant growths. Then I pass through an avenue of cactus plants, which grow to the height of small trees. Their leaves are held out like sharp swords flourished in the air.

*   *   *

But now sunset nears its end, the last light gets dimmer and dimmer; I realize that we must hasten. The path broadens for a few yards to admit a dozen houses which have been built on its side. The mountaineers squat reflectively on their doorsteps chewing coconut husk, that strange Indian substitute for tobacco. Behind one of them sits his wife nursing a baby. She is a woman with pronounced Mongolian features and by birth no doubt half-Tibetan. She has adorned her nose with a silver pendulous ring and her ankles with silver bangles. Her eyelids are painted with black antimony. She has a serious calm face and wears a pink saree around her body.

I try to press the horse to quicker pace, but the animal is already doing its best. The zigzag shape of the uphill trail gives us six or seven more miles yet to cover, with darkness already catching up to our heels. Will it not be wiser to take shelter in one of the huts for the night, than to climb unknown slopes during darkness? No, the journey must be completed today, must come to an end before I dismount for the last time.

The twilight finally melts into blackness, which gives to the cliff-side trees a thousand fantastic forms. Nevertheless, the horse is surefooted and moves unhesitatingly, for this track is an old acquaintance of his. I must perforce trust my life to it now, for the sheer drop below the right edge of this path would swiftly take us both to immaterial existence. It is a strange feeling, this, of complete surrender to a simple four-footed creature, and creates an extraordinary sense of unity and fellowship between us. I pat its shoulder encouragingly as it struggles upward and onward through the still starless and moonless night.

But one must move through this whole Himalayan region with trust, for one is ever at Nature's mercy here. Every year, at this season, pilgrims lose their lives through landslides suddenly tearing away part of the path and precipitating them into space.

Within the hour the first stars show themselves and by their pallid glow the slope becomes faintly visible. We pass a group of enormous boulders, which stand near a bend in the trail like gigantic milestones. What planetary upheaval has cleft them from the main body of mountain and set them up, like a fragmentary and miniature

Stonehenge, to balance themselves thus precariously so many thousand feet above the sea-level?

As we move on I crick my neck and try to catch a glimpse of the starlit horizon above me. The jagged ridge-top, which is the Canaan of my wanderings in this mountainous wilderness, shows itself as not so far off now, but I know how illusory is distance when one has a zigzag path to pursue. Dense forest, which I know must contain a flock of prowling night creatures in its depths, seems to lie ahead.

The thinnest fragment of a moon shows her face. The darkness mocks her with its triumphant power. There is to be no help from that quarter, then.

I try to forget my surroundings and let my thoughts ramble over the most unrelated topics, the while I sit in the saddle and mechanically hold the reins. Someone I know is lying on a deathbed in England and before another moon rises her spirit shall find it Canaan, too. The little pen which she gave me once shall be her memorial, and to me a better one than carven granite. Nearer here, a man in the circle which rules, from Baghdad, the destinies of the youngest of Arab kingdoms, is less blindly fulfilling a prediction of future danger and future power, which I involuntarily uttered once behind the stiff formal front of a Legation building. My affection wings its way at once in protective flight towards him; he is "the bravest of the brave", as Marshal Ney was well called in Napoleon's day, and he shall ultimately put all enmity beneath his feet.

The path winds its toilsome way upward. The miles creep slowly under the horse's hooves. The long and lonely route seems as if it will never come to an end, when we enter the sombre forest. Grim, impenetrable blackness immediately grips us. Even the wisp of light that comes from the starlit sky is cut off by the dense roof of intertwined branches under which we ride. It is so dark that I can no longer see the horse's head.

To make matters worse the ascent becomes unexpectedly and embarrassingly steeper. My mount stops every now and then to catch its breath but bravely continues. And so it plods, pants and exerts itself to the utmost.

A half hour more and a new difficulty is present. The surface of the trail from here has been roughly paved with stones, no doubt as a defence against being completely washed away by the monsoon rains. Evidently we are now near to Pratapnagar. But if the rains could not remove the stones, they have unsettled the foundation and loosened the earth in which the stones lie bedded. The result is a dangerously slippery and totally uneven surface over which the horse stumbles constantly.

It is clear that if I remain in the saddle I shall be thrown within two or three minutes. I jump out of the saddle and lead the animal by the bridle through the inky darkness. Both of us proceed at snail's pace, for we have to pick our way along a route which, as I thought, is nothing but a jagged mass of irregular rocky fragments.

Frogs croak and hop about the path. I feel the dew drip from the branches as I brush inadvertently against them.

I guess the time to be about eleven o'clock. Once or twice the horse chafes at the bridle and then halts, listening with lowered head, dead still, as it catches the not-too-distant growl of a wild beast afoot for the night. I pat its face reassuringly and persuade it to finish this final stretch of our journey more quickly, but I am annoyed with myself for not having thought of removing an electric torchlight from the baggage before parting with it to the coolies. The latter are doubtless fast asleep in some hut for the night and will not arrive till tomorrow.

There is nothing like shooting a beam of glaring electric light into the unexpectant eyes of some ferocious monster. The fear will then be on the other side. The poor beast will call out in its own language for its mother and then do all the running for you! Besides, this method saves one the bother of getting a gun licence—a thing more difficult in India than in any other country. Hitherto I have done all my shooting with a camera by day and a pocket torch by night. The results have been so excellent that I can recommend these weapons to any intending big-game hunters!

At last the troublesome effort of travelling through a pitch-black forest upon billowing broken stones comes to an end. We emerge from the trees suddenly and find ourselves upon the very summit of the ridge. The stars, with their friendly familiar light, show their eyes once again. The ground looks comparatively level. Thirty or forty yards ahead there is the outline of a building and the yellowish gleam of a lantern-light swings before it. I conclude with triumphant relief that this is Pratapnagar.

A few minutes later the horse has been handed over to a groom, and I rest upon the verandah of my new terrestrial home, which possesses ample architectural proportions. My bedding has not arrived, will not arrive till the next day. So as soon as I can borrow a couple of blankets I follow a servant through a huge hall to my room, where, by the light of the brass oil-lamp which he sets down upon a table, I perceive the bed whose soporific comfort will provide me with that delightful compensation to which I now feel myself entitled.

CHAPTER SEVENTEEN

The Snowy Giants of Himalaya—An Attack by a Bear.

THE first few days at Pratapnagar are days of delightful discovery and pleasant realization. I explore my environment in an unmethodical carefree manner, content to find that Nature can be so beautiful and man's improvement upon her so comfortable.

No monsoon makes its unwelcome appearance during these days. The sun shines in so disarmingly brilliant a manner that it is hard to believe any monsoon could ever put in an appearance. My move to this place, however, is a wise one and my earthly life takes on a fairer face. Many of those little comforts which combine to make up the amenities of civilized existence, and which I lacked before, reappear here. True, we have no electric light, no running taps, no motor roads, no streets and no shops, but we have quite enough for a decent quiet existence. And even if those five things are absent, the corollaries which generally accompany them—noise, nerves, political agitation, riots and rumours of war—are equally absent and, so far as I am concerned, may easily be dispensed with. No traffic hoots and toots past my door, no telephone bell rings every five minutes. The news in the gazette which comes by post has already been forgotten by all the other readers when my eyes first light upon it, and perhaps may just as well be forgotten as soon as I read it. Nor do I have to pay for the happy privilege of hearing countless noises coming over the ether under the name of jazz. In short, I ought to praise Providence for her kindly company, which persists even here among the wild mountains of Asia, let alone among the wilder towns of Europe!

I find myself above the clouds surrounded on every side by the lofty ranges and ridges of Himalaya, as in my former abode. But here there are beautiful valleys upon which one can gaze, whilst a lovely flower-garden runs from my house to both sides of the ridge upon which it sits astride. Towards the south stretches the biggest valley of all, along whose deep bottom gurgles the silver line of the turbulently flowing Bhagirathi river. Its lower slopes are covered with pretty green verdure, whilst a little agricultural cultivation, where mountain meets water, appears as yellow patches inlaid amongst the green.

Forests of oak and pine-trees are but a stone's-throw away. I had

171

not expected to hear the warbling nightingale here, but at times its music comes from the trees.

I enjoy an extraordinary good view from the house, which has doors on all four sides and windows on three. Did ever another writer or do-nothing have an outlook like that from my window here? Nature has simply run riot in the profusion which she has strewn for dozens of miles in each direction—certainly more attractive to me than the sanguinous riots in which I have seen human beings engage. The ridges are extremely tangled, first seeming to rush towards each other and then receding just before they touch. Glens, gorges, valleys and hollows alternate in a confused conglomeration with the solid granite mass of barren hills and with dense jungles, thick forests and towering peaks. Two rivers cut their way through the mountains, plunging downwards here and there over the rocks with the wild music of waterfalls.

But finest of all views is that of the snows and the crevassed rock-strewn glaciers looming against a blue sky. I am far better placed now to enjoy them than before. I find them at my very window, so to speak, for it has a northern outlook. The giant ice-clad summits rear themselves in all their grandeur and in all their detail before my eyes. Their nearness provides me with a sense of inspiration which is sometimes overwhelming, whilst the complete clarity of their fronts is irresistibly fascinating.

Some peaks are sharp cones, others are great humps. One by one I pick them out on the long hundred-mile line which confronts me, and which so effectually bars all sight of Tibet from my gaze. On the outermost end, to the left, I catch a glimpse of the last of the Trans-Sutlej peaks. Nearer still is the clean-cut dip of the Baranghati Pass, a 17,000-feet high road into Tibet. Exactly opposite me and largely shutting out my view of Jumnotri stands the queer peak of Bandar-punch, whose top is 20,000 feet above sea-level. The name fits it well and means "monkey's tail". The round body and the curling tail are plainly there, fashioned in snowy vesture and wrapped around a skeleton of rock though they be. It is streaked with glaciers like seas of ice with frozen waves fifty to a hundred feet deep. A few miles away its companion, Srikanta, pierces the sky almost to the same height. The snowy mass of its conventional triangular form rises to a vertical precipice and embodies all one's preconceived notions of what a Himalayan peak should be. To its right a fragment of Gangotri emerges from its sheltering back, overshadowing, at a point eight miles distant and 10,000 feet high, the ancient temple which is the Mecca of the more venturesome of pilgrims throughout the summer, because it is near the glacier source of India's holiest river, the Ganges, or rather of the Bhagirathi, which is the chief feeder of the Ganges and which flows deep below my house at the foot of the ridge. For many centuries flasks have been filled at Gangotri with the sacred Gangetic water, sealed up by the officiating Brahmin priests, and carried by brave traders throughout the plains of India, where they fetch good prices as uncommon treasures.

Still travelling along the white line, my eyes recognize Kedarnath, another sacred mountain group, whilst my ears detect the muffled boom of an avalanche, which has broken and fallen away at some point in the line. The steep scarp cliffs of Kedarnath soar upward to nearly 23,000 feet, although on the other side they dip but gently towards Tibet. Kedarnath protects with its gigantic body of jointed granite the hoary old shrine in the valley below. This shrine marks a place where the story of India's earliest religious epic, the Mahabharata, culminates. It is the favoured resort of the yellow-robed holy men, who come up during the tolerable summer months from all parts of the Indian plain. Here too, they say, came their famous prototype and teacher, Shankara Acharya, two thousand years ago, and falling into a spiritual trance died in perfect peace. His present-day imitators, alas, are less worthy, and one wonders whether they can fall into any trance, spiritual or otherwise, or whether they will die in even an imperfect peace. Be that as it may, those who have the hardiness and courage to come to Kedarnath are the better sort and receive, or believe they receive, for the trouble of their pilgrimage, the blessing of those ancient souls who have made the place historically famous. Their formal ceremony of acceptance is peculiar, and as far as I know unique throughout the whole of India. They enter the temple, which lies less than a mile from the foot of the great glacier which streams down Kedarnath's side, and amid the blaze of butter-lamps and the clang of temple bells bend forward and press their hearts against a carved image of Shiva, the deity of ascetics and Yogis, whose spirit is said to hover over Central Himalaya.

Most resplendent of all the snowy summits which confront my window is Badrinath, which rests to the right nearly twenty miles farther along the line yet seems but a stone's throw, so colossal is its outline. It is really a broad square mass of appalling battlemented peaks, looking like a huge silver castle guarding with chilling grandeur the entry into Tibet against invaders. Here, too, there is a traditional shrine nestling under its protection in the low valley at its base and made famous in Hindu sacred history. Strangest of all, hot springs gush forth into a pool close by, and in a region where ice and snows overlook the valley pilgrims who are willing to be par-boiled may bathe at a temperature of 170 degrees Fahrenheit!

Finally I come to the extreme east of the snows where Dunagiri shows a 23,000-feet snowy coronet, and then, last on the great white line and blocking the vivid blue horizon, the magnificent spire of Nanda Devi rises. It is the highest mountain actually within the British Empire, for Everest and Kanchenjunga are in Nepalese and Tibetan territory. It is beyond the frontier of the kingdom of Tehri and within British Garhwal limits. Nanda Devi's altitude is 25,600 feet.

* * *

Why do I love these mountains? Is it not partly because they tangibly reflect something of that stillness, that beauty, which I find in my intangible meditations?

Thus it is that to look out of my window each morning becomes for me a veritable act of worship. With each glance I give my matutinal homage to Himalaya and enter into a mood of reverent adoration. These mountains stand in symbolic relation to our race. These snow-covered colossi, like stupendous pointing fingers, indicate for me the lofty aspirations which must ever keep man from sinking into the grovelling existence of the gutter, whilst their unsullied whiteness beckon him to a purity which he has yet to attain—not that childish asceticism which the canons of a conventional morality have set up, but that purification from all personal taint which Jesus enjoined upon those who could understand that the highest wisdom is "not my will, but Thy will be done". Only those who have dwelt awhile with such an horizon, filled with an array of shimmering white snowpeaks jutting clear-cut against the sky, can appreciate the intoxication that comes with early morning as one gazes upon it.

The cultivated gardens which set a pretty frame for my house and extend from the strip of green lawn around its walls to the cliff-edges are ablaze with giant flowers whose size and splendour contrast well with the midget wild flowers which I have seen so far. Gorgeous gold and brown sunflowers vie with dainty pink and white briar roses. Slender stems of verbena with a heavy fragrance are comrades to little star-clusters of candytuft, with their whitish flesh-colour petals. One pretty flower-group shows a profusion of blue bell-shaped heads; another is a perennial bearing sprays of sweet lilac petals. Dark-blue hyacinths and flame-like crocuses grow out of the russet ground. Amid the beauty of these and other varieties my colour-loving heart may well be content.

Large funny-looking grey lizards with long rat-like tails and suspicious winkless eyes constitute quite an appreciable population of the crannies and crevices below the sides of the paths in this garden. I like to play hide and seek with them, just as they like to come out, climb on the path, and bask in the sunshine until my intruding human feet frighten them off. But they are stubborn, and the moment they have slipped over the edge they turn and look at me steadily with lidless, staring and somewhat baleful eyes. They are not eager to enter their stony homes whilst the sun shines. As soon as I pretend to withdraw they hop on the path again and seem astonished when I return. They live like little Yogis in their miniature caves!

It is useless to try and pick a spot outdoors for my meditations, because the monsoon may break any day or even any hour. I fix, therefore, upon the spacious shelter of my own room with its walls two feet thick where I can sit with folded legs upon a chair so placed as to provide me with an abrupt view of the heavenly white peaks glistening outside the window. Seated thus, I am both indoors and outdoors! Even the most prosaic of persons must gradually become tinged with poetry amidst such surroundings.

I select the convenient triangular cone of Srikanta as the peak towards which I shall henceforth turn my eyes, when the mind begins to make the first fumbling efforts towards self-abstraction. It is thus that I shall offer my daily sacrifice of the physical senses, drawing the sense of awareness inwards and then utterly away from them as a tortoise draws its head and feet inwards from a threatening world, and not by attempting to immolate them during the hours of active life. To all things there is time and, as I see it, the withdrawal from function of any or all organs belongs to the sacred period of spiritual absorption and not to the secular period of normal physical activity. Physical paralysis is not spirituality. But, of course, I am a heretic.

My treasured Tibetan painting hangs on the wall. Now and then I regard its great central Buddha, with his heavy eyelids folded in meditation.

This cushioned chair, then, shall henceforth enthrone my holiest thoughts; this semicircular window shall open on eternity; these four cream-painted walls shall enclose one man's efforts to fulfil the cherished purpose of his being; the dark oak wooden ceiling shall keep watch over my own vigils; whilst the entire room shall be dedicated to the one whose bidding brought me here. "Be still and know that I am God." That is the penitential theme upon which I shall write my essays during the coming days, not with unreluctant ink but with reluctant life.

*   *   *

Hunters tell me that tigers differ in temperament just as human beings do; not all will attack, some retreat through sheer cowardice. Anyway, there is a whole family of tigers in the grandiose hall which opens to my room. They bare their teeth in a snarl of defiant rage; their cat-like ears are drawn back in fierce alertness; whilst their scimitar-like ivory claws protrude as though ready for a fight.

But these splendidly-coloured creatures will spring upon no one, so well have they been trained by the taxidermist's art to behave themselves and keep quiet! For they are now but mere fleshless skins and nerveless heads, sprawling against a white wall in sheer helplessness.

This black-striped family consists of a handsome father, spitfire of a mother, two sons and one daughter. The male skin measures no less than ten feet in length, its head alone being a foot and a quarter. Alive and filled, it probably weighed over six hundred pounds; dead and empty, it has been reduced to much less than a tenth of that amount. Yet its beauty and majesty still remain. Nature has thoughtfully provided these mountain tigers with thicker fur coats than their relatives of the low-lying plains, I observe. All the family were shot upon the mountain slopes around Pratapnagar some years ago. But now tigers have ceased to trouble the vicinity, whose chief forest population are shaggy black and brown bears, leopards, and those fierce creatures, black-spotted panthers. The prevalence of these animals constitutes such a nuisance that I have been warned from the first morning not to venture out after dark.

The caretaker tells me that a panther once leapt on this peaceful green lawn which stretches around the house and, in broad daylight, attacked three dogs which were dozing in the sunshine. It killed two and dragged the third away into the adjoining forest before it could be rescued.

Even bears came waddling out of their dens grunting and roaming to the very doors after nightfall, searching the garden for tasty roots, or attempting to climb the apple-trees. Every night, soon after I have ensconced myself between the blankets, and sometimes much later, I hear a couple of shots being fired by one of the soldiers who guards the palace and its gardens. The sounds are signals of Brer Bruin's prowling habits, which he cannot change even despite these regular and unfailing deterrent warnings.

In a tiny hamlet a few miles from my former home I had been told of a villager there who had been killed during the winter by a bear. This was most unusual, because bears do not seek to kill but to wound their victims. That unpleasant trait renders them the most vicious of all forest animals. Other beasts attack and kill human beings when driven by the natural hunger for food, but the bear attacks men out of sheer spite and malice and then shambles off again. It cannot bite them successfully because it lacks carnivores, so it claws them instead.

One afternoon a man arrives at the house in a pitiable state. He has been attacked by a rampaging bear only half a mile away and in brilliant sunlight.

His head is broken open, one eye has been torn, his face, shoulders and arms are a mass of ugly wounds. His clothes are in pieces and clotted with blood. The poor fellow has claw-marks and deep gashes all over his breast. Fortunately the palace doctor is still in Pratapnagar, although due to go on leave within a few days. The bear's victim is patched up, his wounds stitched, the bleeding stopped and his head and arms swathed in bandages.

The next day, when the poor fellow has rested and recovered himself somewhat, I hear his story of the encounter. He is a young-looking man and, I surmise, an educated one. He is probably a Brahmin by caste.

"I write letters and petitions for those who are illiterate," he tells me. "Two days ago I left my village to travel on foot to Tehri town, where I had some business to attend to. My servant, a small boy ten years old, accompanied me. Yesterday afternoon, at about five o'clock, I was nearing the point where the mountain path forks into two, one going upwards to the top of this ridge and leading to the palace, and the other turning downwards to the river valley along which lies Tehri. Suddenly I heard a terrific growl. I looked up and saw, high on the mountain-side and among the forest trees, a huge blackish-brown bear with two cubs. The animal rushed down the slope directly towards me like an avalanche, grunting ferociously all the time. Its speed was terrific and I realized that it was useless to run away and that we stood no chance of escape. But as I know the habits of these bears I prepared to defend myself. The only weapon I had was an umbrella. I pushed the weeping boy behind me in order to protect him, shielded my face with the left hand and held the umbrella forward with my right. It seemed only a minute before the bear had descended the slope and reached the path. I saw that it was a female—always more dangerous and more vicious than the opposite sex. It had a thick furry coat, large fluffy ears, a black nose, and a shaggy mane of hair which fell over its forehead and nearly covered one eye. It flew at me, clawed me around the head, the face and the upper part of my body. I jabbed my umbrella into its angry face until the cloth shade was torn to shreds. After the beast had wounded me frightfully several times and when four or five minutes of this terrible fight had passed, the bear seemed satisfied with what it had done and returned to its cubs in the forest. I was glad I could save the boy from being injured. I then managed to stagger here, with the blood streaming along the trail all the way."

Such is this unfortunate man's narrative. It proves plainly what every mountaineer in these parts knows, that bears do not desire to kill a man but will make for him on sight merely to maim and disfigure him for life.

The toll of deaths from wild beasts and poisonous reptiles may be fairly heavy in India, although it is chiefly among cattle, but I do not think that it is any worse, on a percentage of population, than the toll of deaths from motor-car accidents in the West. The average occidental does not realize that nowadays the automobile has become no less dangerous to him than the tiger and the cobra is to the average Indian. In India, where some parts are so infested that snakes and scorpions may sleep behind almost every stone and wild beasts may have their haunts in every patch of jungle or forest, the Western accident and mortality figures can hardly have been exceeded so far as human beings are concerned, although the figure of depredations among cattle must certainly be larger. The truth is that fewer forest beasts will attack a human being who does not hunt them than we think, so long as they can prey on other animals, whilst fewer snakes will bite him unless he accidentally treads on them or touches them, when they bite through fear that they are being attacked, than we believe. In short, the danger of crossing a motor-infested road in the cities of America and Europe is now about equal to the danger of crossing a savage-beast-ridden forest in India!

CHAPTER EIGHTEEN

The Delights of Tea-drinking—How the Monsoon Storms Break Out.

So often during these last twenty years have I sat down to imbibe the good cheer which tea-drinking invariably affords me, so comforting has this habit been to me now that I have carried it into the comfortless Himalayas, that my mind muses in its long leisure upon the philosophy which lies behind it.

No sound is so musical to me as the song of the bubbling kettle, whose contents are destined to be transferred to the round capacious pot which rests companionably upon the white tablecloth so often wherever I wander. I watch with the recurrent reaction of pleasant anticipation the hot vapour flutter out of the elegantly curved spout.

It seems strange that the Western world was bereft of one of the minor pleasures and major necessities of civilized existence for so many centuries. A thousand years before Europe knew of the existence of this fragrant herb the Chinese were sipping its golden extract and gossiping with each other under its gentle stimulus.

It seems stranger still, however, that the land which produces such a huge quantity of the world's tea supply today should have had to wait for the advent of the British before the first roots were transplanted into its soil. Not till last century was tea grown in India, and then only by enterprising British agriculturists. Even now many Indians have never tasted tea, whilst few know how to make it properly. A Chinese poet has sorrowed in verse over the deplorable waste of fine tea through incompetent preparation. No doubt this ignorance will vanish with the new habits which are rapidly being introduced here.

The Buddhist priest who taught me what I know of Buddhism told me that it was the custom in many Buddhist monasteries of Burma, China and Japan to keep the monks frequently supplied with little bowls of fresh tea during their long night vigils of meditation, in order to drive away sleep and thus enable them to extend their spiritual practices to the utmost limits. In that way they hoped to make more rapid progress. He also recounted to me the curious, attractive yet incredible legend of the origin of tea.

He said that a South Indian sage named Bodhidharma journeyed to China about the sixth century and used to sit in meditation before a blank wall. During one of his prolonged periods of mental abstraction he found to his annoyance that he was becoming drowsy.

He cut off the offending eyelids and threw them away. They took root on the spot where they fell and a plant, hitherto unknown, grew up out of them. The leaves of this plant were endowed with the virtue of keeping man wakeful.

The fable is delightful enough, but the only certain thing about it is that the tea-plant did originate in South China, where Bodhidharma landed. He became in time the founder of a great philosophic school, the Cha'an school, or the Zen, as the Japanese call it, whose followers even today drink a great deal of tea along with their imbibing of wisdom, and whose very name embodies the Chinese ideograph for tea.

That the mere steeping of a few leaves should have such stimulating results to both body and mind when drunk so impressed those early tea addicts that one of them, Luwuh, put into poetic prose a veritable *Scripture of Tea Drinking*. His work, *The Chaking*, has led the Chinese tea merchants for a thousand years to adopt him as their patron mascot, such is the profound philosophy he has stirred into the simple act of drinking a cup of tea It is a pity that no one has yet had the discernment to translate this book into one of the Western tongues, for Luwuh has said the last word about tea, from a botanical study of the plant itself to the ideal colour for a porcelain tea-cup, from the assertion that mountain-springs provide the finest water for tea-making to rebukes for the inartistic vulgarity of common methods of tea-drinking.

We who are likewise votaries of the delectable drink would like to have met this man, of whom it was said that the Emperor sent for him several times because one could detect a cup of tea made by him out of all others, so exquisite was its flavour.

Another thing that I like to remember is the Chinese claim to the origin of the custom of offering tea to a guest or visitor. It is said to have begun with Kwanyin, one of the chief disciples of my favourite Oriental philosopher, Lao-Tse. When the latter resigned his Royal service and reached the gate of the Han Pass on his westward journey (after which he disappeared), Kwanyin presented him with a cup of tea—an act of symbolical value, for thereafter it was introduced into social life throughout the Empire. I like to think that the last act of my wise bearded sage was to sip the golden liquid before disappearing from civilization into that simpler life close to Nature which he sought. He was a great soul and nothing but a great drink was fit for him.

In the fifteenth century the Japanese founded an aesthetic cult in its honour, with the most elaborate rituals and ceremonials. In fact the cultivation and preparation of the tea-plant was practically a monopoly of the priests for a long time. The amber-coloured infusion was regarded as a superior and aristocratic beverage and was therefore drunk only by the best classes at first. It was the Dutch trading ships which brought the first tea-chests across the Eastern seas into European waters. Once sampled, it did not take long before a regular craze developed and the new drink was firmly established among the occidentals.

The Japanese gave the most minute instructions for these ceremonies, so important did they deem them. There was a particular way of opening the lid of the kettle; a particular manner of stirring the tea in the pot with a bamboo brush; a particular style of handing the little cup to the expectant guest; a particular importance in drinking up its contents in three and a half sips, and so on.

What fates have hung symbolically upon this delicate bush! The American colonists threw off British rule when they threw the overtaxed tea-chests into Boston harbour, whilst Marco Polo tells us of a Chinese Finance Minister who was overthrown for taxing tea too highly. How much has the Western habit of afternoon tea-parties contributed towards the social amenities, the rounding-off of sharp corners, the smoothing of national asperities and the building of intellectual goodwill between people, even as it did in those more elaborate mores of the mediaeval Japanese! How many have come to know each other and laid the basis for a lifelong friendship in nothing more than a tiny tea-cup! How great are the issues and decisions which have come to final culmination between men and women amid the clatter of cups and saucers!

Every man has his own tastes, his own inborn preferences. He will necessarily carry them into the realm of tea-drinking. My own strong predilection was formerly for the aroma and inspiring flavour of Darjeeling tea. The plantations which throng the hills around that Indian hot-weather station which faces Kanchenjunga, second highest mountain in the Himalayan world, produce a plant which in its turn produces a decoction that seems unrivalled, but others, I know, will disagree. No doubt a part of its enchantment for me comes from the pictures of Himalaya which float up out of the cup before my mind's eye. 'Tis all a matter of taste, and indeed when so many other fine teas are on offer to the world he would be an unscrupulous man who denounced them merely in order to vaunt his own likings. Nevertheless, for many years I have been a convert to drinking the mildest of Chinese teas, because of their smaller poisonous content.

Many writers I know have found their delight in tea, and in this they are but emulating the earlier illustrious examples of Dr. Johnson, who confessed himself to be "a hardened and shameless tea-drinker"; of Charles Lamb, whose words, to my regret, I cannot recall; and of Addison, who found phrases for his essays over "a dish of tea".

I always gain an intellectual stimulation from a cup or two of good tea such as I can gain in no other material way. It seems that the atoms of the brain become revivified and their active functioning greatly enhanced under the stimulating effect of tea. Anyway, I would not dream of tackling a serious job of intellectual work without a preliminary drink of this brain tonic. Were I mathematically minded I might calculate how many pints of tea have gone to the making of each hundred pages of my writings!

My own quiet undistracted existence in the Himalayas enables me to extract the utmost that there is to be had from tea-drinking. I return from my meditations in the late twilight, to sit idly and feel the comforting cosy warmth which the submerged leaves impart to me, the while night's creeping shadows move over my mountain nest. I stir the dissolving grains of brown sugar until they melt rapidly into their Nirvana of liquid nectar, and then sip each mouthful with full appreciation of its worth, for time does not press upon me, work does not harry me and people do not jostle in upon me here. It is in such leisurely manner that one can and should receive all that tea has to offer mankind.

Let the world have its heavier drinks. For me there shall always be but one worthy to touch my palate and to inspire my mind.

'Tis a harmless pleasure this of tea-drinking. What more refreshing in the morning than a cupful? What more useful to the writing man who likes to work at his pages during the calm hours of the night; how else may he repel sleep so effectively?

However, at a certain stage of the spiritual aspirant's self-disciplinary career, he may not take any stimulant without obstructing the way to the inner silence he seeks in meditation. During this special period even tea will have adverse effects and he must guard himself against them by drinking it not often and not strongly.

I think the people who know only one way of preparing tea might usefully experiment with other ways so that they may have the delight of variety in their daily drink. For instance, they might try, instead of after-dinner coffee, a glass of tea in Russian style, made weak, filled up with hot water, well sweetened and with a slice or two of lemon. And as an after-lunch drink, tea in the Persian manner affords an equally pleasant change. This is brewed in the Russian style except that the liquid is scented with mint instead of being made acid with lemon.

Still another pleasant variety is the Egyptian way of placing perfumed rose-petals in a glass of sugared, weak milkless tea. Tea with milk should be reserved for the afternoon tea function proper,

I think, and for breakfast, but here again each to his taste, as the French proverb runs. These are my preferences however.

And now I must sit down to another cup of the "nectar of the gods", as some Oriental person called it, coupled with a slice of toast, and let its delicious warmth flow through my body, lighten my brain, and cheer my heart the while a fragrant aroma ascends from the crinkled leaves.

*　　*　　*

Early one morning there comes the ominous threatening sound of a deep distant rumble, which approaches and develops into angry roars of thunder. The noise is the herald of the monsoon deluge and the presage of India's greatest climatic change.

A cold blast begins to blow through my open window. The arrival of the expected seasonal guest is quite sudden. Five minutes ago I glance up from the table at which I am sitting to view the brilliant sunny scene outside. The green lawn is dappled with light and shade, the chaotic mass of mountains looks pleasant and peaceful, the dark-blue forest-covered ridges smile in the warm rays, and the white-robed summits make a picture of primitive beauty. Gratified, I bend my head again to the page which I am reading.

Now I hear the threatening invasion, and glance up again. The sun has gone. The heavens murmur in prediction. I am astonished to see a vast legion of white fluffy mists appear, as from nowhere, and come scurrying along the valleys towards the house. Above them in the sky a gloomy mass of cumulus heavy thunderclouds hang over the peaks and begin to hide the highest ones under their black canopy.

The dark opaque mists move between the ranges like a squadron of aeroplanes. They blot out from view everything they pass until the whole of the lower landscape is covered with the dense milky vapour, like the full-veiled face of a strictly orthodox Muhammedan lady.

I can still see along the ridge-tops until a chill wind which roars like an express train arises and drives the dark clouds before it. The gale causes them to come in my direction. As it brushes past the branches of the forest trees I hear the swaying of a thousand slim trunk-tops. It sweeps around the room and its sudden coolness cuts my body like a knife, forcing me to slip a thick sweater beneath my thin jacket.

The mists float higher and soon the house is islanded in a white sea. In ten minutes the whole world is blotted out, and the Himalayan mountains turned, as by a magician's wand, into impenetrable

183

sky. I think for a moment of the dreary fogs of London, but I find these here are clean by comparison and not sulphurous in odour.

Then the storm rolls over my head to the accompaniment of thunder and lightning. The grey clouds break eventually into showers of thick sleet. Sheets of lightning descend upon an earth about to be bombarded by three months of tempest. The elements are in a fury and the heavens are rent asunder. The monsoon hurtles its millions of large raindrops from the sky with the speed of a flying machine and amid the roaring noise of a gunfire attack. It avenges its long absence with incredible ferocity.

The terrific downpours which now gush out of the skies in such quantities possess no parallel in temperate Europe. If the energy with which they mercilessly pelt the mountains along the whole length of the Himalayas could be harnessed mechanically and turned into electrical units, the vast breadth and length of half India could be put on an electrically run basis.

For several hours the tempestuous winds drive these torrents of water. The rain is like a solid wall encircling the building. Lightning, at first spasmodic, increases until it becomes almost continuous. Amid the raging tornado outside, the resounding crashes of thunder well nigh cause the ground to shake with concussion.

With the approach of dusk the rains resume their duty. At night I lie in bed listening to the pouring waters or watching the play of lightning upon the walls. Yes, the monsoon season has started and henceforth one thing may unfailingly be expected—rain.

In a few days the square of green lawn which surrounds the house has become a muddy morass. One's feet sink into the mixture of water and earth which hides under the fair face of the grass.

I am not sorry, though. The dry parched ground of the plains will swallow all this wetness greedily and the crops of poor peasants will be assured.

It is this excessive monsoon moisture, too, which jackets most of the storm-tossed Himalayan forest trees with mosses, creepers and ferns.

Yet the weather has its brief fickle moods like a sick and sulky old man. On many a day during this season Himalaya is exposed to great extremes of temperature, from the arctic to the tropical. There are evenings so chilly that I have to hustle into winter clothing in order not to begin shivering with cold, although it is but midsummer. But there are also occasional bright rifts which interrupt the monsoon, when for two or three hours the sun leads the mists away, turning them into dreams that have vanished. It generously beams upon and warms this mountain world and then I bask in the shining satisfying rays. These halcyon moments in the pine-scented air bring compensation for the bleak drenching rains. I discover that even in this season Himalaya keeps a wardrobe of variously coloured clothes, and may dress and re-dress herself a dozen times a week.

So fierce is the momentum of the winds that one morning I find half the zinc roof torn off an outbuilding during the night, to the music of rattling peals of thunder which echo all over the mountains.

The fitful interludes, however, are all the more appreciated and prevent the spectacle of dawnless sunless days wiping away my memories of rosier times.

At this time of the year the monsoon is infinitely preferable to the heats, when the mounting thermometer saps the energy out of white bodies and drives their nerves to distracted listlessness.

Yet must one regret that with the monsoon the Flower of Himalaya folds its lovely petals and hides her beauty under an enwrapping veil of milk-white mists, grey vapours, sombre black clouds and pelting rains.

*   *   *

This tale of my later life in the mountains now becomes entirely the tale of one man's private hours with sacredness, of his inward quest and intimate worship. Nothing and nobody external appears henceforth in its pages. No event needs to be described for it is now only the story of a deepening stillness. What can one record of that sublime Void into which I seek to penetrate? Words fail me, phrases elude me, where once they tripped nimbly at my command. My thought, alas, dies before it reaches the point of my pen. Let me then prepare to put the pen aside and let the further pages of this journal be written on water. I cannot take the world with me into such private precincts, nor do I care to. Let the curtain of silence fall upon them.

EPILOGUE

I HAVE packed my bags and turned my eyes southward and prepared to leave this world of mellow skies and mantled ridges, to set forth once more, a homeless, houseless wanderer. For the season will change, the cold increase daily, and a white rampart of snow will heap itself seven feet high all around my house and all but bury its exits and entrances during the late autumn and winter months. The white flakes will fall thickly upon this familiar scene before long and make the paths impassable. This little kingdom will hibernate in isolated grandeur and the Himalayan heights will once more be cut off from human access until the recurrence of spring.

Yet one does not willingly leave this invigorating atmosphere for the glaring light and stifling heat of the southern plains, even to see the first white faces for a long time when I reach the edge of the plains. I leave my mountain fastness with regret.

For it pains me to remember that I shall soon have to walk into the society of noisy, fidgety, superficial men, whose voices will buzz like flies and be as meaningless to me. How shall I endure the constant cackle of the towns, the endless unnecessary talk? The silence of these mountains seems to have entered my bones: some effort will be required to break it once more. Alas, it must be done. The Overself's eloquent silence must yield to the intellect's babble. But I shall always be able to turn towards the memory of my Himalayan sojourn, which is ineffaceable, and to its divine fruit, which is ineffable. No journey is so profitable as when it is undertaken to find the place or the man who can yield us Truth.

The friend who has read these pages in manuscript and written the foreword thinks that the chronicles will be incomplete if I did not sum up somehow the message of Nature which I learned in the mountains and the message of Himalaya's stillness to distracted mankind. His criticism is a just one. So I add these few lines in the hope that the power of words may convey some hints of the Wordless Power which was and is for me the supreme atmosphere of the Himalayas.

Destiny, I know, sent me across the ocean to my researches; they sent me into the solitude of the Himalayas: and the Himalayas now send me back to the turmoil of the larger world I had forsaken. The circle is now complete. These three turning points make the perfect triangle. A long time must pass before I disappear into external retreat again; before I forsake humanity and abandon the claims of social existence.

And when the day comes for me to prepare to begin a longer journey than that from Himalaya I shall be ready. I know that the stillness here found will pass with me into the world of death and befriend me in a region where riches must fail.

Put into a small packet, the ultimate message of Himalaya is SILENCE, that silence which carries the breath of God in its hush. In that Silence mankind may find its proof of the existence of God, of the reality of a universal Power behind Nature which is ever-present and ever-working. To me life shall ever after be bigger and nobler because I have lived here.

I think the final news which I shall bring away from these peaks is also extremely ancient — that of God's reality. The higher Power is no mere article of belief to me, but a verity—authentic, undeniable and supreme, even though It be so hidden.

I think too that I have learned the highest wisdom is to find and then surrender to this Power. But to discover It we need to go into the Silence every day for a little while, retiring from the outer world to enter the inner world wherein It abides.

God will not lower His mode of speech in order that unfamiliar mortals may comprehend. We must learn His language or go without His message. His language is nothing else than this stillness. And He is no more distant from us than our own selves.

The corollary of this is that man need never mourn his possible extinction. The hope of immortality is the herald of its realization. In his profoundest moments he may feel and experience its truth. Although this thought has been uttered and echoed even by un-percipient persons to the point of platitudinous boredom, it happens to be true. Man's body will pass as certainly as those pale mists which glitter on the sombre peaks before me, but he shall keep the integrity of his own self, for it is divine.

I know this, not because some bible or clergyman has told me so, but because I have entered the Silence. When I sat in my mountain sanctuary, I felt myself being lifted at times out of my body and floating gently upwards into the air. I could see all the landscape around, all the familiar sights and scenes of forest, ridge, ravine and snowy summit. I was not asleep and I was not dreaming, yet once, when a servant came to call me, I was unable to move hand or limb although I heard him. I was incapable of speaking or moving, yet I could quite clearly observe my surroundings in a totally detached manner. My body was as dead, yet *I* was still alive. This convinced me that I shall survive more than a thousand arguments, for it showed one how it is possible for the mind, the inner man, to move in and out of the flesh at birth, sleep and death.

The Divine Power has not deserted its creation, the universe. It is ever silently working. Let us remember and re-remember that in these dark hours of world turmoil. Whatever happens today, I am convinced that the onward history of man shall embody his highest hopes, merely because of this secret working of God. I have this faith, and everyone else may have it too who will go into the silence and listen to its soundless Voice. Let us then hold to Hope, when other things prove not worth holding to. The gods shall and must conquer.

Himalaya taught me so.

I would like, as a last line, to rewrite the Psalmist's sentence and word it thus:

"Be still, and know the *I Am*—God!"

For information about Paul Brunton, his writings and the latest publications based on his work, visit http://www.paulbrunton.org. For reviews, excerpts and a complete detailed table of contents of his posthumously published *Notebooks* series, visit http://www.larson publications.org.

You can also receive information by e-mail from larson@lightlink.com, or by mail from the Paul Brunton Philosophic Foundation, 4936 NYS Route 414, Burdett, New York 14818, USA.

Buy Rider Books

Order further Rider titles from your local bookshop, or
have them delivered direct to your door by Bookpost

☐ **The Quest of the Overself** by Paul Brunton   184413041X £12.99
☐ **A Search in Secret India** by Paul Brunton   1844130436 £12.99
☐ **The Secret Path** by Paul Brunton   1844130401 £10.99
☐ **The Yoga Sutras of Patanjali**   0712655093 £8.99
☐ **The Bhagavad Gita**   0712604383 £10.99
☐ **One Dharma** by Joseph Goldstein   0712659455 £9.99
☐ **The Dhammapada**   0712656847 £8.99
☐ **The Tibetan Book
 of Living and Dying** by Sogyal Rinpoche   0712615695 £10.99

FREE POST AND PACKING
Overseas customers allow £2.00 per paperback

ORDER:
By phone: 01624 677237

By post: Random House Books
c/o Bookpost
PO Box 29
Douglas
Isle of Man, IM99 1BQ

By fax: 01624 670923

By email: bookshop@enterprise.net

Cheques (payable to Bookpost) and credit cards accepted

Prices and availability subject to change without notice.
Allow 28 days for delivery.
When placing your order, please mention if you do not wish to receive
any additional information.

www.randomhouse.co.uk